Routledge Revivals

Pakistani Entrepreneurs

First Published in 1983 *Pakistani Entrepreneurs* covers the role of the entrepreneur within Pakistan. His origins, religious and educational background, and family play a more important part in the development of the Pakistani entrepreneur than is the case with his western counterpart. In particular, the influence of caste was considered in the context of attitudes towards bargaining and credit, knowledge of and information on markets and raw materials. This is a systematic and probing study of efforts at Industrialisation in Pakistan, and of the way entrepreneurs have risen to the challenges of its offers.

This book will be of interest to scholars and researchers of Pakistani economics, South Asian economics, and business economics.

Pakistani Entrepreneurs

Their Development, Characteristics and Attitudes

Zafar Altaf

Routledge
Taylor & Francis Group

First published in 1983
by Croom Helm

This edition first published in 2023 by Routledge
4 Park Square, Milton Park, Abingdon, Oxon, OX14 4RN

and by Routledge
605 Third Avenue, New York, NY 10017

Routledge is an imprint of the Taylor & Francis Group, an informa business

Publisher's Note
The publisher has gone to great lengths to ensure the quality of this reprint but points out that some imperfections in the original copies may be apparent.

Disclaimer
The publisher has made every effort to trace copyright holders and welcomes correspondence from those they have been unable to contact.

A Library of Congress record exists under ISBN: 0709905203

ISBN: 978-1-032-52697-3 (hbk)
ISBN: 978-1-003-40791-1 (ebk)
ISBN: 978-1-032-52698-0 (pbk)

Book DOI 10.4324/9781003407911

PAKISTANI ENTREPRENEURS

THEIR DEVELOPMENT, CHARACTERISTICS AND ATTITUDES

ZAFAR ALTAF

CROOM HELM
London & Sydney

© 1983 Z. Altaf
Croom Helm Ltd, Provident House, Burrell Row,
Beckenham, Kent BR3 1AT
Croom Helm Australia Pty Ltd, First Floor,
139 King Street, Sydney, NSW 2001, Australia
Reprinted 1984

British Library Cataloguing in Publication Data

Altaf, Zafar
    Pakistani entrepreneurs.
    1. Pakistan — Industries
    I. Title
    338.9549   HC440.5

    ISBN 0-7099-0520-3

Printed and bound in Great Britain by
Biddles Ltd, Guildford and King's Lynn

CONTENTS

TABLES AND FIGURES

Tables

Tables and Figures

Figures

To my parents for their unbounden love.

FOREWORD

There are not enough books that make an original contribution to the subject of development economics. Mr. Zafar Altaf's book does so and is therefore most welcome. It is an important addition to the literature and should be read by politicians, academics and indeed all who are concerned with encouraging economic development in third world countries.

Many books and articles discuss the motivation and background of entrepreneurs in developing countries but most of them are based on the intuitive feelings of the author or on a review of the few research studies that do exist on the topic. This book is based on a major research study. In this research Zafar Altaf interviewed a large number of entrepreneurs in Pakistan, including some who had not been successful. He was concerned with such factors as their backgrounds, their motivation, their objectives and their attitudes toward risk.

Zafar Altaf was extremely well-qualified to undertake this research. Not only was he a respected man in his own country who had achieved success in the sporting field and as an administrator, he had also proved his academic abilities in more than one subject area. It was because of the respect in which he was held in his own country that he was able to interview a large number of businessmen from both large and small businesses and to obtain their confidence. The insights he was able to obtain into the attitudes of entrepreneurs and his skilful analysing of the material, together result in a fascinating book.

In this work he corrects a number of misunderstandings which have been built up concerning entrepreneurs and makes a number of

important points that should be of interest to
those responsible for the development of third world
countries. His conclusions are interesting and of
significance. I am sure that in future this book
will often be quoted. Undoubtedly, some people
will disagree with some of the findings but this
does not detract from the overall value of the
work. To repeat this book makes a major contribution to our understanding of entrepreneurs and
should be a great help to those interested in the
problems of economic development.

> Prof. John M. Samuels
> University of Birmingham
> England

ACKNOWLEDGEMENTS

The present study is the result of research carried
out at the University of Birmingham while working
for my doctorate. A considerable portion of that
research has had to be modified to make the data
and the material more manageable.

There were various agencies and individuals
who were responsible in enabling me to break away
from the shackles of public life. My grateful
thanks to the senior bureaucracy in allowing me to
take on this work. Specific mention needs to be
made of Miss. Gulzar Bano and Dr. Tariq Siddiqui,
for their patience, understanding and unflinching
faith. To numerous friends in England who stepped
forward to lend a helping hand and to make facilities available.

I owe to my tutors at the University of
Birmingham a special debt. Patient and encouraging
as they were, they made me aware of points of view
divergent from mine. Prof. J.M. Samuels, Professor
A.L. Minkes were constant intellectual guides and
mentors. Dr. Wilkes who welcomed me to the cricket
nets with a bouncer, gave willingly of his time
and critically appraised my work. To A.H. Kardar
former sportsman and politician, my thanks are
largely due for inculcating in me the attitude that
nothing is impossible. Even when progress is slow
and battles are lost, struggle must continue.
Compromise, no matter what the odds is not the way
to forge ahead, an attitude remarkably strengthened
by Prof. J.M. Samuels in his inimitable way.
Dr. Mohammad Ajmal, Professor of Iqbal at Heidelberg
University for encouraging me to accept life as it
comes and to enrich it with unquantifiable aspects.
I have continued to take on new challenges as they
came my way.

My debt to cricket is immense. This present

Acknowledgements

work can be traced to a telephone call to Professor Samuels, at that time Dean of Social Sciences, Birmingham University from the Edgbaston Cricket Ground where Pakistan and England were playing the first test in]978. I was there as manager of the Pakistan Cricket Team. To Mr. T. Pocock of Faber & Faber whom I met also at a cricket match and who enabled me to meet Mr. Christopher Helm of Croom Helm , my present publishers. He has helped me in improving the text and shown a remarkable combination of patience and efficiency. Above all the game has given me not only pleasure but also more meaning to my life.

My wife has stood by me and read my drafts and gave invaluable suggestions. Invariably the informal system is of extreme significance in developing a frame of mind. The religious zeal of my mother, the argumentative gentility of my father who taught me how to enjoy the simple things of life, to an elder brother who always gave of himself so that I was comfortable and for his help in overcoming frustrations caused by less understanding minds, to sisters who encouraged and stood firm by me.

Time off for this latest draft was allowed as a result of consideration shown by the present Establishment Secretary, Government of Pakistan, Mr. Ijlal Haider Zaidi, who is responsible for inducting me into the rigors of public service, once again. It is possible to belong to two distinct worlds -- the academics and the bureaucrats. One hopes these roles are not mutually exclusive.

Despite all this kindness and help I have researched an area not normally the subject of formal economic theory. In fact there is a socio-psychological interface with economics in this research. In that sense the effort is interdisciplinary. If I have erred in building an argument or if the evidence seems not so convincing the weakness be attributed entirely to me.

The quote extracts reprinted by permission were from: The Dilemma of Mexicos Development -- The Roles of the Private and Public Sectors by R.Vernon, published by the Harvard University Press; Pakistan's Development: Social Goals and Private Incentives, by G.F. Papanek and published by Harvard University Press; The New Vaisyas : Entrepreneurial Opportunity and Response in an Indian City by R.L. Owens and A. Nandy published by the Carolina Academic Press; Entrepreneurship and Economic

Acknowledgements

Development edited by Peter Kilby copy right (c)
1971 by the Free Press, a Division of MacMillan
Publishing Co., Inc.; reprinted from the Journal of
Economic Development and Cultural Change,
Pakistan's Big Businessmen, Muslim Separatism,
Entrepreneurship and Partial Modification, by
H. Papanek , (c) 1972 by the University of Chicago;
The Development of Entrepreneurship by G.F. Papanek
printed in the American Economic Review; Industrial
Entrepreneurship in Nigeria, by J.P. Harris,
unpublished Ph.D. dissertation, Northwestern
University, 1967; Pakistan's New Industrialists and
Businessmen: Focus on the Memons by H. Papanek in
Entrepreneurship and Modernisation of Occupational
Cultures, edited by Milton Singer, Duke University
Press; The Origins of Marwari Industrialists by
I.A. Timberg in Entrepreneurship and Modernisation
of Occupational Cultures edited by Milton Singer,
Duke University Press; Interview with Mrs. Gandhi,
by Anil Agarwal, Daily Guardian; Industrialist and
the Government process in Pakistan by A.L. Fritschler,
unpublished Ph.D. dissertation, Syracuse University,
1965; Pakistan's Development: Social Goals and
Private Incentives by G.F. Papanek, published by
the Harvard University Press; Entrepreneurs in
East Pakistan by H. Papanek in Bengal Change and
Continuity edited by R & M.J. Beach, Michigan
State University Press.

INTRODUCTION

Like other developing countries Pakistan considered
Industrialisation as the basis for creating a
better economic order for its citizens. For a
variety of reasons, industrial policies followed by
successive governments were such that the desired
impact was either not there or was only visible for
a fleeting moment. Invariably policies designed to
take the country to a developed state fell through
creating further chaos and confusion. Interaction
of theory and practise was minimal and far too
often decisions were based on partial appreciation
of facts.

The present study considers the formal and
informal basis of industrial development. Industrial imperatives for Pakistan and there various
ramifications are examined. One finds normally
that policies are devised on the basis of formal
economic logic without due consideration of the
human factor. Policies transferred from the west,
which are developed in a particular cultural setting
are transplanted in developing countries. What is
good for one country is normally considered by aid
donors and world agencies to be good for the
developing countries as well. That is not so has
now begun to dawn on the agencies committed to
bring about a new social order. The resultant
effect of inappropriate technologies, inappropriate
products has indirectly been borne by the common
man. The received knowledge from the west,
appropriate as it was for the home countries, was
not commensurate with Pakistan's requirements.
Under such conditions the role of government assumes
extra sensitivity in as much as it is the bounden
duty of the planners to be able to perceive the
effects of these policies. It is precisely here
that governments tend to break down. Its

information on technologies is limited, its
knowledge on products is inadequate and on
occasions it does not have the ability to aggres-
sively seek what it perceives as its requirements.
On all counts the constraints are unlimited.

A study of the human factor in industrialisation is therefore called for. The central figure
is the entrepreneur and it was apparent that the
human factor as perceived in logic and economic
theory was either hardly examined or if it was the
analysis was only partial and as per going
knowledge of the 60's when some research work was
done at the Harvard University. The only effort in
respect of Pakistan came from G.F. and H. Papanek,
who worked in Pakistan for almost a decade. Their
views were based, naturally on formal systems. The
informal system and networks i.e. of the caste
system was unknown to their logic and theory,
though H. Papanek did look at the Memons and
considered the effects of modernisation on their
occupations. Contrary to normal perception though
the earlier informal system is neither static nor
held in a water tight compartment. So a very
important aspect of the entrepreneur was touched
upon only briefly.

To come to grips with such propositions the
origins and occupations of the entrepreneurs are
examined viz the castes and communities in the
sample. The occupational options which are
available to them. A two generation look at
occupations enabled the analysis of occupational
mobility. The push and pulls and the impact of
government policies in the ultimate determination
of occupations are examined. Informal aspects such
as prestige, power, self confidence, informal
contacts normally never examined have been studied
and argued into existing knowledge.

Occupational mobility assumed in the case of
Pakistan greater significance as in 1947 there was
hardly any industry. Such a large area for investment was available that it was inevitable that the
population at large would respond to the created
opportunities. Even handed policies may have
resulted in a better spread of development.
Important divergences in motivational dynamics have
been examined and a distinction is made between
mercantile and merchant traders. The response of
these two categories of entrepreneurs to opportunities is distinctively different, in size, in
direction and in form. Each category has its own
strong points and articulate themselves into the

Introduction

economy in different ways.

The effects of education is again to be considered not in quantitative terms only but also in terms of informal education where future entrepreneurs develop their work ethics. Education, experience, training all have different roles to play in the ultimate development of the entrepreneur.

The impact of the extended/joint family system on work ethics is an aspect studied when considering the development of entrepreneurs. The influence of the family, its all encompassing role and the manner in which it creates worthwhile citizens as against the role of institutions in developed societies is examined. The roles played by individuals in providing scarce resources is also scrutinised. Whereas institutional funding is available to entrepreneurs in the west based on certain objective and prescribed criteria this is not so in the developing countries. Significant decisions and the availability of resources is dependent on basis other than objective. Time and again elites have been able to obtain scarce resources and plunder financial institutions. Institutional weaknesses, the fact that elites at the top work to each others mutual benefit, has an equally adverse effect on the small scale applicants who are then starved of economic resources.

Despite all this the informal sector does react and does manage to obtain scarce resources. As a response informal methodology is utilised for obtaining scarce resources from informal sources. One such was the savings in foreign exchange of the millions who had migrated to other countries. Religious injunctions were a hurdle for some entrepreneurs because of the concept of usury in Islam, yet for others this was not so. How did some entrepreneurs internalise Islamic tenets into the modern industrial sector.

Caste influences on development of entrepreneurs were considered in the context of bargaining, attitude to credit, knowledge of and information on markets and raw materials. As a result an indication of industrial pattern was obtained. It was found that the response of the agriculturalist, traders, artisans, status oriented, warrior, and immigrant castes was unique to their own ways of thinking and working. Similarly communities tended to have their own unique features. The Memons and Bohras unity, competitiveness, location policy and industrial pattern was unique to themselves and

quite apart from that of the punjabi castes. The
Pathans had their own strong points.

The central theme throughout has been to
consider the policy aspects on highly divergent
groups in developing countries. The formal and
informal sector play a vital role in entrepreneurial
response. To have a vibrant and successful
industrial policy, to help raise the level of
quality of the masses, to lift a nation out of
poverty there are no shortcuts. The path is a
difficult one, growth and development necessarily
slow. That is natures way. There are no forward
leaps, no quantum jumps. That is the reality which
faces countries like ours. Yet it is not an
impossible task. The mill will grind on but hopefully lessons of the past need be kept in mind if
only to have a better future.

I have tried to argue the case differently
then would normally be done in formal economic
logic. There will necessarily be some flaws in the
construction of the arguments. Any shortcomings
whether in the logic or in the argument, or where
a case is not convincingly stated are mine. There
will be many areas which would not be acceptable
to the strictly scholarly. They are requested to
accept it as another point of view and hopefully
worthy of further enquiry. These are areas
studiously avoided by economists as they are not
only unquantifiable but also very hazy. To meaning-
fully analyse developing countries more work in
this area will of necessity have to be carried out.

Chapter One

THE PAKISTAN ECONOMY

Pakistan was created in 1947 from the provinces
formerly part of India that had a Muslim majority,
namely Baluchistan, the Punjab, Sind, the
North-West Frontier Province and Bengal (1). In
economic terms it meant the break-up of a customs
union that had lasted for nearly three hundred
years. Agriculturally, the area was the granary
for an undivided India, and provided cotton and
jute for mills located in the industrial areas of
the sub-continent. Pakistan, an 'economic
monstrosity', had industrial assets worth only
Rs 580 million (approximately $112 million), of
which the Muslims had an insignificant share. The
political leaders of the new state therefore asked
Muslim industrialists in other parts of the world
to help to industrialise the country. The
Adamjees came from Burma, the Fancys from East
Africa and the Habib, Dawood and Bohra families,
who had been close associates of M.A. Jinnah, the
founder of the nation, came from Bombay.
     The desire for industrialisation was the
driving force. The country's leaders realised that
they could move out of an impasse and provide
employment for 6 million refugees (2) only through
accelerated industrialisation. Yet those refugees
could, at best, bring with them only artisan skills,
and most of them were, in fact, unskilled. The
lack of entrepreneurs and industrial investment
during this period is shown in Tables 1.1 and 1.2.
     The reasons for such a lack of entrepreneurs
can be traced to the mutiny of 1857, following
which the Muslims of India were completely
ostracised from public life (3) and relegated to
menial occupations.

1

Table 1.1: Comparison of Occupations of Entrepreneurs

Type of industry	Previous primary occupation		Previous secondary occupation		Father's occupation
	Proportion of industrialists	Present invest- ment	Proportion of industrialists	Present invest- ment	
Large and medium industries	17	16	4	30	8
Small industry and handicrafts	18	6	23	7	17
Traders/importers/ exporters	17	40	30	25	12
Traders/internal	28	29	39	24	34
Employers/ professionals	16	6	4	12	16
Agriculturalists	3	3	–	1	12

Source: G.F. Papanek, 'The Development of Entrepreneurship', in 'Entrepreneurship and Economic Development' ed. P.Kilby, New York, The Free Press, 1971.

Table 1.2: Industrial Establishments: India/
Pakistan 1947

	Total no. of factories	No. employed	Major estab.	No. employed
Pakistan	1,406	206,000	34	26,400
India	13,163	2,936,000	887	1,110,000

Source: A.L. Fritschier 'Industrialists and the
Government Process in Pakistan', unpublished PhD
dissertation, Syracuse University, 1965.

As the migration of populations was a two-way
phenomenon, the departure of non-Muslims from
manufacturing, trade and business activities left
a vacuum. This, then, was the background against
which the search for an entrepreneurial class was
made, strategies for development were created,
great incentives were offered and, despite an
awareness of social goals, inegalitarian policies
were tolerated and even encouraged (4). In a
far-ranging policy statement, the government made
it clear that it would limit its industrial
investment activities to production of arms and
ammunition, generation of hydroelectric power and
manufacture of railway wagons, telephone,
telegraphic and wireless equipment. Reliance on
private enterprise was confirmed when it was
stated that it is the desire of the Government of
Pakistan to associate individual initiative and
private enterprise at every stage of
industrialisation (5).
      Thus reliance on private sector investment to
complement that of the public sector was accepted
in principle, and in 1952 came the nation's first
public sector industries, mainly because the
private sector had failed in certain industrial
fields. The private sector had also failed to
invest sufficiently in East Pakistan. The
Government's intention was to rectify these
shortcomings and to allow ownership to pass to the
private sector, as was happening elsewhere in the
world. The social and egalitarian objectives were
to be fulfilled over a long period, the welfare
implications were considered to be inherent and
the time factor was either glossed over or not
considered to be essential.

In order to accelerate industrialisation the policy instruments used by the government consisted of an overvalued exchange rate, exchange and import controls (direct and indirect), compulsory procurement of food grains at prices below the market level for industrial labour, a low level of direct taxation and a very heavy indirect taxation. During the 1950s and 1960s this policy produced rapid industrialisation at an exorbitant cost to the agricultural sector, where growth stagnated. In the 1960s an effort was made to improve the situation in this sector by an increased inflow of aid. The support price for agricultural products was increased, though they remained below market prices.

In the 1970s some of these economic incentives were removed either partially or completely. For instance, the overvalued exchange rate of the 1950s and 1960s disappeared as the currency was devalued by 131 per cent: the value of dollar immediately more than doubled. A revaluation of the major world currencies coincided with this devaluation, so in fact the revision was really 161 per cent. The response of industrialists in the public and private sectors differed. The private sector took liquid capital out of Pakistan and invested in other Third World countries, notably the UAE, as well as in East Africa, Ireland and Canada. Those in the public sector saw their foreign loan commitments more than doubled, and the repayments of these extra loans were passed on in full to small entrepreneurs.

Review of the Economy

Pakistan's growth rate for the 1950s, 1960s and 1970s indicates a great emphasis on development (Table 1.3). The period of accelerated growth came in the 1960s, with an average annual rate of 6.78 per cent. Growth in the 1950s was significant in industry, when it averaged approximately 20 per cent in the first five years of that decade, declining to only 2.75 per cent for 1959-60. Agriculture was the weak sector in the 1950s, and averaged a growth rate of 1.77 per cent. In the 1960s it reached 5.2 per cent, the highest for the three decades under consideration. In the 1950s per capita income increased by only 0.88 per cent, whereas in the 1970s it dropped to 1.52 per cent from the 3.82 per cent of the 1960s. Weather conditions, as well as movements of population, played an exceptionally large part in these growth rates.

4

The Pakistan Economy

In the 1970s there were two severe floods and one
drought, as well as an earthquake in the northern
region. In a country where industry is so heavily
based on agriculture it is only natural that weather
conditions would be so critical for growth rates.

Table 1.3: National Income and Per Capita Growth
Rates.

Year	Annual average Pakistan GNP	Per capita GNP (% per annum)
1950-1 to 1959-60	3.31	0.88
1960-1 to 1969-70	6.78	3.82
1970-1 to 1979-80	4.51	1.58

The significance of the decline in growth in
the 1970s needs to be explained in greater detail.
Besides weather conditions there was a reversal of
policies in as much as the earlier incentives to
industrialists were no longer available. The public
sector also suffered from the political instability
of the late 1960s and early 1970s, when there was
a civil war which led to the creation of Bangladesh.
No compensation was paid to industrialists, who
were mostly from West Pakistan, for the assets thus
lost. Another period of instability followed,
during which the environment was hardly conducive
to investment in the industrial sector.

The Structure of the GDP
Table 1.4 shows the growth rates for agriculture
and industry during this period. In the first
half of the 1950s industry progressed rapidly,
mainly because it started from a low base-line. Its
growth rate in the 1960s was also substantial but
there was a gradual shift in favour of the
utilities and services sector. Industrial growth
was mostly in consumer goods and the relatively
simpler processing industries. During the 1970s it
would be fair to say that there was an attempt to
create a substantial base of heavy industry with
resultant long gestation periods. As far as the
structural change in the GDP was concerned the
services sector showed a consistently rapid increase
in banking, insurance, shipping and air travel.
The growth of the construction industry was
primarily due to urbanisation and high-cost luxury

housing.

Savings

The Pakistan economy has always been dependent on an influx of foreign capital in order to finance

Table 1.4: Structural Change in GDP

	1949-50	1959-60	1969-70	1976-77
Agriculture	53.2	45.8	38.9	34.8
Manufacturing and quarrying	8.0	12.4	16.5	15.0
Construction	1.4	2.5	4.2	5.2
Utilities and services	37.4	39.3	40.4	45.0

Source: Survey of Pakistan 1976-7.

not only the excess of investment over domestic savings but also to ensure the availability of foreign exchange. The nature of this inflow has changed from grants in the 1950s to grants-cum-loans in the 1960s and finally to loans in the 1970s. Substantial aid at crucial times in the country's economy also came in a variety of forms from the Middle East countries. Currently Pakistan is aided by a rising volume of remittances from its work-force abroad in addition to domestic savings from the private sectors (household and corporate sectors) and public sectors (government). Recent trends in savings are shown in Table 1.5.

On average, private savings stabilised around 9 per cent, while public savings were negative during the first half of the 1970s, probably indicating the large expenditure incurred by the civil war. The stagnant savings in the private sector is explained in terms of 'greater consumption levels induced by foreign remittances, industrial stagnation, a service oriented GNP structure, rising imports and smuggling of luxuries, not to speak of the two-digit inflation rate' (6).

Although tax revenue at current prices rose from Rs 5,645 million in 1969-70 to Rs 29,567 million in 1978-9, indicating a growth rate of 20 per cent, the net effect on savings was negligible because of a corresponding increase in non-development expenditure attributed to greater allocations to 'defence, debt servicing, subsidies, general administration and socio-economic services (7).

Table 1.5: Private and Public Saving as Percentages
of GNP (Current Prices)

Year	Private savings	Public savings
1969-70	8.0	0.9
1970-1	7.8	0.7
1971-2	10.0	0.3
1972-3	11.4	0.5
1973-4	7.2	0.1
1974-5	6.4	0.6
1975-6	9.2	0.8
1976-7	8.7	2.4
1977-8	11.5	1.8
1978-9	9.4	1.4

Source: Planning Division, Government of Pakistan,
Islamabad.

Investment
Prior to planned development from 1955 onwards the
investment ratio was lower than 5 per cent. This
increased sharply during the late 1950s and was
financed by South Korea's rapid economic development
and by the inflow of capital from Muslim communities
residing in former British East Africa. Subsequently
the large profits made by the mercantile communities
as a result of generous incentives offered by the
government were reinvested. The combined effects of
public sector and private sector investment,
financed by an inflow of grants and loans from
consortium countries, tended to accelerate
investment (Table 1.6).

In 1964-5 this investment ratio reached 21.9
per cent but then the first Indo Pakistan War broke
out and finance was diverted towards defence
expenditure. Thereafter the decline in investment
was to continue. At this time came the first
concentrations of wealth and the rising discontent
caused by regional disparities between Pakistan's
East and West Wings. Expenditure was shifted to
the public sector, and for the first time the
'parity principal' (8) appeared in economic
thinking. This, as we know, did not stem the civil
war, the final out-come of which led to the loss of
industrial assets owned by entrepreneurs from the

7

Table 1.6: Ratio of Investment to GNP 1964-78 (million rupees)

Year	Private investment	Public investment	Total fixed investment		Ratio of investment at current prices (%)	
			Current prices	Constant 1959-60	GNP at current factor cost	GNP at market prices from 1969-70 to 1977-8
1964-5	3,200	2,531	5,731	5,351	21.9	–
1965-6	2,985	5,099	4,438	4,438	17.6	–
1966-7	3,133	2,351	5,484	4,469	16.8	–
1967-8	3,137	2,296	5,433	4,163	15.3	–
1968-9	2,981	2,360	5,341	3,862	14.1	–
1969-70	3,493	3,321	6,814	4,667	15.7	13.3
1970-1	3,531	3,514	7,045	4,041	15.5	14.0
1971-2	3,546	3,267	6,813	4,256	13.9	12.6
1972-3	3,726	3,920	7,646	4,279	12.6	11.4
1973-4	3,840	6,774	10,614	4,680	13.2	12.2
1974-5	5,208	11,010	16,218	4,704	15.5	14.4
1975-6	6,484	16,287	22,771	6,163	18.6	17.1
1976-7	7,780	18,897	26,677	6,662	19.3	17.6
1977-8(P)	8,802	20,924	29,726	6,966	18.2	16.5

Source: GOP Annual Survey 1978-9, Finance Division, Islamabad, 1979.

West Wing with no compensation by the government.
In addition, nationalisation followed between 1972
and 1977, which initially meant no compensation and
then deferred payments of compensation in the form
of bonds (at first non-marketable) carrying lower
than market interest rates. This was not conducive
to investment by entrepreneurs. The exchange rate
was also subjected to the massive devaluation
already mentioned. Raids by the internal revenue
department were conducted for tax evasion, in which
the informants generally were the political
supporters of the party then in power (9). The gross
investment ratio in 1972-3 dropped to 11.4 per cent.
This was also the watershed for a shift from private
to public investment (Table 1.7). The major shift
in the public sector industries was in heavy
industry, which India had so successfully launched
in the 1950s. Investment was, however, affected
by the fact that nearly 75 per cent of the programme
was concentrated on capital-intensive, long-gesta-
tion projects, and this created only a moderate
growth rate.
     The consequence of declining trends in saving
and the long-term nature of investment led to an
increased dependence by the economy on an influx
of foreign resources. The financing of investment
by domestic savings accounted for less than half
of the gross domestic investment in the year
1974-8. (Table 1.7). However, the overall effect

Table 1.7: Financing of Investment (Percentage of
GDP at Current Market Prices)

	1974-5	1975-7	1976-7	1977-8
Gross domestic investment	16.4	17.5	18.9	18.2
Domestic savings	4.7	8.7	8.9	8.6
External resource inflow	11.7	8.8	10.0	9.6

Source: Planning Commission, Government of Pakistan,
Islamabad.

of various inflationary economic policies led to
a decline in investment in real terms. At constant
1970 prices the ratio of investment to GDP declined
again to about 12 per cent in 1977-8 (10).

Balance of Payments

Much of the controversy on the balance of payments
and influx of aid centres around the arguments
concerning low price-elasticity of the supply and
demand for primary products. Prior to the civil
war Pakistan was dependent on jute and cotton, but
after 1972-3 there was a move towards cotton and
rice and, to an ever-increasing degree, on
manufactured goods. The export share of value-added
goods has increased in recent years, especially
since 1977-8, but the current account deficit and
repayment of loans have always been met by
remittances from its workforce abroad. These are
now in the region of $2 billion (11) per annum.

Table 1.8 shows the post-civil war data on the
balance of payments. As investment and terms of
trade were adjusted, the requirement for aid tended
to increase as also did the balance of payments
deficit, despite stringent licensing procedures.
The terms of trade also declined as a result of a
steep increase in oil prices accompanied by rises
in the prices of fertiliser, food grains and
machinery, while exports were affected by cyclical
fluctuations and changes in government policies in
importing countries.

Exports were also affected by the failure of
domestic agriculture to maintain a favourable growth
rate, and thus stagnated to around $1.1 million.
On the other hand, Pakistan's rapid industrialisation increased the import of capital goods and raw
materials. The deficit in the balance of payments
was adversely affected by the insistence on the
speedy implementation of capital-intensive
industrial projects. The reality is that Pakistan's
imports continue to be significantly higher than
its exports. The trade gap in 1980 was $2.5 billion
(12) and this was bridged by a combination of loans
and workers' remittances. The latter have resulted
from the rise in the price of oil from the Middle
East, and this may only be a short-term factor in
alleviating the strain on the balance of payments.
Some indirect effects need to be considered to
determine the full impact on the economy. These
remittances do change consumption patterns and
deplete the country's human resources. A preliminary study on the domestic expenditure pattern of
workers' remittances is shown in Table 1.10, and
indicates that only 14.5 per cent of the total
expenditure is in productive channels.

Another survey (13) of 1,150 households
indicates that skilled and professional workers

Table 1.8: Balance of Payments ($ million)

		1972-3	1973-4	1974-5	1975-6	1976-7	1977-8(prov.)
(A)	MERCHANDISE BALANCE	-124	-473	-1,136	-977	-1,286	-1,464
	Imports (FOB)	891	1,493	2,114	2,139	2,418	2,751
	Exports (FOB)	767	1,020	978	1,162	1,132	1,287
(B)	CURRENT INVISIBLES	-7	-76	-51	+30	+235	+863
	Payments	305	445	567	621	661	798
	Freight and insurance	82	154	208	201	229	290
	Interest (a)	92	92	117	157	181	197
	Others	131	199	242	263	251	311
	Receipts	298	369	516	651	896	1,661
	Home remittances	136	139	216	339	578	1,153
	Others	162	230	300	312	318	508
(C)	TOTAL CURRENT ACCOUNT	-131	-549	-1,187	-947	-1,051	-601
(D)	CAPITAL ACCOUNT	+131	+549	+1,187	+947	+1,051	+601
	Gross capital inflow	387	607	1,422	1,354	1,106	1,052
	Payments (b)	-108	-118	-152	-280	-239	-287
	Change in reserves	-148	+60	-83	-127	+184	-164(c)

Notes: a. Include interest payments in addition to debt servicing on foreign assistance.
   b. Includes retirement of loans of less than one year's maturity and other capital payments as well as debt repayment.
   c. Denotes drawdown.
Source: Planning Commission, Government of Pakistan, Islamabad.

Table 1.9: Terms of Trade and Price Indices of
Imports and Exports 1973-8 (1969-70 = 100)

	Terms of trade	Exports	Imports
1972-3	96	273	285
1973-4	106	439	413
1974-5	67	410	615
1975-6	71	411	583
1976-7	83	489	585
1977-8	81	509	628

Source: Key Economic Indicators, Government of
Pakistan, Islamabad. (Figures are rounded).

Table 1.10: Domestic Expenditure Pattern of Workers'
Remittances (%)

Consumption		62.6
Investment		37.4
Real estate	22.9	
Own business	8.3	
Agricultural machinery	3.8	
Savings scheme	1.5	
Industrial schemes	0.7	
Transport	0.2	

Source: Pakistan Institute of Development Economics,
Islamabad.

form the bulk of the migrants to the Middle East.
The initial results show that 42.5 per cent of the
total migrants are classified as unskilled. The
nature of this migration has contributed to
inefficiency in the manufacturing sector, resulting
in reduced exports. The response by industrialists
has been in terms of the substituting of labour by
capital and an increase in capital-intensive
projects in all subsequent investment(14). This
trend may be difficult to reverse and may have
adverse consequences in the long run when the
migrants return.

Influx of Aid
Table 1.11 shows the aid (grants-cum-loan) that
Pakistan has received from the consortium countries.
To this may be added the current IMF (15) extended

12

Table 1.11: Grants and Loans

Year	Pre-1st Plan	1st Plan 1955–60	2nd Plan 1960–65	3rd Plan 1965–70	1970–5	1975–80 (July – March)
Grants	215.6	578.2	1,105.2	703.97	375.4	799.4
Loans	121.2	96.6	1,806.2	2,233.1	3,570.1	4,925.6
Total	336.8	674.8	2,911.4	2,937.07	3,945.5	5,725.0

Source: Economic Survey 1979–80, Government of Pakistan, Islamabad.

credit facility of $1.73 billion, unprecedented in Pakistan's economic history (the loan must be repaid within three years). The value of this loan depends on whether it is productively channelled or is frittered away, and much depends on whether Pakistan has learnt from its past experience. Since this aid is to be used entirely in the industrial sector for the import of raw materials for consumer, intermediate and capital goods, the nature of the import-substitution policies that are followed will be crucial to the country. The support from the IMF is conditional on private enterprise being allowed more incentives and on the liberalisation of import policies.

Pakistan, in the analysis of John H. Power,(16) has already suffered from the rapid increase in the share of income originating in manufacturing. Power blames, the nature of import-substitution especially the replacement of imported consumer goods, for this failure. The policies adopted did not take into account the relative merits of various overseas industries based on comparative advantage, economies of scale, external economies, etc., and he questions '... industrialisation heavily oriented towards production for domestic consumption, some of which could hardly be called essential for economic development'.

Notes

1. The country was conceived as having two separate wings, East & West Pakistan, separated by about a thousand miles of mainland India. Of the five provinces, two, i.e. the Punjab and Bengal, were divided between India and Pakistan, the Muslim majority areas in these provinces forming part of Pakistan and the Hindu majority areas becoming parts of India.
2. A. Gledhill, Pakistan (Stevens, London, 1957), p.26.
3. Ibid.
4. Ibid.
5. M.A. Jinnah, speech to the Chamber of Commerce Industry, Karachi, 27 April, 1948.
6. H. Naqvi, The State of Pakistan's Economy (Pakistan Institute of Development Economics, 1978) pp. 20-1.
7. Ibid, pp. 25-6.
8. The parity principle was conceded by the federal government on the demand by East Pakistan that expenditure should be in proportion to

population. This was not actually conceded, but the quantum of investment in the two wings was made on a basis of equal shares.

9. The Pakistan Peoples' Party drew its support from the masses.

10. World Bank estimates cited in IBRD Report No.2394, 12 April 1979.

11. D. Dodwell, 'The IMF Gives Pakistan a Fighting Chance', Financial Times, November 1980.

12. Ibid.

13. Preliminary findings of World Bank funded project supervised by the Pakistan Institute of Development Economics, Islamabad.

14. The labour-capital shift is visible at the Dawood concerns in Karachi and Lawrencepur, which is said to be of the order of 50%.

15. D. Dodwell, 'The IMF Gives Pakistan a Fighting Chance'.

16. J.H. Power, "Industrialisation in Pakistan. A Case of Frustrated Take-off? 'Pakistan Development Review, Vol.III, No.2 (Summer 1963).

Chapter Two

INDUSTRIALISATION: IMPERATIVES AND CONTRADICTIONS

An emphasis on industrialisation in an underdeveloped economy is understandable and a nation's
hopes and aspirations are indicated in its stated
objectives. Failure to achieve these objectives
and the consequences arising out of their non-
realisation have led to severe social strains in
many countries and in some cases have been
responsible for separatist movements and wars of
independence. In the case of Pakistan, denial
of economic rights to the majority population of
East Pakistan meant that secessionist movements
were given an impetus. Policies that furthered
this denial of rights were upheld as proof of
exploitation and lent to a feeling of hopelessness,
eventually culminating in an independent country.
Since the engine of Pakistan's growth was
industrialisation, we will examine how the various
debates on the issues were identified and resolved.

Choice of Scale (Large versus Small)
Given the relatively small industrial base in 1947
already indicated in terms of assets at Rs 580
million ($112 million), the industrialisation
effort had to be increased and speed was to be of
the essence. What was to be the basis for an
accelerated industrialisation? A few large
enterprises or a number of smaller ones? A number
of smaller enterprises required a level of
knowledge and expertise technical, managerial or
organisational across the country, and the chances
of such knowledge were extremely small given the
social upheavel of the time. The movement of
population across the new frontiers meant that the
initial motivation of the majority of people was
one of survival: existence was day-to-day. The
only people for whom such an existence was not a

16

requirement was the merchant class, and conditions
were conducive for their entry into trade when
import restrictions removed trading profits (1).
The motivating force of these entrepreneurs seemed
to be large profits, made possible by the nature
of government regulations, the inability of the
administration to police these regulations, and,
in the 1960s, by the immense economic power and
influence that was wielded by these individual
industrial groups (2).
    What of small industries? These first found
official recognition in the Second Five-Year Plan
(1960-5) in which the state provided infrastructural
facilities. Despite these assertions, the Fifth
Five-Year Plan (FFYP)(3) indicated that small-scale
industry had been neglected and no effort had been
made to realise its potential. A survey as far
back as 1971-2 indicated that 80 per cent of the
labour force was employed in the small industry
sector. In terms of export earnings the performance,
despite government indifference, has been equally
impressive (Table 2.1). The FFYP(4) accepted that

Table 2.1: Exports by Small-scale Industries

Items	1974-5	1975-6	1976-7
Carpets	527.10	776.10	980.30
Handicrafts	114.00	100.68	90.68
Sports goods	209.10	100.70	223.85
Surgical instruments	130.60	131.30	133.82
Leather products	104.00	131.30	155.20
Clothing (Readymade)	198.80	383.10	417.79
Total	1,280.60	1,623.18	2,001.64
Large sector export (mainly cotton, yarn and cloth)	2,224.0	2,822.0	2,823.0
Small sector export as percentage of large sector	57.5	57.5	71.0

this sector had operated outside the industrial
sector and therefore outside government patronage.
A recent World Bank study(5) analysed the small-
industry sector and recommended its promotion for

the following reasons:
(1) To serve basic local demand at accessible prices
(low overheads and transportation costs).
(2) To employ various types and qualifications of
labour.
(3) To contribute to a regional distribution of
income.
(4) To contribute to a personal distribution of
income.
Despite clear indications of benefits that would
accrue from such a policy, Pakistan has instead
consistently followed a course of providing
excessive benefits to entrepreneurs who could
influence decisions and policy-making (6).

Choice of Industry (Labour versus Capital-intensive)

Pakistan suffers from the same problems in choice
of technique as all other less developed countries.
The reasons for the lack of discussion in Pakistan
on whether to invest in capital-intensive or
labour-intensive industries can be linked to the
country's decision-making process, whose procedures
are cumbersome and time-consuming (7). At the
initial stages of industrialisation, Pakistan opted
for simple processing industries, and, even for this,
technical support was hired from abroad. Given the
overvalued exchange rate and the nature of the
government's policies, there was a tendency to
invest in capital-intensive projects. A recent
survey has indicated that creation of one job could
cost Rs 30,000 ($3,000). In certain industries
the cost could be much higher, as this survey
includes data for some industries which may be
classified as extremely labour-intensive.

The requirement for an 'optimal' decision in
industrialisation are that the range of technologies
are known to (1) the investor, (2) the various
agencies and (3) the ultimate decision makers.
However, current delays in project-examination and
approval are such that the machinery may be obsolete
even before it is installed.

Given Pakistan's shortage of capital and
corresponding abundance of labour, what techniques
need to be employed for her development? Much of
the argument here is coloured by the choice between
economic dependence or economic independence. The
Sen arguments of investible surplus (8) and the Dobb
thesis of growth potential (9) are dependent on the
quality, quantity and availability of other factors
of production in the economy.

In Pakistan, market prices of the factors of

production continue to be distorted by the governments' decisions in the fields of monetary and
labour policies. The result is a preoccupation
with large profits which are not socially optimal
(10). The initial investors in Pakistan were from
the merchant class, who had no technological
expertise and who were attracted by those industries
that posed the least technological problems. This
meant the transfer of advanced, capital-intensive
technology from the developed countries to Pakistan,
with maintenance and other technical skills also
being hired. Such a decision was in keeping with
the Government's cost-plus pricing policies, with
the consumer paying for the co-ordination and hiring.
This also meant that products of capital-intensive
industries, though profitable in home markets, would
not be competitive in world markets. Despite
Pakistan's comparative advantage in the cotton
textile sector, export subsidies are currently
provided to ensure competitiveness in world markets.
An alternative view was that once modern
technology had been transferred to a less developed
country, that country could maintain and develop
the skills required by that technology. However,
this argument was defeated by the lack of development of expertise and skills at the appropriate
level and the undertaking of R&D by enterprises,
either singly or jointly, or under the supervision
of the government. The optimism of this argument
rested substantially on the success of Japanese
industry, but the substantial differences in the
economic environments of Japan and Pakistan were
often ignored. In the latter the choice of
techniques and the range of products were determined
by a given 'sectoral emphasis'.
Since capital was always in short supply, the
nature of the aid available in Pakistan also played
a significant part. Most of this investment was
tied either by geographical factors or by industrial
requirements. Thus, even if the investor had access
to a wide range of technical expertise, he very
frequently had to accept what was available within
the limits of official policy. The cost factor
varied with the range of technologies available.
These, in turn, were dependent on the number of
countries supplying aid. To minimise costs, the
entrepreneur was forced to cultivate connections
with the administration not only to obtain the
latest technology but also to site his factories
near markets and in areas where skilled labour was
available. Thus, given these kinds of barriers to

entry and competition, the amount of the entrepreneur's profit was dependent on the administrative decision-making process.

The justification for capital-intensive projects, the profits from them and the consequent reinvestment of these profits into other projects was advocated by, amongst others, Galenson and Leibenstein (11). Their thesis that profits generated from capital-intensive projects were higher than those from labour-intensive industries has since been refuted by empirical research (12). It has been shown that a higher rate of saving is not necessarily associated with high capital-intensity. To take the argument further, capital-intensity is generally associated with large-scale production. In underdeveloped countries, given the differing natures of markets, the underdeveloped distributional channels, the industrial relations' policies, the weakness in managerial ability, and the particular social milieu, any concentration in capital-intensive projects is bound to be inefficient and costly. Scarce capital is thus wasted and is made more scarce (13). A recent study of textile mills in Pakistan was carried out by the Industrial Development Bank of Pakistan. The recommendations state that (1) to be the owner is not a prerequisite to be the manager; (2) the mill manager should recognise the importance of professional management and should try to learn modern management techniques; (3) cost accounting, personnel management, production management and financial management must be learnt by mill owners (14). In short, Pakistan was still a long way from cost-effective management despite its thirty years of experience in the textile industry.

In addition, when run below capacity advanced technologies can have catastrophic results. For instance, at the moment approximately 40 per cent of the modern textile industry in Pakistan is not in operation. Another aspect, seldom mentioned, is that simple local production techniques may have provided subsistence incomes for many people throughout the country. With the advent of modern techniques local industries may have been completely ruined by their inability to compete in quality as well as in price (15). Besides the acquisition of inappropriate technologies (16) Pakistan has also acquired a considerable amount of inappropriate consumer durables due to a preoccupation with improving building materials for luxury housing (tiles, cement, etc.).

Industrialisation : Imperatives and contradictions

Yet it is conceded that, under certain
conditions, capital-intensive technologies may well
be appropriate due to the linkage affects that such
industries may have, i.e. if machines and basic
materials for the capital-intensive industry were
developed within the country instead of being
imported if the products of the capital-intensive
sector did not displace those of the labour-intensive
sector, and if employment was created in other
areas. Further, the incomes thus generated could
be reinvested locally rather than transferred
abroad (17). A flight of capital or transfer of
property incomes overseas generally takes place
when there is political and economic uncertainty
in a country, and no-one can control the movement
of this form of capital. If the country's house was
in order, this flight of capital would be checked.
The debate on the nature of technology that the
country requires will continue, and Pakistan must
seek the answers after consideration of all the
issues involved.

Public Enterprise Versus Private Enterprise
Since its inception in 1947 Pakistan came out
strongly in favour of private enterprise with a
limited amount of public enterprise (18). In the
1950s, however, the government realised that in
certain sectors private enterpreneurs were not
investing, and, to rectify the structural imbalance,
enterprises were created in the public sector.
These were planned to complement the private sector
and, if successful, were to be sold to the private
sector (19). In 1962 the East and West Pakistan
Industrial Development Corporations were created
both being independent of each other. The objective,
obviously, was to ensure that industrial projects
were also located in East Pakistan and that the
East Wing did not suffer by default. Until 1962,
and even subsequently, industrial investment in the
East Wing was low. By 1962 this situation had
improved slightly, but there was a complete reversal
of policy in 1972-3, when the West Pakistan
Industrial Development Corporation followed Italy's
ENI example (the East Wing of Pakistan had become
Bangladesh). It was hoped that there would be
improved co-ordination and economic management
between the two Wings, but in 1972-3 there were two
further nationalisations in the commodities sector.
The first was the Economic Reforms Order 1972, by
which a political vendetta was satisfied and
thirty-two large industrial concerns were nationalised.

21

Since only the management of the companies was
affected, there was no question of compensation,
although this was later given in the form of bonds
(redeemable in 15 years) under a very restrictive
method of determining the net worth of each
enterprise. Market price evaluation was ignored
and in some cases the net worth of some of the
companies was judged to be negative (depending,
of course, on their liabilities and cost structure).
The second Order passed in 1973 concerned the
edible-oil sector, under which vegetable ghee mills,
which supplied the entire country, were taken over.
The same procedure for determining the net worth
of the mills was followed. The third wave of
nationalisation in 1976, which was much more
drastic, came in the commodity-processing sector,
i.e. in grain milling, rice-husking and
cotton-ginning. This was a movement into a sector
controlled by indigenous entrepreneurs.
     This process of nationalisation came to an
end in 1977 when there was a military coup.
Uncertainty to a very high degree was created
amongst the entrepreneurs while the feeling amongst
the smallest of them was one of fear. To create
stability in the minds of the industrialists the
commodity-processing sector was denationalised, and
this was followed by a strict demarcation of
industrial activities between the public and private
sectors. Under this delineation, basic heavy
chemicals were open for development in the private
sector (although there were some such enterprises
in the public sector). To give further security to
industrialists an ordinance known as the 'Protection
of Rights in Industrial Property Order 1979' was
promulgated. In a period of thirty years the
country had gone full-circle so far as the
objectives of the public sector were concerned.
During this era of nationalisation the government
followed the Mahanlobhis model by investment in
basic heavy industry, which was capital-intensive
and had long gestation periods. The total
investment in the two sectors at current prices
is shown in Table 2.2. The comparison of current
prices in terms of the ratio of public to private
enterprise gives an indication of the emphasis on
public enterprise, i.e. from 1969-70 to 1979-80
the investment in the public sector increased
approximately nineteen-fold.

Table 2.2: Industrial Investment (Current Prices) (million rupees)

Year	Private sector			Public sector (4)	(4) as ratio of (3)
	Large (1)	Small (2)	Total ((1)+(2)) (3)	(4)	
1969–70	1,208	188	1,396	179	0.13
1970–1	1,224	202	1,426	68	0.05
1971–2	1,016	219	1,235	99	0.08
1972–3	763a	256	1,019	111	0.11
1973–4	697a	326	1,022	382	0.37
1974–5	990a	447	1,437	1,065	0.74
1975–6	1,309a	510	1,819	3,181	1.75
1976–7	1,526	585	2,111	4,514	2.14
1977–8	1,539	635	2,173	6,143	2.83
1978–9	1,638	698	2,336	6,647	2.85
1979–80	1,823	789	2,612	6,316	2.42

Note: a. Slightly modified.
Source: Economic Survey 1979–80.

Industrialisation: Imperatives and contradictions

The rationale most often put forward in defence of public enterprises is generally in terms of greater efficiency in resource allocation. Yet decisions are generally hampered by lack of information. A notable example of inefficiency in allocation is the Pakistan Steel Mill, located about forty miles from Karachi. Private entrepreneurs were willing to enter this sector and in fact two of the leading companies had applied for licences as early as the 1960s. One of them had even sent its employees on a course in industrial metallurgy at Sheffield University (20). One company already had a steel mill, providing special steel, which had been nationalised by the Economic Reforms Order, 1972. What, one might ask, were the choices before the country when the decision was made. There were two other areas where iron ore and other non-ferrous requirements could be fulfilled, at Kalabagh and at Baluchistan. The choice was between the two sites, with Chinese and German technical help available at each but using mainly indigenous raw material. The third site, selected in the mid-1970s, was at Karachi, where the original cost was over $2 billion. The three technologies involved in the decision-making process were German, Chinese and Russian. The cost structure of the projects based on German and Chinese technology was at least 40 per cent less than the Russian project, while there were considerable savings elsewhere (21) not to mention the creation of a project based substantially on imported materials as against one based on local raw materials.

The reasons given for denying the private sector from investing were (22) :

(1) Iron and steel were the basic items of importance for the industrial development of the country;

(2) The steel projects required substantial capital investment which was beyond the financial means of private investors;

(3) Both the private sector organisations earlier entrusted with the responsibility of preparing project reports for the steel mills project contemplated heavy reliance on public funds for their financing;

(4) Foreign exchange financing would be more readily available if required by the government.

It is not difficult to see how the decision was made and the lame economic reasons put forward by the government. What in fact, did happen was that at this time there was a public protest on a concentration of economic power in the hands of twenty-two families.

A significant amount of 'socialist' thought could be seen in the decision-making process. In fact, the Economic Reforms Order, 1972 was a result of a trend towards public ownership of the means of production. The reasoning behind this thinking was that, given their profit-maximising attitudes and abilities, private sector monopolies were difficult to handle in Pakistan, and that argument for market economies in developed countries really do not apply to that country, where all costs would be passed on to the consumers. As decision-making in the public or the private sector is difficult, there would be reasonable justification for pressure by the government to improve competition in the marketplace. In reality, however, competitive policies are impossible to implement, as the gap between market efficiency and inefficiency is too large. Raising the point of governmental pressure underlines the superiority of administrative decisions over the combined strength of the entrepreneurs. This administrative power is real, and forces the entrepreneurs to seek protection by the country's authorities.

Another argument put forward against an enlarged public sector is that it would be considered by those in power as a source of employment for their followers. The resultant inefficiencies would also be passed onto consumers in the form of costs. There is no other reason for not denationalising the other sectors of the economy by the present government (23). The balance really lies in trying to determine the best corrective device for the transaction costs of limited or no competition against those incurred by a sluggish and occasionally corrupt administrative intervention.

Industrial Efficiency

The basic rules of economic analysis developed over centuries in a different cultural and social milieu were offered for improving Pakistan's efforts at achieving industrialisation. Competitive national markets did not exist and international markets, with their growing custom unions and non-tariff barriers, imposed further limitations. Given the state of Pakistan's industry at the time of her independence, a protective system for her infant industries had to be devised. The cumulative effect, however, of the incentives provided and the

25

protective tariffs meant that there was an
inefficient utilisation of scarce/resources.

Basic Industry Versus Consumer Industry. Of the two
approaches to industrialisation, i.e. the capital
goods industry or consumer good industry, India
adopted the former, following what is now known as
the Mahanlobhis model to, 'construct machines to
make machines'. Pakistan's options were limited
and followed a strategy based on producing consumer
goods, as those industries were relatively less
capital-intensive. However, the amount of capital
required could be influenced by the choice of
technology involved. The choice of industry in the
consumer sector was important if the Hirschman (24)
linkage effect or the Nurkse (25) effect was
considered. By the late 1960s, the pendulum had
swung towards export-orientated industries. In the
1970s Pakistan changed to the capital goods industry
in the public rather than in the private sector
and around 1975-6 placed an emphasis on export-
orientated industries. The strain on the balance
of payments had, of course, been noticeable since
the end of the Korean War in 1953, but instead of
solving this problem by choice of industry, the
measures adopted were direct controls on items that
were important for foreign exchange. Intially the
concentration on export-orientated industries was
mainly due to the built-in overcapacity in textiles,
and yarn, rather than raw cotton, was exported.
Pakistan further lost a sizeable home market after
the creation of Bangladesh so that survival for
single spinning units was possible only through
export earnings. Thus cotton yarn and cloth
exports earned $222 million in 1974-5, $282.5
million in 1975-6 and $282.3 million in 1976-7.
Ranis (26) found that in 1961 the most efficient
sector was that with companies employing upto nine
workers, but in a subsequent comparison in 1975-6
this moved to companies employing between 50 and
99 workers, indicating that over time productivity
had moved to the medium scale. The higest capital
output ratio was located in the large sector but
for 1975-6 this remained in the medium scale
(50-99 workers), indicating the probable adoption
by this sector of effective technology.
    It was also noticeable that capital-intensity
increased with scale of operation and was more
pronounced in light engineering than in the textile
sector. Up to a point it was also obvious that as
capital-intensity increased, so did labour

productivity. Ranis has explained these imperfections on the basis of inefficiencies in the labour
market.

Appropriate Technology

The strategy of rapid industrialisation followed by
Pakistan did not consider the adaptation of complex
technology to local conditions. It was felt that
the use of modern technology would lead to a
technological 'jump', and would enable Pakistan to
come level with developed countries. In fact, as
far as labour skills were concerned, this created
a wage differential effect resulting in the
inability of urban centres to cope with rural-urban
migration.

Although decisions at the macro level may be
necessary, the impact of such technology at the
micro level must be analysed, and here the arguments
centre on the choice of technique versus the choice
of product (27). In this area there are three
crucial questions:
(1) To what extent are there alternative technologies
which can mix capital, land, skills and labour in
different proportions to achieve the desired
products?
(2) What are the financial returns on these
technologies?
(3) Do the prices attached to the factors of
production actually reflect their relative scarcity
in an economy?
The first priority in Pakistan, and in other less
developed countries, is invariably with industries
supplying the country's basic needs. Two such
industries on which there is controversy on the
appropriate technology are the grain-processing
and the sugar-manufacturing industries. The
technology in the wheat-milling industry in urban
areas consists of modern pneumatic machinery and
the indigenous elevator industry, and in the rural
areas the Chakki type of machine (28). The intermediate industry in such a case would be indigenous
elevators, incorporating the best of both technologies. To the extent that it is modern, this
includes the cleaning and grinding process of
modern pneumatic machinery, and the grinding is
done by roller bodies (29). The cost element between
the intermediate elevator mill and the modern
pneumatic mill is in the ratio of 1:10, (30) whereas
the indigenous stone crushing (horizontal rollers)
system is extremely cheap, though it has no
integrated cleaning process. The end-product of

27

the modern machines is very fine flour (which, according to modern research, has definite adverse medical effects), while that from the elevator flour mills is coarser, or medium to coarse (depending on the number of roller bodies installed). The flour from the indigenous horizontal roller bodies is coarse as it has all the bran in it, there is no separation of bran and flour to make it look white and fine.

In terms of nourishment value today the white, fine flour from the pneumatic mills must be reinforced artificially by vitamins (these are added during the production process to compensate for vitamins lost through cleaning, the separation of bran and flour, or excessive generation of heat). The maximum nourishment value is found in the flour made by the horizontal roller bodies, which does not require vitamins to be added.

The utilisation of ancillary machinery is also different. Modern pneumatic machinery requires sophisticated starting gears and electrical motors, while in the elevator type a single electric motor is needed to take the grain to the top of the machine: the remaining process uses gravity. In the indigenous industry labour is used only for loading the funnel: again, the remaining process uses gravity. In short, intermediate technology is a blend of modern and indigenous, with the processing and other critical factors adapted to local needs. The end-product, too, is a happy medium. Further, the cost factor is a great advantage of intermediate technology, and spin-off from the indigenous capital goods sector could mean the development of local industry. The employment factors are roughly the same for intermediate and indigenous industries and there is a saving of foreign exchange by using locally manufactured machinery. Imported machinery has different specifications, leading to the need for a large inventory of spare parts.

Sen's examples of 'Charka' and the handloom is another example of needs being met in areas where the distribution of modern products is not possible because the markets are either limited or are non-existent.

Similarly, in the sugar industry there is the choice of importing large units with a capacity of 2000 tons or of using locally manufactured units of 500 tons. The approximate cost of the imported units is Rs 320 million while that of the latter is only Rs 25 million (31). Further, refined sugar is produced for use by the urban sector (there being little consumption in the rural sector), and in order to maintain levels of production the indigenous production of sugar by the open-hearth system in villages is banned (32).

It has been established, therefore, that the product from indigenous and intermediate technology is nourishing and healthy, but there are other benefits from this technology. A farmer may sell sugarcane at the farm gate but the preparation and transport of this can could take as much as three to four days, resulting in a drying up of the juice in the cane. This loss could be as much as 2-3 per cent. This could be reduced considerably in the indigenous sector. Moreover, during the three months of mid-December to mid-March, the farmers are not so busy and could provide work for a fairly large agricultural labour force. It is possible to develop this industry along appropriate lines of technology and some signs of innovation can be seen:

Pakistan has local manufacturers around Gujranwala who can produce Mini Sugar Mills ... One of these manufacturers of Gujranwala has been approached by a world famous supplier of complete sugar mills to take up manufacturer of the proposed small units for supply to foreign countries under their marketing arrangements (33).

Some of the other benefits include the establishment of a capital goods industry, a shorter gestation period, lower transportation costs of raw materials and end-products, no inventory on spare parts and minimal administrative overheads.

Thus there is not only a need to identify inappropriate techniques but also to note inappropriate products (34). The desirability of a conscious choice (35) is therefore a requirement of the decision-making process. This is only possible, unfortunately, if the range of technology, the modifications required within each country and the usefulness of the products are known. The options to be considered are so large and may be difficult to implement as they may go against the interests of elites. However, an important point regarding progressive capital-intensive technology in the small-scale sector needs to be made, namely the production of bronze powder for oil-less bearnings by the South Koreans.

Even if criteria are developed, the decisions-makers have to implement them, and, according to Third World observers, 'the single most powerful

reason why this disparity in wealth persists is the
political clout that the affluent in the Third World
have to obstruct change' (36). Even if this were
true, some basis is required for making the choice
of technology consistent with application and
implementation. The determination of the optimal
choice may itself be a matter of contention with
any of the following five procedures:
(1) an econometric estimation of the production
function; (2) an estimate of engineering production
functions; (3) input-output studies; (4) process
analysis models; and (5) descriptive studies. Each
of these methods has its own shortcomings (37).

Other areas for attention are not only capital-
labour substitution but also those of input-
substitution (38). In Pakistan there was actually an
improvement in production capacity, where a local
'recipe' improved imported, capital-intensive
ice-manufacturing machinery (39). Much can be argued
for and against capital-labour substitution and
much would probably depend on the conditions in each
country. In Pakistan, for instance, armature
winding requires copper wire to the proper specifi-
cation, and the tools required are fingers and toes,
but obviously this is one of the very extreme
situations. The options were must aptly stated by
Mrs Gandhi: 'It (appropriate technology) is very
important. But I don't think one excludes the
other. We have to have a mixture of cottage
industry, village industry, small scale industry,
medium industry and heavy industry' (40). Talking
of elites at all levels in relative terms: 'The
people who are more powerful, even at the lowest
level - are the ones who take advantage, (41) and
she sees conflict unless you are all the time
seeing what harm it can do to health, employment
or the poor' (42). She has significantly highlighted
environmental factors and the employment and income
effects on the poor. The real problem is how all
these issues be systematically studied and resolved.
There lies the dilemma of Pakistan, where decisions
are made for the short term. Long-term planning is
unheard of in the administration, which tends
towards the status quo and playing safe. Might it
not be argued that the financial returns on modern
technology, which concentrates on mass production
and economies of scale, are not only more efficient
but also cost-reducing? Besides, there are the
obvious advantages of product improvement and
technology transfers to the Third World.

Financially, the cotton textile industry has

30

continuously needed support. In Pakistan the
industry is now thirty years old and yet the
arguments continue for increasing effective tariffs
and subsidies (43). In the commodities sector (sugar
and grain-milling) modern machinery has certainly
made the industries more profitable but it initially
required large amounts of capital and scarce foreign
exchange. In microeconomic terms, profitability
varies between enterprises. Anne Krueger found
considerable variations in performance and profitability amongst enterprises in the car-accessory
industry in India,(44) and found that it was
impossible, at the micro level, to discover the
reasons for these variation in profitability. Much
depended on government policy instruments and how
scarce resources were provided. However, a
consensus amongst economists on the existence of
excess capacity is widespread (45). No modern enterprise produces to its maximum capacity and some
only work one shift instead of three. Such misallocation in the economy leads to inefficiency
and a demand for import controls. In Pakistan the
modern textile sector suffers from competition
from the indigenous handloom sector, so quality
and product innovation do not appear to be important
to the consumer. Because of rising costs, perhaps
the modern sector has priced itself out of the
market.

  The modern corporate sector should develop
organisational and management practises and R&D
along with the other institutional strengths of a
capitalistic system. Since these benefits are
essential for a modern corporate sector one would
have thought that by now a market for senior
management would have developed in Pakistan. This
has not happened. R&D is almost non-existent, a
complaint voiced by world agencies, notably United
Nations Industrial Development Organisation (UNIDO).

  The argument also centres around the prices
which are attached to the factors of production.
Let us look at these at the very basic levels, land,
labour and capital. Surprisingly, in Pakistan the
factors of production are distorted in favour of the
entrepreneur. Land is provided at below market
prices and in excess. All resources are provided
at below cost. As labour is in excess, one would
assume that this input would be cheap. In the
absence of any regulations, skilled and unskilled
workers are paid wages which do not reflect scarcity
values (46). Capital is at subsidised rates and the
cost of capital is far below what it should be.

Industrialisation: Imperatives and contradictions

Fiscal policies are preferential and there is an overvalued exchange rate.

Location
Pakistan, with its geographically dispersed Wings (until 1972) and the heterogenous nature of its inhabitants, illustrates the problems of location. In addition, there is the problem of four distinct population groups (besides a number of sub-groups) in each of the provinces, the Bengalis in East Pakistan, the Sindhis in Sind, the Baluchis in Baluchistan (further sub-divided tribally), the Pathans in the North-West Frontier Province and the Punjabis in the Punjab. The nature of inter-relationships in all fields is extremely complex. East Pakistan was geographically smaller but its population was greater than that of West Pakistan (East Pakistan was 53,000 square miles approximately while West Pakistan was 373,000 square miles). The maximum density of population according to the 1961 census was 857 persons per square miles while the minimum in West Pakistan was 8 persons per square mile (in Baluchistan). So added to the normal rural-urban bias was another dimension, which had political overtones. The crux of the question was, how were resources to be divided between these provinces and regions? What was the basis, was it to be by population, by area or by sheer economic sense? Was it to be on the basis of foreign exchange earning ability or on the basis of future potential? If it was to be on the basis of mining versus manufacture, how much should be the sectoral allocation? The decision-makers, given the limited resources, were going to be always on the short end of the stick.

The investment in former East Pakistan was never at par with its foreign exchange earnings. Between 1965-6 and 1968-9 the proportion of invest-ment to foreign exchange earnings was 0.07, 0.12, 0.11 and 0.1. The public sector had been specifi-cally brought in for rectifying the shortcomings of the risk-averse private sector. A comparison within the regions comprising West Pakistan indicated the obvious emphasis on the Punjab. Such contradictions in location policy further compli-cated the decision-making process.

Given the preponderance of agricultural workers employed (or underemployed), an industrial policy in the traditional sense would mean that any increase in agricultural productivity would be achieved through releasing excess labour from

agriculture, allowing them to migrate to cities to
be 'badly employed' (47). An urban location has all
the advantages of growth centres in terms of
availability of all kinds of supplies and markets
to ensure demand (48). Administrative access is also
available. When this is balanced against the
expansion of the labour force in rural areas with
their inability to contain this increase, the result
is migration, shanty towns and slum suburbs. All
the major towns in Pakistan are bursting at the
seams, and the social costs of such urban
industrialisation outweigh the financial considerations (49). The examples of even the most progressive
less developed country indicate industry's inability
to provide satisfactory jobs. The answer probably
lies in creating rural industries and rural public
works to cater for the seasonally unemployed.
Industries in the agricultural based sector can
provide the means and Pakistan has proved that it is
possible to do so. For instance, at Mian Channu, a
small hamlet town in the Punjab, thirty-two
agricultural-implement manufacturing units have
developed within one year (50).

Import Substitution

Initially in Pakistan import substitution was linked
with the needs of the nation and the extent of the
market. The problems of definition were later
resolved by stating simply that it was domestic
production of that which would otherwise have been
imported. Thus any import substitution pattern
has of necessity an historical antecedent (which may
be conscious or otherwise) and a conscious development strategy pattern. The implied difference in
the two, of course, is the natural endowment or
resource on which the former is based and the import
content on which the latter is developed.
    The importance of the domestic market is
significant. The determination of the market for
particular goods will determine the Import Substitution (IS) industrialisation policies. Once
consumer goods markets are saturated then further
growth is only possible by investment in the
intermediate or capital goods sectors. If the
consumer goods production structure is to be
maintained then the saturated IS industries must
locate and extend their markets by exporting. The
second stage is difficult. The zero-growth stage is
generally indicated by stagnant growth. The tendency
for soft options usually gains ascendency in
decision-making. This being so, protection not only

continues unabated but does so on a wide range of goods. This is what Felix (51) calls the 'premature widening' of the productive structure, i.e. an expansion into a large number of relatively small-scale activities rather than a concentration on a few. Power (52) notes the inherent dangers of excessive import substitution, a small scale of production or too few firms to enforce efficiency and progress and an easing of the early momentum of the sequence profits-savings-reinvestment.

Too few firms (or even enough to ensure Competition) does not necessarily mean that market forces would ensure efficiency and consumer welfare. Entrepreneurs are able to manipulate policy to their own advantage. There are too many examples but suffice it to say that in Pakistan competition is not to be found as in the marketplace of a developed economy.

Import substitution strategy effectively erodes comparative advantage in international trade. Subsidies and bonuses are provided to enable Pakistani products to be price-effective and it is difficult, therefore, to convert industrialisation import-substitution policies.

It is also evident that the profits-savings-reinvestment momentum is lost, and this gap can only be bridged though increased aid. Nulty provides considerable evidence to prove that the industrialisation effort was decreasingly dependent on the effort and resources of the large entrepreneur. The large entrepreneur had an impressive array of resources to fall back on from diverse sources. In order to steer the economy in the right direction the essential requirement was a movement into production of intermediate or capital goods. A vicious circle results in which the economy is expected to save more in order to maintain its rate of growth but in fact major pressures build up to reduce that rate. In such circumstances, personal relationships, rather than hard economic decisions, generally succeed. Investment decisions also are distorted by an overvalued exchange rate, resulting in capital-intensive investment. Besides reducing employment a level of import intensity is created that is not consistent with the country's foreign exchange earning capacity. Protection and tariff policies complete the picture of distortion (53).

According to Bruton(54) an 'alien' structure leads to underutilisation in the economy, and normal fiscal(55) corrections such as devaluation or raising the price of capital are of no help. Under

34

such circumstances it is difficult to alter the production structure. The IMF suggested solutions which may, in fact, further exacerbate the issues, i.e. devaluation may lead to inflation or raise the loan burden on the small industrialist,(56) and an increased minimum lending rate will reduce investment.

There is a degree of distortion but to unravel this distortion in terms of the evaluation of indirect taxes, direct controls, import and invest- ment licensing and an overvalued currency is difficult. The area is, indeed, very grey. Similarly, a hard look at productivity growth, the deteriorating terms of trade and dependence on import duties as a source of government finance may be a continuous and necessary requirement of our time. Since consumer goods can be taxed and are more easily realisable than direct income tax, there is greater reliance on excise duties and possibly export duties.

The preceding analysis, not surprisingly, lays great store on a critical approach to import substitution. The advantage of such an approach is to develop, albeit with some hindsight, a system more closely akin to Pakistan's requirements, rather than imposing one that may not be suitable. The greatest emphasis has been placed on the aspect of distortion. Not surprisingly, policies need to be developed on an egalitarian basis, and policies and mechanisms which serve the interest of the few instead of those of the many need to be care- fully appraised. The other emphasis has been on 'alienness', and an indication that technology 'adaptation' rather than 'adoption' would seem to suggest itself. This would be in keeping with other characteristics of the economy. A mini- revolution in agricultural implements is very much apparent in Pakistan at the moment (57). A similarly quiet revolution in the tubewell engines took place in the Punjab in the 1960s, curiously without any government aid or patronage (58). Lastly, policies to encourage growth of productivity are essential. A set of policies, based on trial and error, could certainly be developed to give impetus to the industrialisation strategy.

Export-led Industrialisation
The growing initial indentification with a policy of import substitution gave way in developing countries to export-led industrialisation. In some cases, the shift came because of disenchantment

with import substitution policies. The reasons for
this were generally stagnation in the growth of the
industrialisation programme and a growing strain on
the balance of payments, indicating the need to
increase exports. There was also a realisation that,
although in theory a unit of foreign exchange saved
was comparable to a unit of foreign exchange earned,
in practice the former, if carried out under
conditions such as high tariffs and extreme
protection, led to the protection of inefficiency.
In terms of domestic resources cost, the earning of
a unit of foreign exchange is less than saving a
unit of foreign exchange,(59) more so in circumstances typical of Pakistan, i.e. where capital and
foreign exchange are scarce resources and where
there is an excess of labour. The obvious
advantages of export-led industrialisation may be
those of having unlimited markets. Demand is not
dependent on home markets but is exogenously
determined, and may lead to an inflow of foreign
private capital. Foreign investment is likely to
lead to the developing of skills, especially when
labour-intensive production technology is used, the
costs of export promotion are more identifiable to
policy-makers than are those for import substitution,(60) and, if there are significant economies
of scale to be achieved, the size of the market
will enable firms to realise them (61).

Aid-agencies have also taken up this approach
and have distinguished between export-orientated
and export-substitution industries, the former
indicating non-traditional industries and the
latter substituting existing exports of raw material
with processed and semi-processed materials, i.e.
for cotton, export yarn and cloth.

This view is being challenged by the sceptics,
who contend that labour-intensive processes and
component manufacturing for multinationals is
indicative of a dependence in which the host country
has no bargaining power (62). The fundamental problem
is that all decisions of the multinational are
independent of the considerations of the host
country. It is doubtful, though, that the foreign
investor will make a decision otherwise than on
sound economic reasoning. To this extent,
Helleiner's arguments can be refuted. Vaistos,
studying the exports of processed goods by trans-
national enterprises, calls this form of development 'shallow' (63). Pakistan has not had such
experiences with private foreign investment.

What are the characteristic features of

export-led development? First, Pakistan is export-substitution orientated in the sense that semi-processed and processed commodities are being exported, especially since 1972, when the loss of East Pakistan meant the loss of the markets for yarn and cloth, and the only option was to export. The export-orientated labour-intensive industry, on the other hand, is in the small/medium indigenous sector. This sector's share in manufactured exports was 42 per cent in 1976-7, the remaining exports in the manufacturing sector coming from export-substitution industries (semi-processed commodities).

The annual average increase in manufactured exports is 8 per cent (for 1972/3-1978/9). Pakistan has not fared so well when the world's economy was expanding while during world recession the fall in Pakistan's exports has been significant. Any depression in the world economy has a magnified effect on Pakistan's economy, and indicates lack of diversification and depth in the country's exports.

Despite the ever-increasing number of govern-ment incentives, Pakistan's large-sector exports (cotton yarn and cloth) moved from import substitution to export substitution (because of the loss of East Pakistan) and, as a result, competi-tiveness and comparative advantage in world markets was missing. This was compensated by very generous export incentives by the government (64).

The argument for an industrialisation programme is therefore not only that of import substitution versus export-led development but there are also important differences within both strategies. Obviously, the efficacy of a policy is dependent on the performance of large industria-lists and private foreign investors, the relations between multinationals and host countries and the trade policies of developed countries and their attitudes towards tariff and non-tariff barriers.

Economic Power and Industrial Concentration
The question of economic power and industrial concentration was first raised in the National Assembly by a Member of the National Assembly from East Pakistan in connection with the preferential treatment given to West Pakistani industrialists. They were not ostensibly concerned with West Pakistan's economic strength, though this might well have been a motivation (65). (Table 2.3 shows the concentration and ownership of assets of the

monopoly houses). A similar situation prevailed in

Table 2.3: Economic Power of the Monopoly Houses

Authors	No. of industrial houses	Assets (%)	Sales (%)
Papanek	60	60.6	43.5
Papanek	7	24.4	15.6
Haq	22	60	
Amjad	44	70	
		(on Karachi Stock Exchange)	
		35	
		(Large)	
White	43	51-73	
		(Depending on category)	

Sources: Papanek, Pakistan's Development: Social
Goals and Private Incentives: R.Amjad, unpublished
PhD Thesis, Cambridge University: L.White, Economic
Power and Industrial Concentration: Haq, as quoted
in White and Amjad.

the banking and insurance systems: in fact, the
monopoly houses' control of total deposits(66) was
59 per cent of all banks and 86 per cent for
private banks. Similarly, the insurance companies'
assets were 76 per cent of domestic assets and
50.4 per cent of domestic and foreign insurance
companies' assets.
     The logical question is whether other
countries have managed to develop industrial
concentrations without creating such powerful
economic groups, and a survey of the developed
world indicates that concentration in the industrial
sector was very much a question of economic and
industrial power, as the United States, the UK, etc.
bear testimony (67). The difference, of course, is
that in the developed countries a power structure
has developed over centuries, and therefore the
process of industrialisation has been less painful.
In addition, at the time, information was less
available to these countries, the world was not an
'electronic village' as it is today. Again in the
developed world, other sectors have advanced along
parallel lines but there were always countervailing
forces. Economic power was either considerably

reduced or was, in fact, beneficial, since the
community was made aware of social problems. In
the context of less developed countries, Professor
Raymond Vernon has examined the Mexican scene and
concluded:
A dozen or so major groups ... have been created ...
and a large number of the major industrial and
banking enterprises of Mexico belong to one or
another of these groups ... The existence of the
groups is an important and indisputable fact of
Mexican life (68).
Although details of the size of these groups are
not given by the author, their importance is well
established. Chile has undergone a similar
experience, as has Argentina, Brazil, Columbia,
Bolivia, Ecuador and Peru. In these countries the
large groups appear to have emerged from industrial
complexes (69).Chilean groups, however, have
developed around the finance houses,(70) as in Asia,
India, Japan, South Korea, Taiwan, Malaysia and the
Philippines, to name only a few. Are such groups,
therefore, undesirable? One example is that of
Japan and the Zaibatsu group. The rise and fall
of Japan during the Second World War has been
referred to as the rise and fall of the Zaibatsu,
so significant was its impact on Japanese development. According to Yoshino's analysis, in 1942
the percentage of paid-in capital was estimated to
represent 50 per cent of the financial sector,
32 per cent of the (heavy) industrial sector, 11 per
cent of light industry and 21 per cent of other
sectors (71).

After the Second World War, despite the Allies'
insistence on the dispersal of Japanese companies,
the original firms combined to form similar
groupings. In addition, there were other such
associations in post-war Japan, the Zaikal
(business leaders) and the Kankel gaisha (vertically
integrated combines).

There has, however, been some identification
of those who hold economic power in Pakistan. This has
not been possible in India, probably because of
the difference in the periods of industrialisation
in the two countries. India's industrialisation
has taken seventy to eighty years, whereas that of
Pakistan has emerged within the very short period
of fifteen to twenty years. In both India and
Pakistan, economic strength follows caste and
communal lines. Thus in Pakistan the Memons
appeared to have, in 1967, assets of 26.5 per cent
of the total industrial assets in the country

whilst representing only 0.16 per cent of the
population (72). Papanek's survey of 1967 showed
that only 3.5 per cent of assets were held by the
Bengalis (East Pakistan) who accounted for 43 per
cent of the population (73). In India in 1958, two
monopoly houses, Tata and Birlas, accounted for
approximately 20 per cent of the physical assets
of the corporate private sector.

The presence of such disproportionate groupings
is inevitable, or so our brief survey indicates. As
long as there are human differences in entrepreneurial ability, they will remain a consequence of
industrialisation. Perhaps the best way to
circumvent this problem is by trying to direct the
energies of entrepreneurs into other channels which
are particularly useful to Pakistan instead of
allowing a monopoly power to certain individuals,
or to limit them to scale economies and channel
their efforts into other industries which they had
hitherto been reluctant to enter. Given a proper
mix of incentives and policies there is no reason
for assuming that this would not have taken place.

Since these groups are a necessary result of
industrialisation they must be tolerated, and
policies should be devised to adapt them to the
requirements of the country. Over the years, the
developed countries have had their unacceptable
faces of capitalism (74). Japan has had its Zaibutsu,
India its Tata and Birla. Excluding Japan, as the
country has made economic progress, the business/
monopoly houses have tended to decline. Supremacy
in economic power has been balanced by the
development of other sectors.

The Unacceptable Face of Capitalism. The basis for
this unacceptability varies from country to country.
In Japan no such diminution in economic power has
taken place: in fact, it continues to increase. In
Nicaragua, recent events have shown that where
industrial concentration is intense or where it is
closely identified with political power,(75) the
results may well be loss of that political power
and, as a consequence, loss of economic power as
well. In Pakistan the unacceptability was in terms
of regional disparity, and only in the late 1960s
was the 'moral' issue raised, and concern with
morality continues unabated. Underlying the
rejection of capitalism is the rejection of a
concentration of capital in a few hands due to its
far-reaching harmful effects on society. Rejection
of capitalism is therefore based on the presumption

that a capitalist is potentially a social evil (76).
The other side of the coin is very rarely stated.
For example, one of the industrialist interviewed
set up a woollen textile mill in an area where
traditionally nothing grew. There were no skilled
labour force, infrastructural facilities or
agriculture. As a result of his undertaking, in a
span of fifteen years this area is a desirable
industrial location and now has fifty-one units (77).
The social impact on employment in the area has
never been considered by those who were interested
only in the assets to be created and the fact that
someone scratched the surface and took the necessary
financial risk has not been given due emphasis.
Similarly, in 1965 Pakistani textile units visited
indicated the employment possibilities in the
country (78). The examples are only illustrative.
The imponderable still remains.

Impact on Economic Development. One way of
considering the effect of these groups on economic
development is by correlating the rate of a
country's growth with the operations of its business
groups. The rates of growth in Japan, Mexico and
Brazil bear testimony to the influence of these
large groups: the spin-offs are apparent though
these cannot be quantified in the case of less
developed countries.
    In many cases the creation of wealth, if
considered in the light of the incentives provided
by the government, indicates that industrialists
have responded to these incentives. The right of
the government to pick and choose is directly
controlled. Why, then has this right not been
judiciously exercised in Pakistan? The problem,
and the cause of the problem, lie elsewhere. The
crux of the matter is that very few governments
consider the consumer's welfare. They are hardly
ever aware of the market situation. If economic
concentration is a powerful tool, it is so because
the other sectors in society have not developed to
the same degree. In any case, economic power in
the hands of a progressive and socially conscious
industrialist can lead society towards a better
standard of living, as the Zaibutsu have done in
Japan, while in the hands of a decadent elite it
may well be used for exploitation. The extreme
case of Nicaragua may be cited here. It cannot be
denied that the Pakistan entrepreneurs are men with
vision,(79) and in the process of industrialisation
great family wealth has accrued to them as the

financial-industrial axes developed. In the early days they channelled most of their wealth into industry, not into Swiss bank accounts. Only when Pakistan's internal situation became dangerous were there, at best, accusations of a flight of capital. Are policies, then, to be developed on the basis of accusations. If such allegations are correct, the internal house must be set in order, for a country's wealth should be created more by a country's economic policies than by the organisational arrangements of the monopoly houses. A more detailed analysis, however, is required in assessing the impact of such houses on the economy. Such an approach has been made by Strachan (80), and the factors to be examined would include, among others, capital formation, entrepreneurial innovation and social development. It is, in any case, impossible to prove what might have been: the alternative can only be indicated by a series of complex assumptions.

The Role of Government

Papanek (81) points out that in earlier years industrialisation in Pakistan has been made possible by government intervention, mainly due to a lack of entrepreneurs. Government intervention can be justified on many philosophical grounds, to ensure equality and welfare, to make certain that there would be no disproportionate investment, on economies of scale, etc. Such justifications invariably can be countered by citing the opposite case, the side-effects of accelerated industrialisation. In Pakistan, the government's role may be seen as that of a catalyst, an entrepreneur, a strategist/guide and a guarantor.

The Government as a Catalyst.

This phase lasted for most of the period of independence, when the government attempted in its own way, to increase investment in industries. In hoping to achieve industrialisation the government followed industrial policies then favoured by world bodies. No dishonourable intentions can be attributed to the government in the carrying out of its industrialisation strategy. It accepted, in good faith, what was given to it, and the distortions that ultimately occurred in the system were not entirely the fault of the government. In its role of being a catalyst, it gave generous inducements to entrepreneurs. Industrial sites with infrastructures were available at artificially low cost. To ensure

42

equity, the Pakistan Industrial Development
Corporation was involved. Industrial sites were
located in remote areas. The social implications,
even if there were mistakes and some misallocation
of resources, cannot be denied. In providing
location incentives, the government managed to
provide employment for people in areas where such
opportunities had been lacking. The impact of
the arrival of Lawrencepur in a wilderness, around
which an industrial town has since been built,
cannot be denied. Similarly, the government's
incentives for the agricultural implements industry
provided a chance for agriculturalists to go into
large-scale manufacturing. They had tinkered with
home-made gadgets on their own farms for some time
and, as they saw a demand for them, some of them
moved, began manufacturing them. Rural towns such
as Daska and Mian Channu are testimony to the
government's policy here. Misallocation of
resources did take place. For instance, East
Pakistan was given the same number of manufacturing
units as West Pakistan without its resource
structure being taken into account. Sugar and
cotton mills located in East Pakistan either did not
operate or did so for a limited period of time, and
they never became going concerns. Other measures
could have been introduced and more relevant
industrial investments made. It is on such obvious
misallocations of resources that questions on the
decision-making process in Pakistan arise.

The Government as Entrepreneur. Given the assumption
that the system of private enterprise is wasteful,
less developed countries have taken upon themselves
the decision to invest, hoping thereby that the
mistakes of the past could be avoided. The private
entrepreneur was replaced by the government
official. Pakistan decided very early to go into
industry and the Pakistan Industrial Corporation was
created. Besides promoting industry this organisation was to design projects for areas where
factors of production were available. The private
enterprise system continued in parallel, with
substantial encouragement. Although a demarcation
between the public sector and the private sector
was not made, each was aware of their own limitations.
This co-operation came to an end when the private
sector was acquired by the state. A socialist
philosophy prevailed yet the result of such an
action were probably the furthering of political
vendettas. The private enterprise system had also

43

developed its own working methods, which, over a
period of time, became public knowledge (82). To
a certain extent, the acquisition of the private
sector was a result of the unacceptable face of
capitalism. Has the substitution of the market
system been satisfactory? Has the government
official lived up to expectations and directed
industrialisation along the right channels? These
are difficult questions, but it may be safely
concluded that an official's knowledge is certainly
not comparable with the market's traditional
method of dealing with investment decisions. In
the long run, the market system rewards perception
and ruthlessly punishes misallocation. This, for
a variety of reasons, is not possible in a
bureaucratically-orientated industry. The tools by
which investment is made, e.g. cost benefit
analysis, have certain shortcomings, and in the
hands of a government official they can be lethal
weapons. Given human ingenuity, the official
can defend the most outrageons situation. The
fault lies not only in omission, and on occasions
the sins of omission and commission reinforce each
other. In any case, Pakistan's current problems
are too complex to be handled by government
officials.

Given the dynamic nature of the world's natural
resources and of technological change it is
virtually impossible to predict comparative
advantage. This becomes all the more important,
since in Pakistan today there is trend towards
export-led industrialisation. Should this investment take place in the public sector? The answer
seems all too obvious, unless expertise and
management of a very high order could be somehow
marshalled the enterprise is not likely to
progress very far.

The Government as a Guide and Strategist. Once a
broad entrepreneurial base is developed, can the
government then guide and develop a strategy
commensurate with its plans (Five-Year, annual, etc).

An industrialisation strategy emerges from a
number of ministries or departments. In the case of
Pakistan, the Ministry of Industries, the Economic
Affairs Division, the Planning Division, the
National Economic Council and its executive as well
as the executive committee of the NEC are involved.
These ministries consider a projects' feasibility
and the financial institutions advise on the
state of foreign exchange dealings in case such

44

exchange is required. The State Bank of Pakistan ensures that its regulations are followed. When one considers that each of the four provinces have similar departments and further directorates of industries and Small Industries Corporations, the complexity of government decisions may be gauged. A further complication is that, within each of these departments, a document normally travels through four to five hierarchical levels. With each official adding or subtracting items, what are the plan's chances of success? Can the government give guidance? Can it be a strategist? Normally, for a resourceful individual, it can take between three to four years to obtain approval of a document. During this time the cost benefit analysis becomes hopelessly outdated. Therefore not only is a project to be considered in its economic and social context but also in the delay in its administration, for the policy frameworks are usually complex and frequently conflicting.

The Government as Guarantor. Finally we examine the case of the government as a guarantor against risk and uncertainty. To those whom the government is committed to help, such entrepreneurs as had political connections, the policies followed would tend to be of maximum aid. However, where resources are scarce and where the demand for those limited resources is very high, the distribution of those resources becomes distorted in a number of ways, e.g. inequality in income distribution and luxury housing and other preferential treatment given to certain levels of society. It is difficult to question, with hindsight, the basis and need for such preferential policies. Within the framework of certain assumptions they were designed to ensure certain steps towards what was then considered to be essential to progress and self-reliance. These steps required entry into technological areas, modern production processes and modern distribution and exchange relationships. It was felt that by doing this the country as a whole would progress quickly. Pakistan's plans for national integration whereby industries in one wing (West or East) were to be based on the raw materials of the other wing may have been misconceived but no other intentions other than the desire for national solidarity can be attributed to them. How were these policies made attractive? The instruments that Pakistan used included very generous incentives to achieve the country's industrial goals.

Industrialisation: Imperatives and contradictions

The economists brought forth policies, both fiscal and industrial, to stimulate economic environment at all levels, and such policies distorted distribution and exchange relationships and led to exorbitant profits being made. The illusion of profits led to a positive response in the entrepreneurial field, and the government guaranteed all the factors of production to all inputs at less than their market value.

However, the government could not guarantee the continuation of its policies once there was a shift in political power. In Pakistan this power shift has always occurred under conditions of considerable stress, and has often led to industrialists finding themselves on the wrong side of the fence.

Conscious decisions, despite the instability of governments, are essential. There is a large part of Pakistan's economy in which a positive stimulus by the government would be desirable and useful. There are other areas in which more restrictive controls are needed. There are areas in which market mechanisms should be allowed to take their own course. However, whenever governments undertake to control scarce resources through import licences, restrictive direct controls or licensing of new firms there is bound to be some degree of favouritism and misallocation of resources.

Equality and Welfare

In human society extremes of wealth and poverty are the main sources of evil... where a population is divided into the two classes of the very rich and the very poor, there can be no real state, for there can be no real friendship between the classes, and friendship is the essential principle for all association (83).

The fact that Pakistan was created primarily to be economically independent can be questioned. The fact that this was one of the basic causes can never be controverted. This concept is embodied in the literature, the speeches and in the public resolutions at the time(84). Thus, egalitarian ideals and the removal of poverty were the central themes of the early philosophy.

How, then, was industrialisation to deal with the problems of inequality in Pakistan? Why, in the first place, should there be a growing concern for industrialisation, and, having embarked on that programme, what policies would be just and

46

equitable?   The reasons for Pakistan's concern with industrialisation was somehow connected with economic wellbeing and good living.   The answer lies, perhaps, in non-economic thought.   Would the public acquisition of industry be enough to lift the country from poverty and chaos? That is what people thought and that is what was given to them as the panacaea for all ills.   The various decades of reforms in Pakistan (85) bear testimony to this way of thinking.   That these reforms did not necessarily lead to improving the 'quality of life' either never seemed to occur to planners or they were helpless in devising appropriate policies (86).

Under what circumstances,then, does industrialisation alleviate poverty? In broad terms, it can do this when there is efficiency in production.   Anne Krueger would refer to import substitution,which, once the learning process has taken place,leads to a reduction in prices and costs (87).   The choice of techniques, the scarcity value of the factors of production and the degree of combination of the factors of production again have social implications. Is dualistic development in the industrial sector worth-while? Is the experience of Japan(88) and other Eastern countries,as well as that of the United States, where small firms have long term sub-contractual arrangements with large companies of any significance?   To what extent can state intervention take place to ensure that the product of a small, flexible entrepreneur is as good as that produced by the large conglomerates? What are the cost implications? What of the appropriate technology? Has a conscious decision been taken? Above all, where does the balance lie?   Are market forces(89) to be allowed to determine the large versus the small, the enlarging of an industrial structure or the broadening of an industrial base?   Who decides that the textile sector is saturated in Pakistan and that 40 per cent of it should not be operational?   What are the under-currents in decision-making which play such a decisive role and which indirectly have social implications? Can controlled, well-policed policies foster efficient, optimal patterns of industrialisation?

Policies affecting the utilisation of resources by the public and private sectors are important. There are many policy instruments and planners are continually required to have knowledge of factors affecting both.   Locational policies may again be important, especially since the Chinese seem to

have exploded the myth of economies of scale in
certain industrial sectors. A doctrinaire
approach is not conducive to any fruitful analysis.
Each country is dependent to a large extent on its
non-economic factors. What attitudes are held
important by a society? How deprived is it?
What would be conspicuous consumption? Given the
power structure and the elite-reinforcing basis in
less developed countries can there be an awareness
of all the arguments? How and why do inefficient
firms continue to exist? Is it because they are
not dependent on market forces but on 'state
capitalism's'(90) discretionary forces? Krueger(91)
indicates that profitability is not the critical
factor but that maintainence of continued production
is. Virtually all firms operate under a monopoly
or quasi-monopoly and supply never exceeds demand.
Trading arrangements favour the producer, and these
include obtaining import licenses, investment
licences and domestic raw materials(92). Krueger
found immense differences in the cost of the same
product amongst different firms.

The fact that a package of economic policies
eventually led to the creation of Bangladesh
makes it necessary not to repeat earlier mistakes,
but 'bad intentions drive out good intentions'(93).
The question is, are the mistakes driven out for
ever or is there a possibility that the trend will
be reversed, and that the old policies will
return?

Notes

1. G.F. Papanek makes the point in Pakistan's
Development: Social Goals and Private Incentives,
Harvard University Press, Cambridge, Mass, 1967.
2. Rashid Amjad and L.J. White make this point.
3. Fifth Five Year Plan, pp.100-1: 'No
reliable data is available to assess the
contribution of small industries sector to the
economy'.
4. FFYP, p.102.
5. 'Study on Small Scale Industries in
Pakistan', Draft Interim Report, UNIDO Contract
No.80/106, Project No.DP/Pak/79 014, September 1980.
6. L.J.White, Industrial Concentration and
Economic Power in Pakistan, Princeton University
Press, Princeton, New Jersey, 1974, for a detailed
analysis. Also R. Amjad, unpublished PhD thesis,
University of Cambridge.

48

7. In fact all project costs currently, exceeding Rs 1 million (to $1,00,000 = stirling 42,000 approx) are required to have the approval of the Executive Committee of the National Economic Council (ECNEC) and, before it is placed on the agenda of this meeting, be processed by various agencies directly concerned with various aspects of the project, i.e. provincial government for land, financial institutions, etc.

8. A.Sen, Employment, Technology and Development, Clarendon Press, Oxford, 1975.

9. M. Dobb, as cited in E.W. Nafziger, African Capitalism, Hoover Institution Press, Stanford, California, 1977.

10. For details, see G.F. Papanek, 'Pakistan's Investment, Social Goals and Private Incentives, in Robber Barons Progress, pp.27-55.

11. W. Galenson and H. Leibenstein, 'Investment Criteria, Productivity and Economic Development', Quarterly Journal of Economics (August 1955).

12. Pritam Singh, Essays Concerning Some Types of Indian Entrepreneurship, unpublished PhD thesis, Michigan State University, 1966.

13. Keith Marsden, 'Progressive Technologies for Developing Countries', International Labour Review, May 1970, pp.475-80 and 494-502.

14. Z.M. Rizvi, 'Survey Report on the Cotton Textile Industry in Pakistan, Spinning and Weaving W.S.R. to IDBP Financed Projects', unpublished internal mimeo, Industrial Development Bank of Pakistan, Karachi, Oct. 1978, P.15.

15. Sen makes the point in respect of the spinning wheel in India.

16. The term 'inappropriate products and inappropriate technologies' was first given a meaningful analysis by Francis Stewart, 'Technology and Employment in Ldc's, World Development, March 1974, PP.21-3.

17. Harry T. Oshima, 'Labour Force Explosion and the Labour Intensive Sector in Asian Growth', Paper presented at a conference on 'Structure and Development in Asian Economics held in Tokyo under the auspices of the Japan Economic Research Centre, Sept. 1968.

18. Economic analysis indicated that the public sector played a vital role in defence-oriented and telecommunications industries.

19. This led to the creation of the Pakistan Industrial Development Corporation by an Act of Legislature in 1950. It became operational in 1952.

20. The two leading houses were the Dawoods and the Adamjees. Some members of the Dawood Group had studied at British Universities.

21. For example, the construction of new postal facilities, the laying of a railway line and many other projects.

22. Data are based on government publications i.e. the Fifth Five-Year Plan and Pakistan Economic Surveys, 1965-6, 1969-70, 1978-9, 1980-1.

23. This was confirmed in interviews with entrepreneurs.

24. Cf. Hirschman's 'forward and backward linkages'.

25. Cf. Nurkse's 'horizontal linkages'.

26. G. Ranis, 'Industrial Efficiency and Economic Growth: A Case Study of Karachi', Institute of Development Economics, 1961, may be consulted for details.

27. Frances Stewart, 'Technology and Employ-ment in LDC's', World Development, March 1974, pp.21-3.

28. Chakki machinery uses horizontal grinders rather than rollers.

29. At the time of nationalisation of the commodity markets, the author served as Director, Finance and Marketing in the Punjab Flour Mills Corporation. This had 23 modern pneumatic mills and 46 intermediate elevator type mills.

30. Prices pertain to 1976-7.

31. Mushtaq Ilahi, 'Sugar Industry in Pakistan', Research Report Series No. 108, Pakistan Institute of Dev. Economics, Islamabad, P.68.

32. It was held that 3% of Sugar was lost by inefficient crushing (ibid).

33. Ibid.

34. Frances Stewart ('Technology and Employment in Ldc's') supports this contention.

35. The current North, South debate makes this point of conscious choice.

36. Denzil Pieris, 'Who Will Look After the Poor?' Guardian, 3 March 1980.

37. L.E. Westphal, 'Research on Appropriate Technology' in Technology, Employment and Development, ed. L.J. White, Quezon City, Philippines, Council for Asian Manpower Studies, 1974.

38. G. Ranis, 'Some Observations on the Economic Framework for Optimum Ldc Utilization of Technology, in Technology and Economics in International Development, Report of a Seminar,

23 May 1972, Washington DC, Agency for International Development, 1972.

39.   Discussion with an internal revenue officer (the Ice-factory owner was prosecuted for evasion of tax).

40.   Mrs Indira Gandhi, 'New Technology Makes Poor Poorer' (interview with Anil Agarwal), Guardian, August 1980.

41.   Ibid.

42.   Ibid.

43.   At the rate of Rs 40 per bale in 1978-9.

44.   **Anne** O.Krueger, The Benefits and Costs of Import Substitution in India.   A Micro economic Study, University of Minnesota Press, Minneapolis, 1975.

45.   In Pakistan, excess capacity exists in the textile industry and in the commodities sector, in addition to many other industries.

46.   S. Guisenger, 'Wages, Capital Rental Values and Relatives Factor Prices in Pakistan', World Bank Staff Working Paper No. 287, June 1978.

47.   Pope John Paul, on his tour of Brazil in 1981, categorised it well by stating: 'There are only the unemployed, the under-employed and the badly employed'.

48.   P. Streeten, amongst others, makes this point in 'self Reliant Industrialisation', a paper read at the International Seminar on Strategies for Development at Lahore, Pakistan, 1979.

49.   Ibid.

50.   These units are at different production levels.   The most progressive is also the most capital-intensive.   Technology transfer takes place by the sons of the entrepreneurs having taken specialised courses in various universities in developed countries.

51.   David Felix, 'Monetarists, Structuralists and Import Substituting Industrialisation: A Critical Appraisal', in Inflation and Growth in Latin America, Homewood, Illinois, 1961, ed. W.Baer and I. kerstenetzky.

52.   John H. Power, Industrialisation in Pakistan.   A case of Frustrated Take-Off?' Pakistan Development Review, Vol. III, No. 2, 11 (Summer 1963).

53.   For details, reference may be made to the work by Henry J. Bruton, R. Soligo and J.J. Stern, A.R. Khan, Harry G. Johnson and many others.

54.   Bruton uses this term most effectively and views the transfer of the modern sector to less developed in a way that is completely opposed to

Papanek's thinking. For details see H. J.Bruton, 'The Import Substitution Strategy of Economic Development, Research Memorandum and Papanek, Pakistan's Development.

55. As the World Bank and IMF repeatedly found in the case of less developed countries.

56. Interviews with Industrialists from the Small-Scale Sector.

57. Based on the author's own findings.

58. R. Soligo and J.J. Stern, 'Export Promotion and Investment Criteria', P.D.R. Spring 1966.

59. J. Sheahen, 'Trade and Employment: Industrial Exports Compared to Import Substitution in Mexico, ' Williams College Research Centre for Development Economics, Research Memorandum No. 43, 1971.

60. Jagdish N. Bhagwati and Anne O.Krueger, 'Exchange Control, Liberalisation and Economic Development', American Economic Review, papers and proceedings, May 1973.

61. Ibid.

62. G.K. Helleiner, 'Manufacturing of Exports, Multinational firms and Economic Development', World Development, July 1973, P.17.

63. C.V. Vaistos, 'Employment Effects of Foreign Direct Investments' in Edgar O.Edwards (ed), Employment in Developing Nations, New York, pp.339-41.

64. For details of generous incentives see Z. Khan, 'The System of Export Incentives in the Manufacturing Sector of Pakistan, unpublished PhD thesis, Johns Hopkins University, 1979.

65. Rashid Amjad, unpublished PhD Thesis, Cambridge University, takes this view.

66. Ibid.

67. For discussion of links among economic, political and social power See C. Wright Mills, The Power Elite, New York, 1965, and Morton Mintz and Jerry S. America Inc., New York, 1971.

68. R. Vernon, The Dilemma of Mexico's Development, The Roles of the Private and Public Sectors, Harvard University Press, Cambridge Mass, 1965, p.20.

69. Harry Wallace Strachan, 'The Role of Business Groups in Economic Development. The Case of Nicaragua', unpublished Harvard University DBA, 1972

70. Ibid.

71. K. Yamamuro, Economic Policy in Post-War Japan. Growth vs Economic Democracy, University of California Press, Berkeley and Los Angeles, California, 1967, p.110.

72. Papanek, Pakistan's Development.

73. Ibid.

74. This phrase is attributed to Edward Heath, when he spoke of the power of multinational companies.

75. The reference here is to the overthrow of the Samoza regime.

76. Mahfooz Ali, 'Some Aspects of an Interest Free Economy', Monthly Economic Letter of the United Bank Ltd, Sept. 1979.

77. Preinvestment Survey, Directory of Industrial Investment, Government of the Punjab, Lahore.

78. In 1965 the Dawood cotton mill employed 10,000 workers. Over the years because of industrial relations policies the number now stands at 5,000. Capital-intensive machinery and a substitution of capital for labour has obviously taken place.

79. Interviews with the Dawoods, the Adamjees, the Habibs, the Sheikhs, etc.

80. Strachan, 'The Role of Business Groups, pp.14-8

81. Papanek, Pakistan's Development.

82. Mahmood A. Qureshi, 'Professional Accounting and Corporate Reporting in Pakistan, unpublished PhD dissertation, The University of California, Los Angeles, 1969.

83. The oft-quoted quotation from Aristotle.

84. For details see A. Gledhill, Pakistan, Stevens, London, 1957: the speeches of Quaid-i-Azam: the Pakistan Resolution, Hodson 'The Great Divide'.

85. During the presidentships of Ayub Khan and Z.A. Bhutto, eulogies on developments and reforms appeared in the press frequently.

86. G. Myrdal in Asian Drama and C.F. Black, Dynamics of Modernisation, New York makes these points in great detail.

87. A.O. Krueger, 'The benefits and Costs of Import Substitution in India, A Micro Economic Study', University of Minnesota Press, Minneapolis.

88. Susame Watanabe, 'Entrepreneurship in Small Enterprises in Japanese Manufacturing', International Labour Review, Dec. 1970.

89. Krueger makes the point that market forces tend to reject inefficient firms, whereas this is hardly the case in an overtly protected economy. It is more a case of state capitalism.

90. Professor Emile Dupres makes the point forcefully in 'Foreign Exchange Purchase Systems', PIDE, Karachi, 1965.

91. Krueger, 'The Benefits and Costs of Import Substitution in India', p.108.

92. Ibid.

Chapter Three

THE CONCEPT OF ENTREPRENEURSHIP

Problems and Historical Review

The entrepreneur is a very contentious subject in economics. Few scholars have agreed on the place that should be given to the entrepreneur in formal economic logic. Everyone, though, is agreed that '... by ignoring the entrepreneur we are prevented from accounting fully for a substantial portion of our historic growth ... and ... our body of theory as it has developed offers us no promise of being able to deal with a description and analysis of the entrepreneurial function'.(1) Penrose reinforces this by stating that 'Enterprise or Entrepreneurship, as it is sometimes called, is a slippery concept, not easy to work in formal economic analysis, because it is so closely connected with the temperament or personal qualities of individuals' (2).

Penrose thus indicates the complexity of the subject by indicating the overlap between economics and the other disciplines such as sociology and psychology. The research student must therefore study these other disciplines and to decide whether the methodology utilised elsewhere can help in determining aspects of the entrepreneur hitherto unknown. Recent ideological and religious trends need to be taken into account, if only to determine their impact on entrepreneurial performance. In a given social milieu cultural factors are difficult to ignore. In this grey area much earlier discussion was focused on economic and non-economic factors, on human and non-human resources, on supply and demand and on the need to evolve quantitative measurements in development economics. Entrepreneurs given the complexity of human beings, have managed to defy any kind of quantification. Scholars have failed to arrive at consensus on their attributes or activities.

The Concept of Entrepreneurship

The Views of Early Economists

Despite its interdisciplinary nature, it is in the field of economics that the entrepreneur has been the subject of much study. As early as the eighteenth century, Cantillon defined the entrepreneur as one 'who buys factor services at certain prices, with a view to selling their products at an uncertain price in the future, and as such becomes a bearer of an uninsurable risk (3). He went on to agree that, as risk-acceptors, 'all entrepreneurs seek to secure all they can in their state'(4) (and hence maximise income). Cantillon excluded princes and landlords from his studies and divided the rest between entrepreneurs (which included farmers and merchants) and hired labour. Put simply, then, entrepreneurs were to carry on the production and exchange of goods. It was when the demand for goods was depressed, bringing the danger of bankruptcy, that the risk factor appeared.

J.B. Say developed this argument and provided a key role for the entrepreneur. To him, the entrepreneur may have provided capital but it is his functions that makes him different from the capitalist. For Say, the functions attributed to the entrepreneur were the application of acquired knowledge to the production of a good for human comsumption. In order to be successful, Say maintained, the entrepreneur must have the ability to assess future demand (a factor of judgement), to determine the appropriate quantity of goods and their timing (market research and analysis), to calculate probable production costs and selling prices and to possess the art of administration (management) (5). In terms of giving functions to a skeletal form, Say was definitely a forerunner of modern economists, although he completely missed the concept of innovation when he said '... the adventures (the entrepreneurs) were a kind of brokers between the vendors and the purchasers, who engage a quantum of productive agency upon a particular product proportionate to the demands of the product'. Say added the concept of management in a form with which modern industry is all too familiar.

Walras probably gave the most exalted, position to the entrepreneurs by calling them the 'fourth factor of production'. The role and functions assigned to them consisted principally of hiring others. In this capacity they were buyers of productive services from the market and sellers of the goods produced. This was compatible with the

The Concept of Entrepreneurship

General Theory of Equilibrium propounded by Walras
whereby under free competition, the entrepreneurs
as profit-maximisers ensured that free markets move
towards equilibrium. Walras thus provided a blending
of the French school of thought, which had until
then considered the entrepreneurs as workers charged
with the special task of managing firms, with that
of the English economists, who equated entrepreneurs
with capitalists (6).
     Although Walras had managed to bridge a
significant gap between the English and French
economists, few English economists have written on
the concept of entrepreneurship. The classical
economists did not distinguish between interests and
profits, and therefore did not differentiate the
capitalist from the entrepreneur. The belief of the
classical school that economic relationships were
dependent on natural laws may well have been
responsible for this attitude and lack of identification of the entrepreneur as an acceptable
concept (7). Although this may be so, the influence
of these economists was profound. The belief of
Adam Smith that, by furthering their own selfish
ends, individuals would unwittingly and inevitably
be adding to the wealth and welfare of the nation,
freed industrialists from the stigma of exploitation
and instead presented them as agents for social
improvement. However, despite Adam Smith's powerful
influence on economic thought, the general failure
to differentiate between profits and interests
remained.
     With the growing division of labour, Alfred
Marshall(8) introduced a fourth factor, which he
called 'organisation'. The concept was vague and
the functions attributed to entrepreneurs very
diverse, ranging from the co-ordination of capital
and labour to superintending minor details. These
'organisers' (entrepreneurs) introduced improved
methods, thus increasing their earnings, only to
have these earnings reduced when competitors
entered the markets. The concept of improved
methods was to be forerunner to the Schumpeterian
idea of innovators and which has had such an impact
on the study of entrepreneurs.
     In the Schumpeterian system(9) the entrepreneur
engineers change and is a special type of co-ordinator
in that he provides new services notably (1)intro-
ducing new goods or an improvement in their quality,
(2) discovering new methods of production,
(3)finding new ways of marketing goods, (4) discovering new sources of raw-materials supply and

(5) reorganising production methods.

Accordingly, economic leaders were individuals motivated by a will to found a kingdom and to conquer with the joy of creating. Only with the motivational condition, 'a will to found a kingdom', does Schumpeter consider the profit motive to be important. This has the added advantage of providing a quantitative measure of success and was used as a criterion of succes in the many research studies that followed.

Of the early economists, F.H. Knight(10) projected Cantillon's concept of risk further by stating that entrepreneurs bear the responsibility and consequences of making decisions under conditions of uncertainty. Knight's entrepreneurs specifically commit their capital and bear the resultant uncertainty and risk. The control and decision-making lie with the entrepreneurs and, although in the modern corporate state risk can be covered through institutional insurance and decisions may lie with management, Knight felt that uncertainty defied definition, as every uncertain condition was unique and depended on a number of imponderables in the marketplace. The subject was not pursued further as economists became preoccupied with the Depression and the Second World War, but it was raised again in the late 1940s and early 1950s culminating in the setting up of the Entrepreneurial Research Centre at Harvard University through the efforts of A.H. Cole, who had continuously advocated that 'to study the entrepreneur is to study the central figure in modern economics'.

Activities of the Entrepreneurial Research Centre

During the three decades that the Centre was in operation the entrepreneur was studied in great detail as well as on a broader scale. Besides Cole, Schumpeter, T. Cochran and F. Redlich were involved and, in time, the Centre moved away from the Schumpeterian concept of 'innovator-prime mover', despite Schumpeter's presence.

This systematic method of study enabled scholars to identify and differentiate entrepreneurs in terms of functions. It became apparent that variations in types would appear, dependent on the economic environment, and different areas of study emerged, e.g. landowners as entrepreneurs, the aristocracy in Sweden, the effectiveness of entrepreneurs in France and the Industrial Revolution and its entrepreneurs in Britain. Redlich found artisans and merchants amongst the early

European industrialists, and a craftsman's son with
commercial training often went into manufacturing.
Cole emphasised decision-making, while Alexander
graded the entrepreneurial styles into primitive,
commercial progressive, modern organisational and
technological. He also noted that artisans became
primitive industrialists while traders became
commercial industrialists. The important findings
may be listed as (11)
Environment-oriented. Entrepreneurs respond to
population growth, evolution of methods of production
due to technological change, protected markets.
These entrepreneurs find technical expertise by
travel and hiring and by forming joint stock
companies.
Opportunity oriented. Entrepreneurs appear in
response to opportunities perhaps caused by wars
or other major social upheavals.
Origins. Entrepreneurs come from diverse social
backgrounds depending on the economic environments
and different stages in economic development.
Innovational. Innovators are distinguished by their
inventiveness, energy and vitality.
Organisational. Entrepreneurs build an organisation
that can sustain the introduction of an invention
into the economy.
Motivational. The motivations of entrepreneurs are
remarkably varied and the most basic motives are
security, prestige, power and service to the
community.

Relevance of Theories to Pakistan and Other Less Developed Countries

Of all the findings and theories examined so far,
some of the major concepts must be examined in the
context of Pakistan and other less developed
countries. For simplicity, three concepts will
be considered, (1)Walras's fourth factor in
production, (2)the Schumpeterian innovator and
(3)Knight's entrepreneur who commits the capital
and bears the risk.

In the Walrasian definition entrepreneurs are
examined within the concepts of the General
Equilibrium Theory, entering and leaving the
industry at will and dependent, of course, on their
profit-maximising abilities. As the fourth factor,
he hires land, labour and capital. Considered from
the academic point of view the definition is
difficult to apply empirically because of the
complexity in identifying such people (12). Again
the concepts of a free market and of entering and

leaving industry at will are difficult to apply to Pakistan. Schumpeter's entrepreneurs would be innovators under all conditions, but since require- ments of Pakistan can be viewed in terms of less complex adaptation, entrepreneurs here could hardly be termed innovators. So far as new markets are concerned, every product that was adapted for a particular market would be an innovation. Depending on the definition of the word 'innovation', one would have considerable leeway in defining any number of actions as innovations. Schumpeter further considered innovation in the context of competition, where there would be a continuous effort by entrepreneurs to improve on a marketable commodity, bearing in mind the consumer's preference of the entrepreneurs' ability to influence this choice. Although there have been empirical studies using this concept, notably by Sayigh,(13) it is difficult to agree with Schumpeter's concept of innovation.

Berna(14) confirms that a country with little or no industry is incapable of producing innovators until a large number of small entrepreneurs are developed. Owens and Nandy(15) make a similar point with much more force when they state that the traditional Schumpeterian behaviour associated with adventurous, expansive business activities may be an attractive variable in economic history, but at certain stages of economic growth it may be less critical from society's point of view than the less spectacular, small-scale, survival-orientated entre- preneurial activities of socially deprived communities. Hans Singer(16) states that the Schumpeterian system is not really a theory of how economic development starts from a very low income level but how it continues and proceeds once it has reached a stage which is characterised by the creation of innovating private entrepreneurs. Knight, in speaking of decision-making and risk- taking, is probably nearest to the concept of the entrepreneur in the Third World, where modern ideas of ownership have not yet been developed, where management has not evolved, where accounting techniques used by the corporate sector in the West are completely lacking and where ownership and management are more or less synonymous. In the Third World, capital markets are not yet fully established and credibility relies on personal contact. Decisions under such 'risk-orientated' conditions assume paramount importance.

The Concept of Entrepreneurship

Recent Economic Thought
In the 1960s a second attempt was made to determine
the characteristics of entrepreneurs in less
developed countries and ideas were challenged once
again. Scholars studied contemporary markets in
the light of supply and demand requirements. It was
considered that such a model, if adequately
developed, would be a dynamic one. Leibenstein(17)
pointed out that it would be modified by the way in
which entrepreneurs determine their own supply and
demand. Despite this shortcoming, a study based
on supply and demand determinants offered promise.
     Baumol(18) pointed out yet another problem,
notably the difficulty in classifying supply and
demand. For instance, was an insufficiency of
entrepreneurs to be viewed as inadequate opportunities for them or as a straightforward lack of
entrepreneurs. Where markets were imperfect and
entrepreneurs less mobile, lacking in knowledge
and varying in skills, any increase in demand was
not likely to be satisfied automatically. Entrepreneurs were therefore to be identified and studied
in terms of their activities and not of their
attributes.
     Economists such as Papanek and Harris constantly
emphasised that the greatest motivating factor for
entrepreneurs is the desire for financial gain, to
maximise real income. Given certain essential roles
which the entrepreneur has to perform, the aspect
of supply is coloured by the desire for profit. Any
activity which reduces profit would restrict these
essential roles and would reduce the supply of
entrepreneurs. When introduced into the economy
this reasoning led to the creation of a limited
number of entrepreneurs. The policy instruments
and incentives that followed resulted in a
concentration of wealth in the hands of these
entrepreneurs (19).
     But it was Kilby,(20) who, in attempting to
study the entrepreneur in greater detail, gave a
comprehensive list of activities critical to an
entrepreneur's success.

Exchange relationships
(1) Perception of market opportunities.
(2) Obtaining control of scarce resources.
(3) Purchasing inputs.
(4) Marketing the product and responding to
     competition.

Political administration
(5)   Dealing with bureaucracies (concessions/
       licenses, etc).
(6)   Management of human relationships within the
       firm.
(7)   Management of the customer-supplier
       relationship: management and control.
(8)   Financial management.
(9)   Production management (control by written
       records).

Technology
(10)   Acquiring and overseeing assembly of the
       factory.
(11)   Industrial engineering, minimising inputs with
       a given production process.
(12)   Upgrading product and product quality.
(13)   Introduction of new production techniques and
       products.

In an effort to be all-encompassing, Kilby generalised for the modern corporate sector, not for the
humbler entrepreneur of Berna or the 'New Vaisyas'
of Owen and Nandy.

Current Empirical Studies
These studies have indicated different motives for
the entry and development of entrepreneurship. All
assert the importance of different factors at
different points in time for increasing the supply
of entrepreneurs. As the supply of such people is
critical for less developed countries it is
important to determine the kind of entrepreneur
that responds to the economic environment created
by governments. Is it the entrepreneur with
commercial motives, looking at the short term,
making a quick turnover and investing a minimum
savings, or is it the entrepreneur with a long-term
plan, investing a major part of savings and having
other long-term objectives? The impact on the
development of a less developed economy would be
dependent on such attitudes.
     Sayigh's study(21) of 207 Lebanese entrepre-
neurs was designed to test Schumpeter's theory of
innovation. In doing so, Sayigh broadened the
innovative base by including advances in technology,
derivation or adaption. He concluded that
occupational and social mobility was significant,
and found indications of the concentration of
economic power in Lebanon.

The Concept of Entrepreneurship

Carroll's survey(22) of 92 indigenous industrial entrepreneurs in the Philippines was based on a detailed analysis of socio-economic background and mobility. The critical factors included an awareness of the possibility of entrepreneurial success which results in living in large cities which, in turn, is dependent on the greater access to opportunities in urban areas. Carroll also found great mobility in the Philippines, which was consolidated by continuous entrepreneurial activities and investment.

Alexander's studies(23) of Greek and Turkish industrialists indicated the importance of the merchant class in the supply of entrepreneurs. Former craftsmen tended to have smaller firms. Greek refugees who migrated from Turkey in 1920 were very well represented in the sample.

Papanek(24) studied 250 industrialists and found that government incentives stimulated entrepreneurship. He found that the minority ethnic castes comprising less than 0.5 per cent of population provided 43 per cent of Pakistan's industrialists. For Papanek, economic incentives were supremely important in as much as, on the one hand, these created a basis for monopoly power and hence financial gain and on the other, allowed entrepreneurs to have a congenial environment.

Berna(25), Mcrory(26) and Owens and Nandy(27) confined their research to particular areas in India: Berna dealt with Madras State, Mcrory with a town in north India and Owen and Nandy concentrated on the Howrah area in the city of Calcutta. Berna decided that traditional occupations and sub-castes have little impact on determining the entry of an entrepreneur. For him, economic factors such as access to capital, possession of business experience and technical knowledge were of prime importance. Mcrory found that industrialists with a mercantile background viewed a rapid turnover as the sole source of profit and were thus unwilling to tie up more than the absolute minimum of capital in plant and machinery. Owens and Nandy confined themselves to a particular community and concluded that small firms were linked to well-developed large-scale industries. Entrepreneurs had ease of entry and were highly efficient because of the competition thus generated. They were from the agricultural class but the economic environment created by a large industrial city was such as to enable them, over a period of time, to become entrepreneurs and develop an indigenous industry.

The Concept of Entrepreneurship

In their conclusions, Owens and Nandy linked
competence (and hence efficiency) with education.
     What were the conclusions of research carried
out in other disciplines? Sociologists established
the importance of religion, of ethnic groups that
had lost their importance, while psychologists held
that the basis for formation of attitudes was
important. A brief survey of these findings would
be useful in establishing some of the salient points.

Sociologists' Views
The earliest and probably the best-known concept is
that of Max Weber, who linked the driving force of
industrial entrepreneurs with the Protestant ethic.
This link between religion and industrial practise
enabled entrepreneurs to explain some of the
attitudes which society would otherwise stigmatise.
Cochran(28) followed Parsons' system of social
roles and social sanctions. These roles are dynamic
and change according to economic development, the
direction and pace of such change being dependent
on the acquisition of new skills, the expectations
of new rewards and the sanctions by society on such
behaviour. Thus the entrepreneur would change
as society changes, and although these changes may
not be quantified, by historical analogy it may be
possible to measure these social variables in terms
of above or below a certain norm or as correlates
of other variables.
     Hagen(29) explained the emergence of industrial
entrepreneurs by means of the concept of 'status
deprivation'. A social group may lose its status
and succeeding generations, in a state of tension,
may turn to industry to recover this. The critical
factor here is tension, as this causes changes in
personality (in terms of needs, values and world-
cognition) and thus leads to creativity and
retrieval of the position that was lost.
     Hoselitz(30) viewed blockage of careers as
critical. In such situations 'marginal men', who do
not belong to any influential groups, turn to
industry as a way of succeeding in society. Young
(31) analyses a socially reactive group with no
career opportunities but which has resources the
utilisation of these resources generally triggering
social change.

Psychologists Views
D. McClelland, R.Levine, J.Kunkel and Collins and
Moore considered entrepreneurial behaviour on the
basis of personality patterns. McClelland(32)

64

viewed child-rearing patterns as critical in
developing personalities orientated towards
achieving success (need-achievers). In such cases,
the stress is on self-reliance and an ever-increasing
urge for inner standards of excellence as benchmarks,
which individuals overtly try to maintain.
Empirical measurements are obtained through Thematic
Apperception Tests (TAT), fantasy essays, childrens'
stories, myths, etc. By using these methods
McClelland arrived at the view that there was much
in common between high-need achievers and entrepreneurs. On the basis of empirical results in India,
he concluded that if achievement motives were
latent these could be developed with suitable
training. Levine deviated from McClelland's thesis
by stating that high-need achievements were characteristic of parents seeking higher status.

Kunkel posits that conditioning was the
essential requirement. Behaviour is straight-
forwardly rewarded or punished by the existing
social and economic environment. Therefore, the
pressing need was to increase the stimuli which
lead to the desired modifications in behaviour. A
change in selected elements of a man's social life
which were conducive to the learning of new
behaviour was all that was required.

Collins and Moore, using TAT and extensive
interviews developed life-histories of entrepreneurs.
A typical case would be an escape from poverty and
acute insecurity and an early training in self-
reliance. Their entrepreneur was a restless social
reject, who enters industry having been psychologi-
cally and socially blocked from more traditional
and socially accepted careers.

The Pakistani Scene

Research on entrepreneurs is limited to that by
G.F.Papanek(33) and Hanna Papanek(34). In terms of
resources Muslims in the sub-continent had played
an insignificant role in industry. In fact, of
the seven million people who migrated to Pakistan,
only three families had any significant industrial
background. Two of these were in leather tanning
and one in the match industry (35).

G.F.Papanek concluded on the basis of his
empirical research in 1959 that in Pakistan there
were strong economic incentives and it was the
attraction of financial gain which induced traders
to move to industry, particularly as the banning
of consumer goods meant disincentives to any
further trading. Because of their knowledge of

markets and their available marketing channels,
these traders were very valuable to industry. As
further evidence, Papanek refers to their continuous
ability to reinvest not only in the same industry
but in other industries as well. His analysis was
in terms of 'push' and 'pull' factors. The 'push'
factors were falling profits in their current
occupation and the pull factors were the incentives.
These factors reinforced each other and worked
towards a common objective, financial gain (36).

However, he indicated some non-economic reasons
that were a prerequisite to the development of
entrepreneurship. These he listed as (1) a civil
service able to maintain law and order, prevention
of a massive flight of capital, enforcing of import
controls and provision of reasonable facilities,
(2) a proportion of the population responding to
economic incentives, (3) a value system and
institutions which were not hostile to entrepreneurial activity and (4) a political system which did
not collapse despite high prices for the consumers,
high profits for industrialists and the presence of
many foreign technicians. The lessons that Papanek
deduced from the Pakistani situation were threefold:
(1) development should be by large firms, (2) a
transfer of technology is necessary, and (3) generous
incentives should be available. In his opinion one
hundred industrialists were all that were required
for a population of 100 million. Important
distinctions and considerations of equality between
different geographical areas had been completely neglected: for instance, the different economic
environments of East & West Pakistan had been ignored,
as had those between the North West Frontier
Province, Baluchistan and urban and rural Sind and
the more affluent areas of Karachi and the Punjab
(37). If the entrepreneurial response was according
to 'push' and 'pull' factors, where was the shortcoming? The answer may be partially, if not wholly,
in what Hanna Papanek had to say: 'The emergence of
a new class of industrialists from among the
citizens is determined by political and economic
oppurtunities to which members of some strata
in the population respond more readily than
others' (38). To this may be added the Carroll
hypothesis (39) that in large cities the perception
of oppurtunities was greater and therefore the
probability of response more likely. The factors,
though, were many. First, the business class had
connections with politicians who were demanding a
separate homeland for the Muslims (40). Their

connections repeatedly enabled these businessmen to take the larger share of available credit as well as scarce foreign exchange. Second, the location of the capital at Karachi and the development of credit institutions in that city meant that industrialists based there had access to sources of credit. Otherwise, it is difficult to explain why two of the three industrialists who had moved to Pakistan after migration should transfer their head-quarters from East Pakistan to Karachi. The third factor 'was the manipulation of credit which the trading classes are so adept at'(41) coupled with H.Spodek's(42)' a closely knit ethnic community with expertise in finance rather than technology'. The early Pakistani industrialists certainly had these qualities; they were closely knit (the ethnic minority was an extension of the extended family system) and they were competent in matters of finance and in the manipulation of credit and foreign exchange. In comparison, the inadequacies of the inhabitants of East Pakistan were obvious, with a different language, limited markets, the population at subsistence levels and with no appreciation of opportunities. Given these conditions, it was not surprising that a response was lacking. The technology advocated was capital-intensive, with all other facilities hired at an exorbitant cost. Since high tariff protection was recommended this meant that inefficient industries, or rather high-cost industries, were installed in which the needs of consumers were completely ignored.

There were few financial incentives besides the evasion of income tax, which, after five tax-free years ('tax holidays') was in the region of (for the textile industry) Rs 1 per spindle per day. This meant that for a textile spinning unit(43) of 12,500 spindles the net profit per day was Rs 12,500 ($1 = Rs 3.00).

It has also been argued, specifically for the small entrepreneur,(44) that, once in trade, one can obtain a good knowledge of the extent of the market. In the case of entrepreneurs in the modern sector this knowledge is not a basic requirement and their risk is very limited, as their equity is generally 10 per cent. It is the credit institutions who, when failure is writ large, clamour for tariff protection to safeguard their credit contributions. The degree of tariff protection plus the barriers to entry and the shortage of foreign exchange (which again acts as a barrier to entry) ensures monopolistic profits for all involved. So far as the smaller entrepreneur is concerned, such profits are not there. Their knowledge is of a more substantive nature, based on risk and uncertainty. They not only have to asses consumer preferences and the extent of the market but also obtain resources from the private sector on the basis of their known competence in handling such resources. With such reputations acquired over time, the transfer from trade to manufacturing seems a logical step.

Papanek's 'generous incentives' worked for these industrialists who managed entry early, who moved with ease amongst the higher echelons of bureaucracy and who influenced government policy on all industrial matters. A comprehensive sphere of influence was at work. The interpersonal links which had their roots in pre-partition days were consolidated. H.Papanek makes the point 'whatever else might be said about the achievements of Jinnah and the Pakistan movement it does seem to be evident that the actual alignment between at least some big businessmen and the Muslim League leadership had begun long before partition' (45). This relationship was further cemented through contacts with the administration. The civil service in Pakistan wielded power behind the scenes and was responsible for a continuity in policy.

If these economic incentives had universal appeal, why was there not the same kind of response from other regions? This lack of universal appeal had catastrophic results for Pakistan. Economic opportunity was never even-handed: it was highly discriminatory.

The pace and direction of industrialisation plus the domination of some large economic/industrial houses having their origin in West Pakistan but industrial ownership in both Wings, so cherished and put forward as an example for other less developed countries to follow, led White to say:(46)

To the extent that industrial concentration worsened income distribution generally, and the extent that the Bengalis resented the foreign ownership of East Pakistan by West Pakistan indus- trialists and resented having to buy overpriced West Pakistani manufactured goods, the industrial policies may have contributed to the ultimate Bangladesh split (47).

One has to go back to partition to understand the importance of the economic grievances. The split with India was partially, if not entirely, on this matter. This economic exploitation was extreme before partition, in which the Hindus were the main culprits, and was continued by the industrialists of West Pakistan towards East Pakistan. The question, though, is too complicated for a simplistic explanation but suffice it to say that this exploitation increased internal instability. Pakistan lacked social engineers to devise policies and programmes which were not discriminatory. What were accepted were economic concepts. The failing, if any, was entirely of their own making.

Industrialists span a broad spectrum, from the large to the small. A country such as Pakistan, with little or no industrial tradition in 1947, can hardly produce and develop innovators without first producing the smaller type of entrepreneur in large numbers (48). The commanding heights of the industrial world can be reached only by sustained effort. Great innovators,(49) like great scholars, are always an exceptional few, who appear at the summit of a broadly based pyramid.

A total of 196 entrepreneurs were interviewed by the author, and the sample contained successful, unsuccessful and barely surviving entrepreneurs. Therefore what follows is based on empirical research.

Notes

1. W.J. Baumol, 'Entrepreneurship in Economic Theory', American Economic Review, May 1968, pp. 66-8.

2. E.T. Penrose, The Theory and Growth of the Firm, Willey, New York, 1959.

3. R. Cantillon, 'On the Nature of Commerce in General' in Early Economic Thought, ed. A.E. Monroe, Harvard University Press,Cambridge, Mass., 1951.

4. Ibid.

5. J.B. Say, A Treatise on Political Economy, 4th edn, translated by C.R. Prinsap, Wells and Lilly, Boston, 1824, as in E.W. Nafziger, African Capitalism: A case Study in Nigerian Entrepreneurship, Hoover Institution Press, Stanford, California, 1977, p.7.

6. L. Walras as cited in Nafziger, African Capitalism, p.8.

7. M. Tyagarajan, 'The Development of Theory of Entrepreneurship', I.E.R., Aug. 1959, pp.135-50.

8. Alfred Marshall as cited in Nafiziger, African Capitalism.

9.   J. Schumpeter, Theories of Economic Development, Harvard University Press, Cambridge, Mass, 1934.

10. F.H. Knight, Risk Uncertainty and Profit, Harper and Row, New York, 1921.

11. M.P. Rowe, 'Indigineous Industrial Entrepreneurship in Lagos, Nigeria', unpublished PhD dissertation, Columbia University, 1972.

12. Nafziger, African Capitalism.

13. Y.A. Sayigh, Entrepreneurs of Lebanon, The Role of A Business Leader in a Developing Economy, Harvard University Press, Cambridge, Mass, 1962.

14. J.J. Berna, Industrial Entrepreneurship in Madras State, Bombay.

15. R.L. Owens and A. Nandy, The New Vaisyas, Carolina Academic Press, Durham, North Carolina, 1978.

16. H. Singer 'Obstacles to Economic Development'. Social Research, Vol.XX, Spring 1953. F. Redlich makes a similar point in his 'Entrepreneurship in the Initial Stages of Industrialisation' in Weltwirtschaftliches Archiv', Vol. 75, 1955.

17. H. Leibenstein, 'Entrepreneurship and Economic Development', American Economic Review, May 1968.

18. J. Baumol in 'Entrepreneurship in Economic Theory' American Economic Review, May 1968.

19. Y.A. Sayigh, for Lebanon and R. Amjad and L.J. White for Pakistan, illustrate this point. There are many examples of such a concentration in other countries, e.g. Nicaragua, Mexico, Brazil.

20. P. Kilby 'Hunting the Heffalump' in Entrepreneurship and Economic Development, P. Kilby (ed), The Free Press, New York, 1971.

21. Sayigh, 'Entrepreneurs of Lebanon'.

22. J.J. Carroll, The Filipino Manufacturing Entrepreneur. Agent and Product of Change, Cornell University Press, Ithaca, 1965.

23. A.P. Alexander, Greek Industrialists. An Economic and Social Analysis, Athens Centre of Planning and Economic Research, 1964: 'Industrial Entrepreneurship in Turkey: Origins and Growth', Economic Development and Cultural Change, Vol.VIII, No. 4, Part I, July, 1960, 349-65.

24. G.F. Papanek 'The Development of Entrepreneurship' in 'Entrepreneurship and Economic Development', ed. P. Kilby, The Free Press, New York, 1971.

25. Berna, Industrial Entrepreneurship.

26. J.T. Mcrory, Small Industry in a North Indian Town, Case studies in Latent Industrial Potential, Government of India, New Delhi, 1956.

27. Owens and Nandy, The New Vaisyas.

28. T.C. Cochran, 'The Entrepreneur in Economic Change', in Entrepreneurship and Economic Development, ed. P. Kilby, The Free Press, Ithaca, 1971.

29. E.E. Hagen, 'The Transition in Columbia', in ibid.

30. B. Hoseltiz, 'Entrepreneurship and Traditional Elites', E.E.H, IInd series.

31. F. Young, A Macrosociological Interpretation of Entrepreneurship, in 'Entrepreneurship and Economic Development' ed. P. Kilby, The Free Press, New York, 1971.

32. D. McClelland, 'The Achievement Motive in Economic Growth' in Kilby (ed) Entrepreneurship and Economic Development, p. 151.

33. G.F. Papanek 'Pakistan's Industrial Entrepreneurship, Education, Occupational Background, and Finance' in Development Policy II, The Pakistan Experience, eds. W.P.Falcon and G.F. Papanek, Harvard University Press, Cambridge, Mass, 1971.

34. H. Papanek, 'Entrepreneurs in East Pakistan', in Bengal: Change and Continuity, eds. R. and M.J. Beech, Michigan State University, East Lansing, 1972: 'Pakistan's Big Businessmen; Muslim Separatism, Entrepreneurship and Partial Modernisation', Economic Development and Cultural Change, Vol. 21, No. 1, Oct. 1972.

35. Interviews with industrialists. The two in the leather industry were the Monnoos and the Saigols. The former moved initially to Dacca (East Pakistan) and the latter to West Pakistan. The Adamjees were in the match industry and they moved to East Pakistan. All three own substantial industrial assets and are amongst the most vigorous of the industrial houses.

36. G.F. Papanek, Pakistan's Development: Social Goals and Private Incentives, Harvard University Press, Cambridge, Mass, 1971.

37. Pakistan at that time consisted of five Provinces: the Punjab, Sind, Baluchistan, North-West Frontier Province and East Pakistan. The most populous was East Pakistan and the largest in area was Baluchistan.

38. H. Papanek, 'Entrepreneurs in East Pakistan'.

39. Carnoll, The Filipino Manufacturing Entrepreneur.

40. H. Papanek, makes a similar point in her article 'Pakistan's Big Businessmen; Muslim Separatism, Entrepreneurship and Partial Modernisation' in Economic Development and Cultural Change, Vol. 21, No. 1, Oct. 1972.

41. T.A. Timberg, 'The Origins of Marwari Industrialist' in Beech, Bengal.

42. H. Spodek 'Manchesterisation of Ahmedabad' The Economic Weekly, Vol. XVII, 13 March 1965, 483-5.

43. Interview with a 'feudal' entrepreneur.

44. Interview with an 'aspiring' entrepreneur.

45. H. Papanek, Big Businessmen.

46. L.J. White, 'Industrial Concentration'.

47. A view definitely confirmed by the author who was in a senior position and served for two and a half years in field positions in former East Pakistan. Not only was there overpricing but the quality left much to be desired. Import of competitive goods was banned. The net result of such discriminatory monopoly positions was the existence of a 'no-option situation', i.e. a situation in which there was only one seller, unsatisfied demand and no substitutable products.

48. Berna, Industrial Entrepreneurship, p.7.

49. Ibid.

Chapter Four

THE ORIGINS AND OCCUPATIONS OF ENTREPRENEURS

The more significant findings in this chapter will
be considered in the light of existing theory and
of the actual world of the entrepreneur rather
than being abstracted from secondary sources.
References to concepts developed in other
disciplines will also be made.
    There are any number of ways in which the
world of the entrepreneurs may be interpreted.
To consider their development from a point where
they enter industry is to use an arbitrary point
of reference. Much has happened in the economic
and psychological life of entrepreneurs to take
them to the brink of a new era. What is it that
takes them to the cross-roads of life and to
accept significant risks? There is much
cumulative experience given that any individual
is unique. The societal influences add further to
the elements of uncertainty in the environment.
With so many factors working together any
interpretation of all that has happened may be
inadequate. Some of the origins, mobility,
experience, education and training of entrepreneurs
will be examined and the informal influences of
family, caste and community and their effect in
the making of entrepreneurs will be discussed. The
aim here is to examine entrepreneurs in as wide a
context as possible.
    The majority of entrepreneurs in the sample
are from the textiles and products sector (19 per
cent) followed by metal machinery (14 per cent),
electric fans (12 per cent), and agricultural
implements (8 per cent). In all categories a
total of twenty industrial sectors are represented.
Although the majority of the entrepreneurs were from
the textile sector there is much diversity in this
industry that they reflect all forms of enterprises,

from composite weaving and spinning units in the
large modern sector to calendering and finishing
units in the small one. The technological span
varies from the most indigenous to the most modern.

The geographical spread of the sample was
the entire length of Pakistan. The only province
where no entrepreneur was interviewed was
Baluchistan, as the conditions for entrepreneurial
growth in Baluchistan may not be relevant for the
rest of the country. Baluchistan exists in the
tribal world of the eighteenth century. Cut off
from the rest of the country, the province has a
population density of eight people per square mile
(1). The number of literate people, i.e. with a
rudimentary ability to sign their own name, in the
five major tribes (2), according to a special census
of Baluchis (3) carried out during the early 1970s,
was 1,846 (4). The main town is under occupation
by inhabitants from other provinces. There is no
industry and hardly any infrastructure.

The spread of entrepreneurs by industry
covered a substantial part of the industrial field.
Here entrepreneurs are analysed as members of
distinct communities. Four such communities were
identified in the sample, with a fifth other category
to show miscellaneous communities. The communities
are migrants from pre-partition India who have
retained their individuality. They are not
adequately represented to be dealt with separately.

Two of these communities are identified by
ethnic origin and two by region. The Memon and
Bohra communities, in the former category, come
from areas which are now in India. Although they
have been in Pakistan since 1947, they have been
able to maintain their identity and have not
integrated with the local population. Papanek states:

This tradition extends ... also to an
associated complex of values and attitudes which
might be called their work ethic and the supportive
social structure of the group, including kinship
relations, the marriage network, systems of training and education, internal communication network,
and internal system of social controls (5).
So strong is this cultural base and so well
integrated is it that one rarely hears of any
dispute or scandal involving any member of the
Memon community. Similarly, the Bohras pursue
their occupations with single-minded ability, and
rarely allow themselves to be drawn into any
disputes. What is important is that, despite the
pressures of the modern world and the increasing

74

levels of aspiration, there is rarely, if ever, a
conflict at any social level. The two regional
communities are the Punjabis and the Pathans,
residents of the province of the Punjab and the
North-West Frontier province, respectively
(Table 4.1).

Table 4.1: Communities in Industry

Communities	No
Punjabis (a)	152
Memons	6
Bohras	3
Pathans	3
Others	7
Missing observations	31

Note: a. The number of Punjabis seems to be
excessive in the sample. (The Punjabi sample is
further examined under the caste system heading).

There was a preponderance of Punjabis in the
entrepreneurs interviewed. These were
geographically dispersed. The reason for this
dispersion of Punjabis goes back to the period of
migration of refugees in 1947. Of the two
provinces that were most affected by the migration,
the Punjab and Bengal absorbed the majority of the
refugees. The exodus into East Pakistan (now
Bangladesh) was largely by the Biharis, who, prior
to migration, had been employed on the railways and
in other public services. The refugees into the
Punjab were largely craftsmen and agriculturists.
The lack of professionally skilled people and a
shortage of administrators meant that, the first
reaction to uprooting and the resulting insecurity
was a search for a regular income, at least until
life became stable again. This response was a
natural reaction to great insecurity caused by the
Second World War and the demands for independence.
Constant threats, each more frightening, produced
different reactions. The imminent invasion of
India during the Second World War meant that all
industries became suppliers for the first priority,
the war effort. The second priority was determining
price differentials, and to assess whether it
would be profitable to supply goods to the army.
This was least risky. On occasions the transaction

was completed within the credit period allowed by
manufacturer to the initial purchaser or, as he
came to be known, the contractor. Some of the
later industrialists became contractors and others
were Muslims because of the religious laws for the
Muslim troops concerning the eating of meat which
was not hilal, or the equivalent of Jewish Kosher
meat. The Indian army had seen a mutiny in 1357
based on the twin problems of hilal meat and pig's
grease (which was used for cleaning weapons). The
result was that, over a period of time, a number
of Muslim contractors were established. The
Muslim industrialists were located in the Punjab,
and other areas which are now Pakistan, and the
rise of the country's industrialist entrepreneurs
is mainly a result of these activities. At least
two of the twenty-two families, the Alis of the
Punjab and the Sheikhs of Multan - give this as the
reason for their moves into industry. According
to them, this not only enabled them to assess price
differential gaps but also allowed them access to
important members of the bureaucracy.

The Memons had such contact with the political
authorities who, for them were the link with
bureaucracy. They have maintained this link over
a long period, as it enabled them to seek favours
from those in authority and has substantially
increased their security and economic benefits.
The method invariably employed was to seek the
favourite projects of those in power and to
contribute substantial finance for the completion
of these projects. In Pakistan, the spin-offs
from such investment are immense. Such donations
are a passport to a much larger world of economic
benefits through important inside information and
contracts which may lead to windfall gains. Once
established, further cementing of the link was
dependent on the ability of the entrepreneur to
'cultivate' these relationships. Bureaucratic
faces are powerful ones and seldom change. Once
established, friendship lasts in perpetuity and
a two-way relationship develops. For benefits
guaranteed and insured by the bureaucracy, the
entrepreneur, in turn, is the creator of goodwill
for the bureaucrat, and this he does by praising
the efficiency and honesty of the bureaucrats
before their political bosses. Whereas in West
Pakistan this went unnoticed, in East Pakistan it
came to be regarded as yet another coalition of the
'western unholies', West Pakistani exploiters, and
further accelerated the demand for secession.

The Origins and Occupations of Entrepreneurs

Occupational Options at Partition
At the time of Partition the intial response of the
majority of the migrants in the Punjab was to seek
a secure occupation which would enable the family
to subsist and perhaps ensure a reasonable standard
of living as well as educational opportunities for
their children. The first option therefore was
either the civil service (which included higher
government positions) or military service (6).
Such jobs were powerful ones and were identified
with the former representatives of colonial
authority. Since colonial power was absolute at
that time, those who replaced the administrators
were deemed to be equally powerful. Such a transfer
of authority followed, though with one exception.
The colonial administrators were not interested in
acquiring productive assets in the form of real
estate in an alien country, and when it came to
dispensing material benefits, they could do so in
a reasonably objective way. Their replacements
found themselves unable to do this because of the
nature of their social responsibility, and,since
most of the real estate belonged to the Hindus who
had since migrated, the new administrators started
to pass these assets on to their relatives,
friends and connections. The response for jobs
came in particular from the city of Lahore in West
Pakistan and specifically from the Government
College, where every year a number of students
entered the civil service through competitive
examinations. In these examinations success was
synonymous with excellence. In terms of education
Lahore had an edge over all the other towns in
Pakistan. While the Punjab University is more than
hundred years old, the Government College is older
still. Until 1947 Karachi was of no significance
educationally and other cities were even further
down the scale. This meant that the inhabitants
of these other cities had to find inferior positions
in the civil service and local councils or, as in
Karachi, were forced into other areas, e.g. trading,
stevedoring or catering, from where, over a period
of time,they progressed either vertically in these
jobs or left them to go into more lucrative
situations such as manufacturing. In the North-
West Frontier Province, the nature of the terrain
forced the major entrepreneurs to go in to
transport, the only exception being the influential
tribal chief who, in response to government
exhortations, went into manufacturing. In
Baluchistan all industries and industrial estates

have been located near Karachi. This has meant
that entrepreneurs have come from other parts of
the country and not from the province itself.

Occupations of Entrepreneurs' Fathers
The statistics from a sample of 196 interviewees,
collected in September 1980, are given in
Table 4.2

Table 4.2: Entrepreneurs' Fathers' Occupations

	No	%
Agriculturalist	23	12
Civil servant	22	11
Private employment	4	2
Trade	39	20
Industrialist	98	50
Professional	8	4
Others	1	1
	195	100
Missing observations	1	

The surprising fact is the large response by
agriculturists and civil servants. In these two
occupations parents had to contend with serious
problems and, since the father always decided his
children's occupation, it is not surprising that a
significant number encouraged their offsprings to
go into industry. Why should the agriculturist
want a different occupation for his son? The
answer lies in the decline of the agricultural
sector not only economically but also in terms of
a loss of prestige.

A spate of land reforms (7) and the
anticipation of more legislation in this area meant
a steady whittling away of land-ownership.
Holdings continued to become smaller because of the
new laws of inheritance (8), and landlords had
either to sell the estimated excess land, distribute
it between the family members or allow it to be
expropriated by the government. Such an
expropriation was to be avoided by all means and
would only happen if unexpected land reforms took
the agricultural community by surprise. Of greater
significance in this sector were the changes in the
tenancy system (9), whereby the responsibility for

agricultural inputs (10) was now that of the landlord and not the tenant. When land was permanently
acquired by the government it was given to the
agricultural tenant, free of cost, for building
houses. This meant, of course, that the tenant was
no longer residing in quarters provided by the
landlord, and he was therefore no longer subservient
to him. This produced a rapid transformation in
the landlord's attitude; he no longer wanted to be
an absentee landlord and, rather than suffer
further humulitations, the landed gentry sold their
excess land, including that which was likely to be
subject to further reforms. The finances thus
obtained were used for building textile mills in the
majority of cases. The sugar industry was again an
obvious choice.

As the feudal system in Pakistan created
most of the political links it was not difficult
to deal with official requirements. Since 1960,
excluding the first Governor-General all senior
political positions have been occupied by
agriculturalists, and employees in the civil and
military services, even if they had no agricultural
background, have supplemented their income by
acquiring landholdings. This resulted in a growing
disenchantment of the landlords with agriculture
and their desire to diversify if only to keep their
positions intact.

Over the period civil servants had also lost
prestige. It was no longer true, as Papanek had
stated that, 'After 1958 the civil service and
military were dominant even at the political level
of government. Traditionally power, prestige and
competence lay with the Civil Service, not with
political leadership' (11). He goes on to state:
'Great responsibilities at an early age made for
self-confidence, decisiveness, and an ability to
work hard' (12).

Action by successive governments looking for
reasons for the country's failure led to punitive
action against corruption and inefficiency in the
civil service. This was well publicised in the
media and it eroded what little self-confidence and
conviction was left in the administration. Overnight,
civil servants, praised by the previous government,
became the villains of the present government.
After 1958, when the precedent was established,
successive governments have dismissed many civil
servants within a month of taking office. Thus the
Yahya government dismissed 302 officials and the
Bhutto government 1,300. The elimination of

corruption and inefficiency continues to this day.
Successive governments have seen this as a means
of controlling their administration. Vacancies
thus created had to be filled, and loyalists of
various kinds were brought in depending upon the
regime in power, it all depended on how insecure
the decision-makers felt. Suffice it to say that
the ratio of newly recruited to dismissed personnel
is on the increase and leadership of the civil
service is no longer provided by families with a
traditional background of government service (13).

Surprisingly, the majority of dismissed civil
servants (36 per cent) went into the electric-fan
industry and another 14 per cent entered the
textile industry. The choice of industry is not
surprising as in both there was no shortage of
expertise and demand. Pakistan's order books for
fans are usually full for nine months ahead and
that there is a continuous need for clothing, and,
given favourable government policies, the chances
of doing well in these industries were more than
even.

Not surprisingly, another 20 per cent of the
civil servants went into trading. In the total
absence of any kind of marketing services, the only
way to meet demand is through trading. With the
state of Pakistan's foreign exchange and the
variability in granting commercial licences for
the import of consumer, intermediate and capital
goods, there are occasions when depletions in
foreign exchange are reflected in the shops. Under
such circumstances traders either obtain foreign
exchange and goods in the black market or purchase
industrial licences so paying the industrialists'
substantial goodwill premium. The next hurdle for
trader is customs clearance. At times, given the
right mix of graft, even an elephant can walk
through customs, while an insignificant article can
be held up. Over a period of time the traders'
options to maintain trade are by (1) obtaining
import licences from the government, (2) purchasing
licences in the open market and having to pay
goodwill premiums and (3) purchasing industrial
licences at an exorbitant premium and facing
further increases in costs of the informal payments
required by the customs.

What is the net effect of all these additional
payments? The traders, if they can still sell
their goods, find that the demand for them is
stable, and the difficulties of increased payments
and premiums often force them to start manufacturing

the goods that they have traded. Their experience
of obtaining import licences from the authorities
is very valuable, particularly in finding their
way through the intricate procedures involved in
starting up a manufacturing company and replacing
the trade which they may have lost.

On the other hand the response from the
industrial sector was very refreshing and augurs
extremely well for the industrialisation strategy.
Fifty per cent of the sample had fathers in
industry. Thus sons were following in the footsteps of the fathers, creating a cumulative
industrial experience. The entrepreneurs were
dispresed across a wide range of industries,
perhaps signifying a conscious development of
opportunities where a demand had been created. The
sample did not determine the number of enterprises
that each entrepreneur had developed, either
formally or by extending help to the members of
his family. Conglomerates were not only to be
found in the modern corporate sector but also in
medium and small-scale industries. There are
obvious advantages in this. The smaller unit often
escapes notice by government authorities and is
therefore free of the imposition of rules and
regulations. The unit is kept within organisational
and management capabilities, thereby reducing the
need for specialised management. The response to
a greater demand is met by creating another unit,
rather than increasing existing capacity. This
allows industrialists to offset their profits
against this other unit and it provides a bargaining
position for tax on profits. More important,
genuine fears were raised in the 1970s when
industry was subject to a massive nationalisation,
and the entrepreneur with the ability to expand
did so by means of creating more units.

During the early stages of a manufacturing
company decisions are usually made by the father
or by the head of the joint family while the son
undergoes intensive training. With craftsman
entrepreneurs this informal training takes place
throughout the educational life of the son,
generally after school hours - leisure is considered
to be a waste of time. In the large corporate
sector the emphasis is usually in providing
management skills. Thus contrary to Papanek's (14)
determination of educational levels, present
entrepreneurs are more literate (15) and possess
the relevant technical or management education.
Table 4.3 and 4.4 gives details of the sizes of the

Table 4.3: Size by Employment of Entrepreneurs'
Father's Firm

No	Size	Total no. of firms	%
1	0-10	15	18
2	11-50	34	41
3	51-100	7	8
4	101-200	10	12
5	201-1,000	11	13
6	1,001-5,000	6	7
7	5,000+	1	1
	Total	84	100

Table 4.4: Size by Sales of Entrepreneurs'
Fathers' Firms (rupees)

No.	Size	Total no. of firms	%
1	0-50,000	7	11
2	50,001-250,000	13	20
3	250,001-500,000	4	6
4	500,001-1,000,000	7	11
5	1,000,001-2,000,000	5	8
6	2,000,001-5,000,000	10	16
7	5,000,000+	18	28
	Total	64 a	100

Note: a. Twenty entrepreneurs could not recall the
sales figures.

firms run by the entrepreneurs' fathers. The
really small firms composed 18 per cent of the
total sample and 59 per cent of the sample was
composed of firms with up to fifty employees. The
sales of this category of firm may be rather high
for the period as shown by a comparison of the
sales figures with the low number of employees.
Medium-sized firms (51-100 and 100-200 employees)

form 20 per cent of the sample while large firms
(201-1,000, 1,001-5,000+employees) constitutes
21 per cent. The size by sales category shows the
vigorous nature of the transactions and the demand
for products at a point at a time. It was
difficult, however, to obtain sales figures for the
firms for the pre 1947 period in the absence of any
record.

If companies with sales of up to Rs 50,000
are considered to belong to the small firm category
then those comprise only 11 per cent of the sample
and medium-sized companies i.e. with sales of
Rs 50,000 to 2,50,000 form 20 per cent. The
majority of firms are those in the large-firm
category, i.e. with sales of more than Rs 2,50,000.
Some 69 per cent of the firms are in this category,
the implication being that the number of employees
is not always related to sales figures (and hence
profit) and that, provided that the demand for
goods continues to increase, this cumulative
experience will encourage an ever-increasing supply
of entrepreneurs. This is the impression that
entrepreneurs have, by and large, of the industrial
efforts of their ancestors. However, people
interviewed did mention that government rules and
regulations were not so restrictive for their
ancestors as they are now, and in earlier times
there was little attempt by the government to
stipulate the direction of industry or the amount
of industrial output. One's efforts were dependent
entirely on ones work ethic and competitiveness in
the market place. Data for the years in which
these firms came into existence are shown in
Table 4.5.

It is not surprising to note that the supply
of entrepreneurs increased during the period
of (1) forced import substitution and (2) demand
created by the requirements of the Second World
War. The period from mid-1920 to 1950 was also
one of maximum environmental instability. The
'quit India' movement had already started, then came
the depression of the early 1930s, the Second
World War and the disturbances before and after
the partition in 1947. Despite this instability
and of the unrest on the subject of law and order,
industry still thrived.

Table 4.5: Year of Founding of Father's Firm

Firm founded	No. of firms	%
1900-10	3	3
1910-19	4	4
1920-9	14	16
1930-9	19	21
1940-9	33	36
1950+	18	20
Total	91 a	100

Note: a. Missing observations: 7.

Growth in Inherited Industries
With the above figures in mind, we will study how
sons of industrialists have progressed in terms of
increasing employee numbers, assuming technology
to have been constant in a simplistic way. Tables
4.6 and 4.7 indicate the growth of the firm in both
categories, i.e. by size of employment and of
sales and significant differences can be seen. For
the heirs, the 0-10-employee category has
disappeared, indicating growth. The implication
for employment is significant, as the large sector
of the firm had shown an increase from 18 per cent
to 24 per cent in this limited sample. Greater

Table 4.6: Comparison of Father's Firm with Sons'
Firm (by number of employees).

Son's firm	Father's firm						
	0-10	11-50	51-100	101-200	201-1,000	1,001-5,000	5,000+
11-50	6	19	3	4	4	–	–
51-100	3	7	1	4	–	3	–
101-200	3	1	1	–	–	1	–
201-1,000	1	5	–	1	2	2	–
1,001-5,000	–	1	1	–	1	–	1
5,000+	2	1	1	1	4	–	–
Total	15	34	7	10	11	6	1
	18%	41%	8%	12%	13%	7%	1%

Table 4.7: Comparison of Father's Firm with Son's
Firm (by sales)

Son's firm	Father's firm						
	1	2	3	4	5	6	7
0-5,000	1	-	-	-	-	-	-
5,001-250,000	-	1	-	-	-	-	-
250,001-500,000	-	-	1	1	-	1	-
500,001-1,000,000	1	4	1	-	1	1	2
1,000,001-2,000,000	1	4	-	1	1	1	1
2,000,001-5,000,000	-	4	1	1	1	1	1
5,000,001+	4	-	1	4	2	6	14
Total	7	13	4	7	5	10	18
	11%	20%	6%	11%	8%	17%	28%

employment opportunities have therefore been
provided by the second generation of entrepreneurs.
The large sector has also increased in money terms,
showing increased sales and profits.

Occupational Mobility
A substantial proportion (44 per cent) of the
entrepreneurs had changed their occupation. The
six areas of employment from which the majority of
the mobile entrepreneurs transferred into
manufacturing are shown in Table 4.8. The higest
proportion came from private employment (or 42 per
cent), mostly at middle mangement levels. These
people were usually poorly paid, although the jobs
that they performed were often important, usually
essential co-ordinating tasks on behalf of owners,
e.g. interpreting industrial relations policies
with law and order agencies and handling law suits
at labour tribunals. With this experience and an
awareness of the requirements of the production
process, all the employees needed to enter industry
was finance. They usually took production and
some maintenance staff with them, and 42 per cent
of the entrepreneurs who had shown mobility in
occupation came from this group. Access to a
large number of co-ordinating functions was thus
provided by the 'odd jobs' nature of their previous

The Origins and Occupations of Entrepreneurs

Table 4.8: Occupational Mobility

Occupation	Occupational mobility	
	Number	%
Agriculture	1	1
Civil servant	15	17
Private employment	37	42
Trade	31	35
Professional	3	3
Others	2	2
Total	89	100

employment. They had learnt, informally, enough about the technical managerial, and marketing aspects in their roles as trouble-shooters. They had also discovered that the technical aspects of their work could be performed by indigenous consultants who, although lacking formal training, were endowed with mechanical ingenuity. They were too proud to work for anyone else, but they were readily available to help, for a suitable fee or retainer, in the setting up and maintenance of a factory. They operated from, what in colloquial language, is known as Adda (16), which was either the office or home of someone else. The contacts were personal and dependent on the whims of the consultant.

The next largest profession in Table 4.8 is trade, roughly 35 per cent of the sample. The trader has always been considered important in industry primarily because of his ability to obtain credit/and manage finances. There are a number of studies in praise of trading and its spin-offs. In Pakistan the Papaneks (17), on the basis of an empirical study carried out with the help of 250 Pakistan industrialists with twenty or more workers, came to the conclusion that the country's remarkable results in the industrial field were due to the response of certain merchant classes. Previously, the main occupation of 45 per cent of these new industrialists had been trading. In trying to explain the basis of their results, Hanna Papanek found 'occupational specialisation in business' as the most useful variable. She states that 'this implies a host of associated institutions, values and attitudes different from what the term applies in most other

settings' (18). Similarly, Sayigh (19) found for
Lebanon that 31 per cent of the fathers of the
industrialists were in trade. Alexander (20),
in his study on Greek industrialists, found the
preponderance of large merchants and small merchants
(21 per cent and 14 per cent, respectively) in the
industrialists' sample. Only Berna (21), while
interviewing fifty-two entrepreneurs in the light
engineering industry found that the majority
(twelve) were graduate engineers. Sharma and
Singh, who studied the sports and light engineering
industry in two provinces of India (The United
Province and the Punjab (22)) found empirically that
the business castes were in a majority in the
industrial sector. They further determined that a
business family's propensity to enter industry was
greater than if one belonged to a functional caste
such as artisans. Owens and Nandy (23) traced the
occupational heritage not only to the father but
also to the father's father. On the basis of their
findings, they found that 65 per cent of the
respondents were from the business community and
that 52 per cent of their fathers were in
agriculture. The transfer established by Owens and
Nandy is not from business to industry but from
agriculture to factory worker or small business and
then into industry. The area that these two
authors were studying had distinctive features
and may have been a special case, namely the
district of Howrah, west of the river Hoogly, where
land was always in short supply and where, because
of Howrah port, opportunities abounded. It was
therefore obvious that the Mahasiyas, who were
originally agriculturists, would move first to
small business, then into the service industry and
finally into manufacturing.

Having established that traders do play a
significant part in industrialisation, do these
entrepreneurs have distinct significant
characteristics. First, in the Pakistan context
a distinction needs to be made between merchants/
traders and traditional small merchants. The two
professions have become confused but it is not
only necessary to define and provide a frame of
reference for each but also to deal with them
separately. To equate a small bazaar merchant
from Gujranwala (24) or Gujrat (25) and to devise
policies for him similar to those for a Chiniot
Sheikh or a Memon mercantile trader would be
impossible. During the course of the interviews
the mercantile traders were allowed free discussion.

Each trader's perception of the business was
different and their aspirations were no longer
profit-oriented. They confessed that they had never
had a hedge against risk, but their record of great
social responsibility could not be denied. However,
an effort to channel their resources and energy
though would be useful. The second generation of
entrepreneurs, as well as the pioneers, were
interviewed. Papanek may have found education
irrelevant, but its relevance to trade and industry
would probably have to be analysed differently.
The emphasis on industrialisation by the second
generation coincided with specific issues of
Pakistan's increasing wealth and inequality of
opportunities. Never arrogant, always
supporting their arguments with reason and logic,
never short of bargaining ability (in fact bargaining was their strong point) the second generation
have seen industry differently. The second
generation of traders have taken precautions against
nationalisation. Their long-term perspectives are
different from those of the first generation, and
the more progressive have covered their potential
risk by transferring their resources, to other
countries or by becoming Third World multinationals,
investing in the industrialisation of those other
countries. Pakistani entrepreneurs looked to the
Middle East with its expanding markets, or to the
new nations of Africa, which provided valuable
testing grounds. These large houses competed in the
international sector, where tariff protection was
no longer available to them. Others, firmly
entrenched, decided that group identification was
dangerous, and their industries were split up:
although joint responsibility still remained with
the family, on paper the units were, as far as
possible, not given names that would link them with
the family. No group financial statements were
issued, interlocking directorates were reduced,
taxation policies were not established on a group
basis or tax returns that would reveal these units
submitted. A loophole in the law, it may be
countered, can be overturned by another law, but
this kind of separation of identity provided the
ability to take on the system with the succeeding
governments. A low profile was adopted when
circumstances were not favourable, with self-
assertion when conditions allowed.
    The consequences of these policies were as
follows:
(1) The entrepreneurs decided that small was

acceptable, and that they would invest in medium-/
or small-scale, highly capital-intensive industries.
(2)   The equity patticipation should be reduced
as far as possible, which meant that more
institutional funding was required.
(3)   To esnure this the entrepreneurs had to
manipulate policies in such a way that the financial
institutions (26) came within their sphere of
influence, and what better way to do this than to
be on the board of directors, with a chairman for
each instituition from amongst them.
(4)   Tariff protection and other benefits and
incentives should be increased so that profit/
margins of profit should continue to rise.
(5)   Every major policy decision was to be attacked,
so, after due consultation with them, whatever the
government offered would be considered as
un-acceptable. For instance: 'The government has
given an amnesty for holders of non white money
at least thrice in the past (on popular demand by
the entrepreneurs). Last time the holders of such
money were required to pay 30% tax on their hidden
income. It appears that these exercises have not
yielded a fruitful result. It would, therefore, be
helpful if this time a tax incentive is provided to
the holders of such money for investment in certain
selected industries, and such investment should not
be subjected to search or enquiry. This would
bring the non white money into productive channels
and would greatly contribute to the promotion of
investment in some well defined industry' (27).
(6)   Since industry had been nationalised in
1972-3, an attempt at denationalisation had to be
made. This was achieved in some cases and in
others it was proposed that the nationalised
industry's board of directors should be drawn
entirely from the private sector, with only the
managing director of the unit co-opted as a member.
        Entrepreneurs in the large modern industries
have come a long way since 1959: they have grown in
confidence and subsequent generations have been
extremely well educated.
        What of the small merchants? What are their
characteristics and how are they to be distinguished
from mercantile traders? Perhaps the most
significant distinction is their limited access to
information beyond their immediate environment.
Their success depends upon their ability to sell
and to see price differentials. They can foresee
periods of shortage and obtain the maximum scarcity
value from hoarded consumer products, e.g. prior to

budgets, which tend to raise prices. They
understand the fluctuations of the bazaar, due to
long experience. Cash accumulated over a period
of time provides the initial financing and their
limited market transactions, which are mainly
credit-oriented, establish their credibility, so
that when they move into industry, credit facilities,
though limited, are available to them from sources
outside the normal capital markets.

The major distinguishing point between large
and small entrepreneurs is the difficulty that the
small merchant has in dealing with government
agencies. Manipulation aside, in thirty-three
years the major industrial towns of Gujrat and
Gujranwala do not have representation by the major
industrial finance houses. Applications are
considered only once every three months by a
committee, and sometimes more infrequently. Why
does such a gap exist between the large entrepreneur
and the small trader? One reason is that the nature
of commercial transactions in Pakistan are such that
the former can only sustain their import trade by
carrying out large transactions, while the latter
must rely on traditional sources of credit.
Therefore the occupational mobility of the small
trader needs to be examined not only in terms of
movement from an earlier occupation but also by the
size of the firm established (Tables 4.9 and 4.10).
Small traders comprised 3 per cent of the firms in
the smallest sector (0-10 employees), 47 per cent
were in the 11-50 employees category, 30 per cent
were in the medium category with the number of
employees ranging between 51 and 200 and 20 per cent
were in the large category. The preponderance of
small and medium-sized firms (50 per cent and
30 per cent, respectively) is indicative of the
preponderance of merchants in the small-firm
sector. The sales figures are worth noting because,
by our definition, only 10 per cent of firms
qualify for the small-firm scale, 13 per cent for
the medium-firm scale and 77 per cent for the
large-firm sector. The merchants, it is obvious,
have enjoyed windfall profits, and the industries
in which they initially invested generally make
products which they had previously sold in the
marketplace. Industries in which they invested
were textile (two), furniture (four), glass
products (two), chemical products (three), steel
rolling (two), metal machinery (four), electric
fans (two) car equipment (two) sports goods (one),
agricultural implements (three) and cycle and

Table 4.9: Change in Occupation and Size by Employment

Own occupation	0-10	11-50	51-100	101-200	201-1,000	1,001-5,000	5,000+
Civil servant	–	5	1	1	2	2	1
Private employment	4	18	6	3	4	1	–
Trade	1	14	5	3	4	1	–
Professional	2	–	–	–	1	–	–
Others	–	–	–	1	1	–	–
Total	7	37	12	9	13	4	1
	8%	45%	15%	11%	16%	5%	1%

Table 4.10: Occupational Change and Size by Sales

Occupation	1	2	3	4	5	6	7
Civil servant	1	–	–	1	1	4	5
Private employment	–	6	4	3	5	8	9
Trade	1	2	2	2	2	13	8
Professional	–	1	1	–	–	1	–
Others	–	–	–	–	–	–	2
Total	2	9	7	6	8	26	24
	2%	11%	9%	7%	10%	32%	29%

Key: 1=0-50,000, 2= 5,001-250,000, 3= 250,001-500,000, 4= 500,001-1,000,000, 5= 1,000,001-2,000,000, 6= 2,000,001-5,000,000. 7= 5,000,001+

Parts (two). The results of these preferences became
known to other traders and possibily led to their
desire to emulate the market leaders. In Pakistan
traders are undaunted by adverse circumstances,
although they do not seem to have the advantages
of leading business houses, who enjoy and have the
traditional backing of property, influence, status
and other privileges which are taken for granted
by those in power.
   Is this because the traders desire to have a
regular supply of goods, or is it because of some
comparative advantage,as happend in the industrial
links with the Green Revolution when agricultural
production increased substantially because of
industrial developments in the small sector in
Pakistan and as is happening now with the vanishing
of the traditional washerman,the indigenous manufacture of washing machines, which were hawked on
the roadwise? Was the environment suitable or was a
government incentive scheme responsible? The answer
will probably depend on specific areas. In some
instances merchants saw 'demand' growing and brought
the factors of production into play. In others, they
wished to maintain a regular source of supply and
yet others they saw an oppurtunity for increased
profits. Why was there not this response in
former East Pakistan? Most studies have ignored
the issue of entrepreneurs in former East
Pakistan. Some have explained it in political
and economic terms, while others have linked this
with the question of readiness of response and
societal characteristics (28). Hanna Papanek's
analysis suffered from not appreciating the
importance of the trader/merchant. First, we must
consider the nature of the market committees, which
regulated outlets in the large towns and collections of
small shops and which were completely controlled by
Hindu merchants (29). These traders were in complete
control of economic decision-making until the 1970s (30).
The Muslim merchant did not exist and since they did not
even sell on a small scale,how could one expect
Muslims to be involved in large-scale trading? The Hindu
trader in East Pakistan maintained a relationship
familiar to the Chinniotti Sheikhs of the Punjab, i.e. they
left their families in the villages, mostly in
India, and made periodic visits across the border.
   Second, the nature of markets in East
Pakistan was such that many areas were self-
sufficient through satisfaction of basic needs from
the surrounding countryside. Given the terrain (31),
no regular distribution channel was either possible

or available. The merchants who made windfall
gains were from Sialkot, who sold sports goods
at exorbitant prices. Public wrath eventually
turned against them and they were shot in Jessore,
Dinajpur and a host of other outlying towns during
the civil war. In East Pakistan the Sialkotis were
the only traders to challenge the hegemony of the
Hindus. Third, given the extreme poverty of the
area, the average Bengali was always in debt. This
created opportunities for the proverbial Pathan
moneylenders, who recovered their impossible debts
by demanding, and receiving, young Bengali girls as
concubines. The principal was never written off
but the interest on the debt generally was. The
moneylenders met their fate in the riots of 1968,
when the majority of them were hanged from trees,
while the remainder fled the country. Circumstances such as these dampened the response side.

Fourth, on political and economic matters
West Pakistan enjoyed many advantages from the
customs union. All goods of low quality or at
uncompetitive prices were dumped in East Pakistan,
which the ban and tariff protection for local goods
made a captive market for West Pakistani
industrialists. Finally, Papanek's study suffers
from the major disadvantage basing her study of
importers on the list of East Pakistanis to whom
import licences were granted. In fact, these
people were not genuine importers-the East Pakistan
trader did not exist. These 'traders' were
vociferous individuals to whom the government gave
certain benefits in order to placate them. The
licences were never used by the original applicants
but were sold at a premium along with a general
power of attorney. The only way to confirm this
would be to compare the issue of a licence register
against the port where the goods entered (even this
would have to be modified). Traders did move into
industry in East Pakistan, but these were the
Ismailis (the followers of the Aga Khan), the
Adamjees, the Chiniotti Sheikhs, the Memons and
other large industrial houses. What made the
situation even more explosive was the tendency to
employ a Bihari (Urdu-speaking) against a local
man (Bengali-speaking). It was at these levels
that the situation was tense. The vociferous
Bengali was purchased by the federal government,
and projects in the late 1960s were granted on the
'parity principle', which meant that for every
industry set up in Pakistan a similar one would be
developed in East Pakistan, irrespective of

resource-endowment. The 'parity principle' was
used as an economic and political instrument (32).

The Virtues of Traders and Merchants

Having highlighted their differences let us examine
their strong points. The first must surely be
their ability to save and live within their means
combined with their credibility and creditworthiness.
Merchants and traders are men of their word.
Seldom is anything produced in writing. The spoken
word is rarely ambiguous, as the manner of speaking
and intonation of the voice impart much to the
hearer. The voice is the document which is incapable of many interpretations. A broken promise
spreads quickly through the entire community and
can lead to social ostracism.

Although accumulated capital or its surrogate,
credit (33), has been considered important by the
majority of writers one cannot help but observe
that this importance was given to it because of the
view in the 1960s that capital accumulation could
lead to development. Thus wherever a gap in
resources was found, foreign aid was provided. The
importance of capital accumulation led to an
inordinate emphasis on the saving, investment
function (34). Very few analysis, however, have
emphasised the need for securing raw materials (35)
and the right market. Timberg writes of induced
'import substitution' in consumer goods, where the
government has possibly played a key role in the
establishment of the industry. The raw materials
for these industries, as is now well known, are
imported and this creates balance of payments
problems, leading to further restrictive practices
by the government.

The nature of financial assistance varies not
only according to the industry but also to the size
and nature of the firm, and any number of
methodologies can come into play:
(1) The extended family may provide the capital.
(2) The socially high caste may provide the
financial requirements without any interest, though
it is understood that this must be paid back on
request.
(3) A 'chit' system may operate between a group
of local industrialists with those in need bidding
for the cash against the others. The bid goes into
the next cash collection and thus a circular flow
of spare money is available at short notice.
(4) Working capital is provided by the purchaser.
(5) Usually the request for finance, if it is not

too high, would be met either by the local men of importance or, if a community exists, by a general fund.

The next in the sample's category of occupational mobility was the civil servant. Seventeen per cent had experience in government employment either in the higher civil services or the commissioned military service. Some 37 per cent of the civil servants had entered the textile industry, 13 per cent moved into pharmaceuticals and the rest were distributed between the manufacture of hosiery and garments, electric fans, surgical instruments, sports goods, agricultural implements and marble products (approximately 7 per cent in each). The majority, it will be noticed, have entered the capital-intensive area of the industrial field, the part which is the most lucrative and in which expertise is readly available. Of this sample, 41 per cent are in the small-firm sector, 16 per cent in the medium-firm sector and 43 per cent are in the large-firm sector (when assessed by employment). In terms of size by sales, 8 per cent are in the medium-firm sector and 84 per cent are in the large-firm sector.

We note here a curious anomaly. If traders are to be in the largest category, how does one account for the civil servants, who, despite their lack of expertise, are in capital-intensive industries and have the highest sales figures? What enabled the civil servants to do this? The question can be answered in terms of the levels of prestige, authority and responsibility between the civil servants of the early period and those of the later ones. Although no measure of the erosion of authority is possible, a relative assessment can be made. Papanek maintains:'The primary loyalty was to the nation, the government, their service, their family or themselves, not to one of the major pressure groups seeking to 'influence government decisions' (36). All this subsequently changed, as is bound to happen in a developing country. The civil service was identified with colonial administrators, and they were called neither civil or servants or Pakistanis.

The result of a continuous whittling away of authority and salaries meant that civil servants were forced to seek other careers. For those who had served the country in discussions with world agencies the movement was outwards, migration. For others, believing in their ability to organise, the response was to go into industry. This move

paid immediate dividends and the earliest outcasts
of 1958, within a couple of years, had such success
that they entered not only the industrial field
but also that of insurance and even tried to compete
with the media by publishing a national newspaper
(37). Others went into consultancy and, because of
their contacts with former colleagues, reaped rich
harvests. There were lesser known civil servants
who went into small-scale industry, and the
qualities they brought with them were an ability to
organise, to manage men and to perceive opportunities. They were invariably short of capital but
they had the ability to locate sources and to
manipulate money or credit. Their elite army
counterparts had similar strengths. In some ways
these were even better equipped for man-management
and some have shown themselves to be excellent
entrepreneurs (38). Important connections and bonds
developed in marriage were also utilised. The
environment was also conducive to their activity;
as a result of forcible removal from service the
response from their colleagues was sympathetic. It
was the public which wanted scapegoats. Years of
comradeship in service meant a very strong
relationship between members of the services and
any technical short-comings were immediately
rectified. These civil servants, with their
generalist training, are convincing and articulate,
and their greatest ability is persuasion. These
'young men' are referred to by Papanek as (39):

Members of the administrative elite were selected
in their early 20's, largely on the basis of a
competitive examination. The ideal was a well
adjusted, intelligent, all round individual.
Participation in sports, an ability to write and
talk well and to respond quickly on a wide range
of subjects were more important for selection than
a deep understanding of a new field ... By his
middle 20's, one of these officials could be the
administrators of, and the most powerful person in,
an area with a million people ... From then on he
advanced regularly in the hierarchy, typically
shifting between the administration of an area and
the Provincial or Central Governments ... Great
responsibilities at an early age made for self
confidence, decisiveness and ability to work hard,
of great importance when a tiny group administers
the affairs of a large and complex country.
Papanek does not go far enough. The 1960s was
the age of the technocrats in Pakistan, just as the
1970s had been the age of the chartered accountants.

97

The Origins and Occupations of Entrepreneurs

In the 1960s the economists were considered to have
the cure for all ills. In the late 1960s and early
1970s engineers were given priority on account of
their detailed technical knowledge. In the 1970s
came the chartered accountants, with their
pulse-reading ability and appointments as managing
directors in industry. This was the normal reaction
to the criticism of the civil service by Papanek
and others (40):
The weakness and limits of the group stemmed from
the same set of circumstances. Self confidence
often changed to conceit and contempt for technical
staff. The selection and promotion process did not
penalise the incompetent, nor did it rapidly advance
the brilliant individual.
The criticism that followed was possibly a reaction
to that which the Papaneks experienced themselves.
The civil servants were so far ahead of the pack
that it was difficult to contain either their
reasoning or their arrogance which resulted from
their confidence. They further miss out an
essential feature of the civil servants' training,
especially that of the elite civil service. Given
the elite's position in the service from the day
they started, their experience has been of a very
diverse nature. Field officers serve their first
eight years in the country (or what is known as the
field). The normal working habitat is the district
town, but they must spend eight nights out in the
district, in conditions of discomfort, where they
come into contact with different kinds of people
and problems (41). Over a period of time they
develop a knowledge of these problems and, given
the right conditions, provide pragmatic solutions.
They are thus utilising knowledge for appropriate
decisions under different conditions at the
grassroots level. This pragmatic ability is
critical at that level. Civil servants must undergo
continuous and rapid transfers to be given a broad
knowledge of people and their problems, and the
wider the span of experience the better. Since
technically they are working twenty-four hours a
day they are provided with a residential office and
are in constant communication with the area under
their administrative control.
    Suffice it to say, though, that such pressures
on the civil service began to take their toll.
The job was neither well paid nor did it have any
prestige, and it did not entail the in-service
training which was a hallmark (42). Administrative
reforms provided a further disincentive. Although

the principles of these reforms could not be
contested, what actually occurred in their
implementation was patronage of one kind or another
political, connective, career-advancement.
     The net result of the combination of these
positive and negative factors, i.e. the political
(43) authorities' rejection, led the civil
servants to either a 'crossroads' (44) or a
'challenge' (45) led to increased effort and immense
financial benefits in the process, but most
important of all, they were elevated to their
previously high status.   It is difficult to
conceive of 'picking up the pieces' and reconstruct-
ing the original vandalised possession.   Yet that
is what took place.   The 'spirit' had taken hold.
Roughly 17 per cent of those who went into industry
after an earlier occupation came from this source.
The mix of the industrial field into which they
ventured indicates their flexibility and ability to
weigh choices.

The Professionals
On the other hand although they had a relatively
small share in the sample (only approximately
4 per cent), the 'professionals' were in highly
technological areas and generally provided
intermediate goods for industry, for example,
spindles and accessories for the textile industry.
All these entrepreneurs and their concerns, usually
private limited companies, had no relatives as
partners but rather relied on technically comparable
people with long standing friendships.   Usually
these were entrepreneurs with 'crossroad' decisions
who felt that there was not enough job-enrichment,
or who thought that decisions by entrepreneurs who
were 'co-ordinators' of factors of production were
not acceptable, or that, given the kind of technical
expertise required, they were superior to the
general run of people.   The skills which they
brought with them were a deep understanding of the
production process and a knowledge of technical
developments.   However, ironically these
entrepreneurs were inadequate at cultivating
contacts.   Each of them was thus living with a
serious problem but, despite this, they were people
with a considerable amount of will and pride.

The Agriculturalists
As far as agriculturalists were concerned, only
1 per cent had changed their occupation and gone
into industry.   The bias may well have been due to

the fact that entrepreneurs in rice, cotton and wheat-processing units were not included in the sample. This is the area in which the agriculturalist is found almost to the total exclusion of all others. However, when the entrepreneurs' occupations were compared with their fathers' occupations, roughly 19 per cent of the entrepreneurs were from backgrounds which were agricultural. Table 4.11 compares fathers' and sons' occupations. It is obvious that, apart from industrialists, the categories consistantly supplying entrepreneurs are civil servants and traders. Professionals are in the high-technology areas, which may hold interesting possibilities for those who have temporarily left the country and who may return to play their part in its economic development.

Table 4.11: Comparison of Father's and Sons' Occupations

S.no.	Occupation	Fathers occupation	Own occupation
1	Agriculture	19	1
2	Civil servant	21	17
3	Private employment	1	42
4	Trade	29	35
5	Industrialist	23	–
6	Professional	7	3
7	Others	–	2
Total		100 a	100 a

Note: a.   Rounded to nearest whole number.

The most significant increase can be seen in the private employment sector. This is to be expected, as, once insecurity had receded, rising expectations forced individuals to take action to provide them with increased status, as well as with adequate living standards, Experience and ability developed during this period served as an apprenticeship for furthering themselves. The most significant decrease is seen in the agricultural sector, but that has been already explained as sample bias.

Since the occupationally mobile as a class are different from those who begin their career in

industry, it will be worth while to see how they
were initiated into this new occupational venture.
Typically, by size and by employment (Table 4.9)
these entrepreneurs started from humble beginnings.
As many as 53 per cent of them were in the small
category (less than 50 employees), 26 per cent in
the medium sector, (51-200 employees) and only
22 per cent were in the large category. But when
comparison is made in terms of sales, only
13 per cent are in the small category and 9 per cent
in the medium category, the remaining 78 per cent
being in the large category. The majority of the
entrepreneurs have, therefore, despite keeping
their enterprises to the minimum size, had excellent
sales thus increasing the possibility of substantial
profits.

Table 4.10 indicates that civil servants have
used their persuasive powers significantly, for
approximately 92 per cent have sales over
Rs 500,000, which is a significant improvement on
their own fixed-salary positions. Similarly,
72 per cent of the private employment category are
in this sales bracket and 83 per cent of the traders.
Significantly, then irrespective of experience and
entrepreneurial input, Pakistan does have
opportunities for attracting entrepreneurs.

The period when entrepreneurs went into
industry is indicated in Table 4.12. Of the
entrepreneurs who invested in industry, only 6 per
cent did so before 1949, another 24 per cent
between 1950 and 1959, while 25 per cent invested
in the period considered as the decade of reforms,
i.e. 1960-9. Despite the upheavals of the

Table 4.12: Occupational Change and Year of
Founding

Occupation	1930-9	1940-9	1950-9	1960-9	1970-9	1980+
Agriculture	-	-	-	-	1	-
Civil servant	-	1	4	3	6	-
Private employment	1	2	6	8	20	-
Trade	1	-	10	8	10	1
Professional	-	-	-	2	1	-
Others	-	-	1	1	-	-
Total	2	3	21	22	38	1
	2%	3%	24%	25%	44%	1%

1970s (47), 44 per cent set up enterprises during
this period. The response from three categories,
traders, private employees and civil servants,
during this period was very positive. Entrepreneurs
came from private employment, which could certainly
be an indication of the times. Jobs were secure
but problems concerning law and order arose during
this period. Again, the 1973 oil crisis led to an
inflationary rise in prices, resulting in acute
difficulties for the salaried person. Survival
could only have been possible by substantial pay
rises, which were not possible under the circumstances. At that time, the authorities were concerned
entirely with social welfare, and no-one cared very
much about white-collar workers. The circumstances,
adverse though they were, required a response which
would not have been possible under conditions of
security or high salaries. The response to such
conditions led to 54 per cent of this category
investing in industry in 1970-9. The traders were
more or less evenly spread in the three decades,
i.e. 1950-9 33 per cent, 1960-9 27 percent and
1970-9 33 per cent. Therefore the response of
traders to the environment was more stable and the
general atmosphere of insecurity did not affect
them as much as in certain other occupations. In
fact, during periods of insecurity traders tend to
maximise profits, as demand far outstrips supply.
The scarcity value of goods may increase
substantially, and the entrepreneurs who manufacture
the product and have trade openings available to
them, then occasions may arise when curtailing
production may be more profitable. For the small
trader entrepreneur shows:
'... his commercial skills in how effectively he
dupes or overcharges his customers, not how much he risks
capital or moves into new lines. The concept of
sizing up consumer demand to make profit is only
entertained in the form of black marketing
operations during time of scarcity. To vantage
but not to venture is the motto ...' (48).
In doing so the traditional merchants are behaving
rationally: they may be 'leaden of mind and of
technique' but their exploitation can only be
reduced if factors affecting supply and demand are
considered. Pakistan's experience of using
short-term administrative measures tend to have a
completely adverse effect. Under conditions of
martial law, district commissioner's head committees
known as fair price committees, and punishment is
by a summary military court. Invariably the

commodity in scarce supply and great demand is even 'scarcer' to obtain and is in even greater demand. To the black market price, therefore, is added a 'premium' for the uncertainty and risk which the traders have undertaken and which is dependend on the repressive measures in force. If these measures are extreme, the variation in price varies in direct proportion. Given these profit margins, why do such traders change their occupations? The move is generally in two stages: the trade is not completely abandoned but is continued by someone else while the new occupation is developed. This process involves other cumulative experiences, such as the success of another entrepreneur, the status allowed to the manufacturer or even pressure from unmarried daughters, for whom marriage proposals from a wealthy caste will only follow if their family is improving their occupation and hence their standard of living.

The response of the mercantile traders was different. All along, trading continued in parallel with their entrepreneurial activities. Furthermore, their products were sent into trading channels through the managing agency system (49). This was often only a mythical body with certainly, in the majority of cases, no offices and no work. The creation of the managing agency system, peculiar to the Indian sub-continent, was never taken very far, except in a minority of cases; for example the Memons developed a very capable management base in the mid-1970s. The probable reason for this was the influences generated by business schools on the second generations. Nearly all the young men of the leading families have graduated from Western business schools. They were no longer 'leaden of mind or of techniques'. Instead of using the managing agency system to siphon off profits and/or increase the price of the product, the Memons utilised it to remain market leaders. The 'siphoning off' varied from 2.5 per cent to 7.5 per cent (50) of the sales as far as other corporate sector entrepreneurs were concerned.

Thus we see parallels between the traditional merchants who use a differential price system in periods of scarcity and the mercantile merchants who, because of their control of the market, use a more sophisticated methodology. The mercantile houses have, in fact, scored a major victory. The managing agency system has been allowed to operate again in 1981. The private sector has been given to understand, tacitly, that '... the government

has revived the managing agency system which was
undone in 1972 (51)'. Also, accepting the
contention of the private sector that the
organisation which supervised this system has
performed badly, the government has decided that
corporate laws such as the Monopoly and Restricted
Trade Practices Ordinance 1970, the Security and
Exchange Ordinance 1969, the Capital Issues Act
1947 and the Companies (Managing Agencies and
Election of Directors) Order 1972 be amended to
reduce governmental control and to simplify
procedures relating to the conduct of companies (52),
and that a single organisation, the Corporate Law
Authority, be set up to administer these and other
corporate laws (53).

Private employees have shown an increasing
percentage of movement towards industry: in 1950-9
16 percent, in 1960-9 22 per cent and in 1970-9
54 per cent (Table 4.12). The growing percentage
can only be explained by the fortunate experience
of these entrepreneurs. The increase between
1960 and 1969 and 1970 and 1979 is substantial and,
despite the uncertainty of the times, one can only
attribute this to non-satisfaction of certain
demands as well as to increased opportunity. The
combination of these two factors has meant breaking
the stranglehold of the existing occupations and,
given an opportunity to be a troubleshooter for
someone else, to be a troubleshooter for oneself.
The successful outcome of such troubleshooting,
of course, is unprecedented profits.

The civil servants' pattern was similar: in
1950-9 29 per cent, in 1960-9 22 per cent and
1970-9 43 per cent (Table 4.12). The period
1960-9 was one of unprecedented stability for the
civil service (though it was less stable than in
1959). The civil service had come to terms with
the political authorities and their period of power
was almost as long as in any period in Pakistan's
brief history. However, in the 1970s this was not
to be: circumstances had drastically changed.
Assumption of critical positions by loyalists was
the order of the day. The response to these factors
plus the accumulation of experience over a period of
time already referred to enabled civil servants
to seek 'greener pastures'. The other option, of
course, was to train themselves academically to
widen their opportunities. This is difficult for
the normal civil servant, who, after entering the
service, considered himself secure for life in a

vocation which he considered to be the culmination
of his ambition.

Motivational Dynamics

Entrepreneurs who have changed their occupations
need to be differentiated from those who have
entered industry directly, either straight from
school or inheriting from their forefathers.
Entrepreneurs were asked to give their reasons for
changing their earlier occupation. The majority of
them gave one reason only: others put their reasons
into an order corresponding to their positions at
the time: The four reasons listed in the answers
were: (1) Did not like the job, (2) low pay,
(3) work on one's own, and (4) the profit motive.

In an earlier study in 1959 Papanek (54) had
empirically determined an overwhelming emphasis
amongst entrepreneurs on financial motives. His
results are shown in Table 4.13 and the initial
responses in this study are in Table 4.14.

Although Tables 4.13 and 4.14 are not comparable, the motive for going into industry for high
profit seemd to have been reduced considerably.
Whereas in the Papanek sample, expected profits
averaged 22 per cent for large and smaller firms
and 35 per cent for poor prospects in trade (a
negative reason but one linked with financial
motives), in the case of the latter sample the
expectation of high profits was only 16 per cent.
The category which seemd to have motivated the
majority of entrepreneurs was the desire to work on
their own (50 per cent). Less pay in salaried jobs
provided 10 per cent with the desire for change,
while 9 per cent moved because of not liking the
particular job they were doing. Why is it that
such a majority of the sample have overwhelmingly
sought independent work? The reasons are to be
found in the historical context and in the
traditional job orientations in the various
regions and provinces of Pakistan. In the four
provinces, the emphasis on jobs varies substantially.
In the Punjab, almost the first priority is to get
a son into either a coveted civil service position
or the army. This decision arises after ten years
of education. In the Punjab, at least, a
considerable amount of prestige is attached to
positions of authority and at partition (1947) the
majority of Muslim civil servants who opted for
Pakistan were from the Punjab. Similarly, the army
consists entirely of Punjabi soldiers and officers.
It is the wish of every Punjabi parent of any

105

Table 4.13: Reasons for Entering Industry

		All firms (%)	Larger firms (5)
(1)	Family or individual in industry before	25	16
(2)	Poor prospects for trade	25	45
(3)	Expected profits	27	14
(4)	Incidental to trade	5	6
(5)	Industry superior, patriotism	9	5
(6)	Government policy, accidental, other	10	14

Table 4.14: Reasons for Change in Occupation

		All firms (%)
(1)	Did not like job	9
(2)	Less pay	10
(3)	Work on one;s own	50
(4)	Expected high profits	16
(5)	Other reasons	16

Note: Total does not add as to 100, rounding error.

consequence to see a member of the family in these highly prestigious positions. Failure to obtain one remains with a person for life, despite the low salary involved. Working in the private (55) sector carries with it a constant stigma. There is no security and one is considered to be subsurvient to the boss. To be subjected to orders in a private sector, whether large or small, is to be at the beck and call of the owners of the unit, with rarely any spare time at one's disposal. Consequently, if we see which occupational category in the sample has opted for this change to independent work it may be possible to test the assumptions stated above.

The Origins and Occupations of Entrepreneurs

Those in the employment category (civil servants, of both higher and lower levels, and army), those in private employment and employed professionals together constitute 38 per cent of the 50 per cent who wanted to work on their own. In fact, about 27 per cent of these were from private employment, about 9 per cent from the civil service. So far as the Punjab was concerned, negative factors in these two vocations were responsible for the supply of entrepreneurs. Their initial experience either provided them with the expertise and/or confidence to try new ventures. Surprisingly enough in this category 11 per cent of traders/ merchants also appear. These, however, were bazaar merchants, who had been making a killing as and when the market provided a premium for scarce goods.

The next category in the sample is the high-profit one (Table 4.14). It is not surprising that of the 16 per cent who gave this as a first response, 12 per cent are from the merchant/trader category. This comes as no surprise, and is in keeping with the earlier findings of Papanek, who determined that the Pakistani traders are almost exclusively profit-orientated. That the entry of the merchant/trader into industry is a foregone conclusion is contested by empirical research indicating that other characteristics may be important. Thus Mattison Mines considered that 'merchants do not play as significant a role in the initial stages of industrialisation as one might suppose' (56), and Berna (57) suggests that merchants enter industry in the greatest number only after the point of sustained growth has been achieved. Redlich (58), writing on industrialisa- tion in Western Europe, spoke of a similar situation.

The analyses of Berna and Mines follow special cases. Berna was dealing with the engineering sector, where traders would be very wary of entry as they do not have the ability, the expertise or the skill to control a specialised production process, especially if competition comes from highly skilled and qualified entrepreneurs already in that area. We know from Berna that this was the case. So far as Mattison Mines' merchants were concerned, they were Muslims in a bazaar environment and were in the category of extremely small firms. They were reluctant to take risk and did not seem to have the ability to develop either the new personal ties required in the manufacturing sector or the ability to develop long-term credit needs.

Occupational Mobility and Popularity of Industry

Which industries found favour with the entrepreneurs who had sought occupational mobility? For those who had chosen to work on their own, amongst the civil servants the textile sector was the most popular, whilst those who had moved to industry from private employment, metal machinery, electric fans and the textile sector (in that order) seemed to find favour. The preference for the private employee seeking industries in which the method of production ensured survival meant that these entrepreneurs, over the years, had developed skills which were considered to be critical to those particular industries. Traders who had moved to industry solely on the basis of the profit motive were evenly spread in the textile, furniture, steel rerolling, electric fans, auto equipment and sports goods industries. This wide range of industries indicates the ability of traders to perceive gaps in the market, and, in the absence of adequate supply facilities, to make the most of the situation.

Occupational Specialisation in the North-West Frontier Province, Baluchistan and Sind.

Baluchistan and the North-West Frontier Province are tribal and nomadic, though the latter is now urbanised and 'settled' (59). The Sind is a special case, highlighting the two extremes of entrepreneurial and non-entrepreneurial talent, with Karachi providing the former and the hinterland of Sind the latter. In Karachi, the tendency towards occupations is diametrically opposed to that in the Punjab and the greatest number of entrepreneurs tend to move into trade and/or industry.

The Memons and the Bohras have been segregated from the rest of the entrepreneurs because of the degree of occupational specialisation that they brought with and, although they settled in Karachi, they maintained this distinction and remained ethnically and culturally apart. The Kashmiris' occupational specialisation fell into two categories, i.e. weaving and as guides or porters for tourists. The weavers excelled in craftsmanship and indeed some of them still carry on their work today. The occupational specialisation of the Memons (60) and the Bohras was trade, and, despite having gone into the large-scale modern sector, they still maintain their trading activities. Their ability to bargain allows them to drive home an advantage

The Origins and Occupations of Entrepreneurs

skillfully and without hindrance.

Age Profile
The extended family system, the caste and community
play vital roles in delegating authority. What is
responsibility, and how can it be understood in
different social millieus? The age of the
entrepreneurs is certainly indicative of levels
of authority, responsibility and effectiveness of
a class. What, even if we determine the age
profiles, is the consequence for the economy?
Would it be fair to deduce that the younger the
entrepreneurial element, the greater the chance of
progressive technological improvement? Would the
emergence of too many younger elements constrict,
the economy and deter others from entering industry?
At this stage it is difficult to answer these
questions but, by analogy, it can be said that the
early entrants by age and by industry, although
they held off competition for some time (for
example, in the textile industry), they could not
do so when political factors modified the economic
environment. Others with political connections
entered the textile industry only to find that
profits were not for the picking: making a profit
entails a certain amount of effort. Waves of
entrants into industry came via the back door and
left just as quickly. Figure 4.1 shows the growth
in the textile industry, the periods of a steep
rise in investment being 1951, 1953, 1955, 1962,
1966, 1968, 1973, 1974 and 1977 in the spinning
units. The number of looms installed also followed
a similar pattern.
     Up to 1955 the economic reasons for entering
industry were apparent: between 1962 and 1966 came
the first group of politicians seeking an economic
base, and this phenomenon was repeated between
1968 and 1973 and between 1974 and 1977. The basis
of economic resource allocations was simple. The
sanctions (61) were directly proportional to the
political authority wielded, so early entrants did
have an advantage though their most significant
advantage lay in the inability of new entrants to
manage their units effectively. This has been the
cause in industry since 1962. The position
concerning closed capacity is shown in Table 4.15.
     The years in which the units came into
existence is not, however, shown in Table 4.15, and
this would have indicated a possible reason for
poor performance, e.g. run-down machinery. During
the present survey newly installed units in the

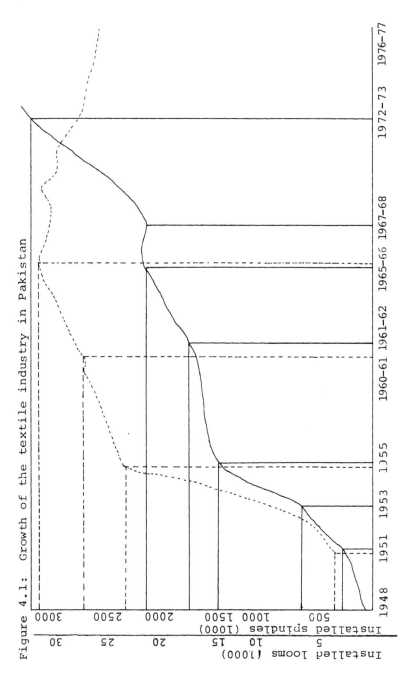

Figure 4.1: Growth of the textile industry in Pakistan

The Origins and Occupations of Entrepreneurs

Table 4.15: Closed Capacity

	Province	Spindles (%)	Closed looms (%)
(1)	Sind and Baluchistan	32	46
(2)	Punjab	6	9
(3)	NWFP	21	40
Non-members (all provinces)		35	38

Source: All Pakistan Textile Mill Owners Annual Report, 1977.

Jhang (62) district were found to be closed.
        The other unexplained discrepancy is, of course the percentage of closed spindles. In Sind 32 per cent of the spindles and 46 per cent of the looms were closed, while in the Punjab there was the least closure. For Sind the period 1972-7 was politically favourable for the province and the maximum number of units were installed there. Similarly, the North-West Frontier Province was to be won from a regional party. Political bargaining of this kind is economic disaster, yet government analyses tend not to look for the most obvious reasons for this. Seasoned entrepreneurs seize opportunities and benefits from government policy, and the more competent enhance their profit margins at the expense of failed units. So competition never came from those who were competent in industry and had a proven track record but rather from political opportunists.
        The age profiles of entrepreneurs is shown in Table 4.16, and the sample contains a greater number of entrepreneurs in the higher age groups. Only two age groups, 20-9 and 30-9 will be analysed, as these are considered to be critical for the future supply of entrepreneurs.
        The majority of the 20-9 age group were in the electric fans and agricultural implements industries while the 30-9 age groups were predominant in the textile, furniture, steel rerolling, metal machinery, electric fans and sports goods industries. In the level of responsibilities that they have, 83 per cent of two groups (ages 20-9 and 30-9) managed 30 per cent of the small-group

Table 4.16: Entrepreneurs by Age

No.	Age	No.	%
1	20-9	12	6
2	30-9	50	26
3	40-9	72	37
4	50+	61	31
		195	100

Missing value 1

enterprises (less than 50 employees). The youngest
age group is significant, because it is indicative of
entrepreneurs being thrown in the deep end and being
forced to survive. This figure, however, is not
corroborated when company size by sales is
considered. For a number of reasons (among them
careful supervision) this age group does well
economically. Table 4.17 indicates the age group
and size of the enterprise by employees. The
11-50-employee category seems to find favour with
the majority of entrepreneurs, and this may be
attributed to the conditions originating in the
economic environment, i.e. (1) in the period 1972-7
the threat of the nationalisation of industry was
real and (2) the policy adopted by the government
gave benefits which increased in proportion to
the labour force in a unit. The pattern would be
best understood by the types of formal and informal
inputs that were responsible for the development of
the age profiles of the entrepreneurs. In the
youngest age group, i.e. 20-9, almost 92 per cent
had fathers who were industrialists, and their
induction was predictable and closely supervised.
These men had been brought up in an entrepreneurial
environment, so their trial period included a period
of extended family supervision in the outside world.
Surprisingly, 8 per cent were from two agricultural
castes, notably those who were status orientated and
the immigrants. Craftsmen, who would have been
expected to be prominent in early entry, were third.
When questioned on the issue of supervision by
senior family members, 83 per cent replied in the
affirmative, 8 per cent had had no guidance and 8
per cent had been only loosely supervised, i.e. they
had set up independent units and had worked their

way up.

Table 4.17: Age of Entrepreneurs and Size of Firms

Age	Age and size by employment						
	0-10	11-50	51-100	101-200	201-1,000	1,001-5,000	5,000+
20-9	3	7	1	–	1	–	–
30-9	1	24	10	3	8	–	1
40-9	8	27	14	7	5	4	5
50+	2	27	7	4	11	6	2
Total	14	85	32	14	25	10	8
	7%	45%	17%	7%	13%	5%	4%

Entrepreneurs in the 30-9 age group had fathers who were already in industry, but other groups, i.e. traders, civil servants and agriculturists, were also represented. For this age group, the textile, furniture, steel rerolling, metal machinery and sports goods industries were most popular, a greater range of industries.

Education of Entrepreneurs
References to education, experience and technical training have already been made when we considered the impact of the extended family system. A more detailed examination is called for simply because in Pakistan early empirical research indicated(63) that education was not critical to either entry or to success. This was contradicted by empirical findings elsewhere. Is education a requirement of our times at this stage of our economic development? How is it related to success? Does the number of years at school have a bearing on the quality of education?

Primary Education. With the average Pakistani child education at the primary level is supplemented by religious teaching, i.e. initiation to the Quran and the teachings of Islam. However, there is significant difference between rural and urban sectors. Religious teaching is uniform as the Imams are charged with this responsibility. They have had a very structured training at their Dar-ul-Ulooms (schools or institutions) under qualified religious teachers. This has been carried out under a private

113

and self-financing independent scheme. The various divisions(64) within Islam cater for their requirements in similar ways. So whereas the religious institutions produce a fairly consistant standard of instructors for both the rural and urban sectors, the secular educational system, divorced from religious systems, has important qualitative differences. Again, secular education in the large urban areas is different from that in the small district towns. Moreover, some of these secular institutions have no religious teaching.(65) This only happened after the 1978 educational policy, in which the objectives were 'To develop and inculcate in accordance with the Quran and Sunnah, the character, motivation, and conduct of a true Muslim through effective elimination of gaps and contradictions between the professing and practice of Islam'.

These qualitative differences are reflected in the entrepreneurs. For example, with the industrialists Papanek interviewed survivors(66) in the large scale sector were not only educated in Pakistan institutions but also outside the country, most of them having professional management or business school qualifications. The second generation, who had received formal education in large towns, also supplemented their children's education with a certain amount of formal technical education at university. In terms of quantity and quality, their education depended on the level of development of the enterprise. At the medium-scale enterprise level, education would be of a general nature. With the craftsman/entrepreneur, where education is at a bare minimum, religious education is probably at a maximum. Unaware of market forces, unaware of any production difficulties except those that they have learnt to deal with on an informal basis, they continue to operate, despite high odds. What is more, they survive. The religious exhortations of honesty and sustained hard work are drilled into them at a very early age. To compare the secular education in large towns with that in small towns in terms of 'quality' would be difficult. To compare the quality of education between the urban and the rural areas is inconceivable: it would be like comparing 'one portion of our nation living in an ancient age, another in a medieval and a third in a modern age (67). The general situation in Pakistan may not be as sharply differentiated but it is certainly variable. To that extent, education may be responsible for variability in

usage, requirements of resources and in performance.
     The other significant difference, only appli-
cable to large towns, is the Western style mission
schools compared with local schools. Whereas the
former emulate the teaching methods of the West,(68)
the latter utilise learning by rote, as in religious
schools. So the methods of teaching vary, even in
urban centres. The mission schools are limited in
number, and only a handful of new pupils can be
admitted each year, while the local schools are
usually overcrowded. These differences have been
mentioned only to explain the environment for
entrepreneurial effort and to give reasons for their
attitudes and characteristics.
     Table 4.18 shows the years of education cross-
tabulated with those spent in industry. Entrepreneurs with up to five years of education are to be
found in the (small) textile sector,metal machinery,
furniture, footwear (leather), chemical products
(soap), metal machinery, electric fans, car
accessories, ceramics and agricultural implements
industries. The textile sector at this level is a
service industry, and is neither a composite nor a
spinning unit. All the remaining industries require
some form of skill rather than formal education.
The ceramics industry is a family-orientated
industry, with every member in the family, as soon
as he or she is capable of working, involved.
It is an extremely labour-intensive industry in
Pakistan and uses a low-temperature process for
glazing. For many years the potters used red clay
but have now switched to white table-ware. One of
the craftsman entrepreneurs is totally illiterate,
yet he is President of the Soap Makers Association
in Sialkot (otherwise known for its manufacture
of sports goods and surgical instruments). He has
unquestioned ability in this industry and, despite
the fact that he is illiterate or self-educated,
he has an immense knowledge of chemistry and the
chemical reactions of fatty oil substances.
     In these industries economies of integration
exist but economies of scale appear to be relatively
unimportant. What is important, though, is the ease
of entry into these industries and their relatively
low capital requirement.
     In the ten-year educational category are to be
found textiles, hosiery, furniture, chemical
products, steel rerolling, metal machinery, electric
fans, car accessories, sports goods, ceramics,
cutlery, agricultural implements and cycle parts.
In this category these entrepreneurs are seen to

115

Table 4.18: Education in Industrial Sectors

Sector	0	1-5	6-10	11-12	13-14	15-16	Total
Misc	1	-	3	2	5	1	12
Commodity	-	-	1	1	1	-	3
Marble	-	-	-	-	1	1	2
Cycle	-	-	2	1	1	-	4
Agricultural implements	1	2	8	-	2	1	14
Pharmaceutical	-	-	-	-	3	1	4
Cutlery	-	1	3	-	2	-	6
Ceramics	-	1	4	-	-	-	5
Sports	-	-	1	1	3	-	5
Surgical	-	-	-	1	2	-	3
Car equipment	1	1	1	-	3	-	6
Electric fan	-	1	6	5	6	5	23
Metal machinery	-	4	7	6	8	3	28
Steel rerolling	-	-	6	2	5	1	14
Chemicals	1	-	3	3	1	-	8
Glass	-	-	-	1	1	4	6
Furniture	-	1	5	1	1	-	8
Hosiery	-	-	2	1	-	-	3
Footwear	1	-	-	1	1	2	5
Textile	1	3	5	8	13	7	37

The Origins and Occupations of Entrepreneurs

be using mechanical industrial process.
    In the categories of more than ten years of
education the industry seems to be progressively
more capital-intensive and orientated towards
economies of scale.

Education and Size of Firm. There is a positive
relationship between the size of firm by employment
and education, as can be seen in Table 4.19.

Table 4.19: Size and Education

S.No.	Size class (By employees	No. of firms	Average education of entrepreneur (years)	
1	0-10	14	10.7)	10.1
2	11-50	85	9.4)	Small
3	51-100	32	11.6)	11.4
4	101-200	14	11.1)	Medium
5	201-1,000	25	11.6)	
6	1,001-5,000	10	14.5)	12.6
7	5,000+	8	11.8)	Large

The differences between the various firms in terms
of education follow a systematic relationship
except for the two categories at the smallest level
(0-10 and 11-50 employees). The period of years of
education for the 0-10-employees category compared
with the 11-50-employees category is greater by
about fifteen months. This quantitative increase
may be explained by the fact that all entrepreneurs
in the 0-10-employees category are following in
their elder's footsteps. On the other hand, the
11-50-employee category, which comprised the
maximum number of firms, includes entrepreneurs
who have progressed from a relatively small base
over a number of years. The majority of them belong
to a class that has progressed on the basis of their
technological and production expertise. The highest
category, i.e. 5,000+ employees, have obtained
quantitatively less education than the 1,001-5,000-
employee category. These entrepreneurs were early
entrants into the industrialisation process and
this partially confirms Papanek's findings in that
the most noticeable difference in education at the
highest and middle level entrepreneur was at the

11-50-employee range. The difference in education
was five years. This does mean that the large,
complex firms (the large category, approaching
thirteen years of education) were in the higher
educational category, where entrepreneurs would be
classified as graduates. The medium level was at
the secondary school level (equivalent to 'A' levels
in the UK) and the small sector had matriculated
(equivalent to 'O' levels in the UK). There was
thus a positive relationship between educational
attainments of its employees and the size of the
firm. There is a need for large, complex firms to
be able to communicate within the company as well
as outside it. In Pakistan this ability needs to
meet the government's ever-growing 'informational'
and other requirements. Firms unable to communicate
limit themselves and have a rather simple kind of
organisation.

Table 4.20 shows the profits declared in the
sample. Ten per cent of all categories of firms
with educated entrepreneurs were running at a loss,
another three per cent were barely breaking even and
12 per cent were performing approximately at a level
commensurate with the earnings of a fixed salary
group (Rs 12,000 - 50,000 per annum). After this,
the categories continue to increase. When the
company's performance is related to the educational
level of its entrepreneurs, there is no failure, and
only one poor performance in a company with
entrepreneurs with less than five years of
education. In fact, poor performance is linked
with the higher educated employees (13-14 years
and 15-16 years). The other significant result is
that, although the less educated entrepreneurs seem
to hold their own at the middle-income levels, it is
the 13-14 year category who seem to be in the
maximum income bracket. The indications definitely
show that, for production-orientated entrepreneurs
with relatively simple technology and organisation,
the ranges of six to ten years of education are
critical, and for the more complex modern sector
the 13-14 years and 15-16 years categories seem
to be relevant.

However, the relatively less educated
entrepreneurs seem to reach a point beyond which
they do not have the ability to make profits, and it
is here that one sees the strength of those who have
been educated. Although some uneducated or poorly
educated entrepreneurs do reach the top, they are
in the minority. There are increasing numbers of
educated entrepreneurs who are more articulate and

Table 4.20: Education and profits

Education	Own profits (Rs)						
	Less than 0	1–12,000	12,001–50,000	50,001–100,000	100,001–500,000	500,001–100,0000	100,0001+
O	–	1	–	1	2	–	2
1–5	–	–	3	2	7	1	1
6–10	3	2	10	9	18	4	11
11–12	4	1	4	1	9	5	10
13–14	8	1	4	4	13	5	24
15–16	5	1	2	–	5	1	12
Total	20 10%	6 3%	23 12%	17 9%	54 28%	16 8%	50 31%

have the ability to succeed. At the very highest level, where professional management is available, the government needs to be persuaded that such men can produce rich rewards.

The difference in the rates of profit is related to the ability of an entrepreneur, a group of entrepreneurs or an association to persuade governments. In the large corporate sector, government incentive policies for entrepreneurs are helpful, and these policies have developed through connections at various ministries. Those entrepreneurs who have no influence do not get anywhere. The small entrepreneur, by virtue of his poor education has another limitation imposed on him, notably an inability to perceive opportunities. Entrepreneurs in the smaller, indiginous sector are not so widely travelled as those from the large sector, and consequently perceive less product differentiation, fewer consumer preferences and less technological differentiation. Even if they do perceive these opportunities they do not have expertise in production methods nor the authority to act. Smaller entrepreneurs also may have considered formal education to be not only a waste of time but also a waste of money and effort, and may well have considered on-job training or experience in industry to be more relevant. The negative association of education with success though may indicate that formal education may be insufficient or may conflict with the kind of training required for industry. In Pakistan it is common to find parents complaining, that since their sons had successfully completed their education, they were unwilling to soil their hands, and would prefer some vocation which has some status in the eyes of society (69).

Education and Entrepreneurs' Concept of Profit.
Entrepreneurs were asked whether they considered their profits after tax to be substantial. The relatively less educated (primary level) stated that their profits were substantial and indicated a level of satisfaction with the industry. In the 6-10 years' category they were evenly balanced, but as the level of education increased the dissatisfaction with profits after tax increased proportionately, with the highest figures being recorded for the graduate level, i.e. while 10.5 per cent considered profits to be satisfactory, another 19 per cent considered that the profit level was unsatisfactory. At the post-graduate level,

5 per cent considered profits to be adequate while 8 per cent thought them to be not so.

Why was this growing disenchantment at the higher level? This response can be explained by the experience of the immediate past. The corporate sector cannot conceal its profits and is vulnerable to the revenue-raising authorities. Entrepreneurs (70) stated that, on average, they received one letter per week from the various revenue-collecting agencies of the government. Another explained that there were, in all, nineteen government departments relating to various aspects of industry who constantly interfere.

The period 1972-7 was one when nationalisation was being put forward under the doctrine of socialism. In fact, it was obvious, that the basis for nationalisation was different for each industry and had been discriminatory. The Economic Reform Order 1972, the vegetable ghee industry in 1973, the commodity processing industries in 1976 all revealed the policy of a carrot and stick. The compensation terms were so regressive that the net worth in 90 per cent of the units proved to be negative (71). It was obvious to entrepreneurs that, henceforth, safety lay in small capital-intensive units. Even though these policies no longer exist, the fear still remains, and finds expression in the state of continuous dissatisfaction by entrepreneurs.

In some cases greed may explain this tendency. In an unstable environment there is a tendency to pull out as much equity from the firm as possible. This helps in two ways. First, it allows entrepreneurs to place their case before their association, who then take up the matter with the government for added benefits or incentives. Second, it keeps away marauding government departments.

Community and Caste Response to Education. If the extended family is a hindrance to economic development, what role do caste and communities play? Economists, have examined the role of these informal institutions in the context of expenditure, and their analysis has been deficient on the informal ' props' and strengths that these institutions possess. How do, these informal institutions view levels of education? Table 4.21 shows the community's preferences for education and Table 4.22 outlines that of the Punjabi castes (72). These tables indicate a positive

The Origins and Occupations of Entrepreneurs

Table 4.21: Community Education Preferences (%)

Years of education	Memon	Punjabi	Pathan	Bohra	Others
Less than 5	-	9	-	-	2
6-10	1	23	-	1	10
11-12	1	13	1	-	2
13+	2	33	1	1	3

Table 4.22: Caste Response to Education (only Punjab) (%)

Years of education	Agricul- turalist	Trader	Status	Crafts- man	Immi- grant
Less than 5	1	2	4	4	1
6-10	6	9	7	3	5
11-12	7	4	2	3	1
13+	9	13	10	5	8

Note: Details of Punjabi castes are given in Chapter 5.

response to education in the Punjabi community as well as in the categories of the Memons and others (mostly immigrants). The effect of education will, no doubt, have to be borne by the traditional occupations. In the Punjab, where education has considerably increased, the traditional occupational structures no longer appear. Surprisingly, the status orientated castes (Rajputs and Qureshis (73) have probably the pooorest response, indicating perhaps a rigidity in coming to terms with education. Since these castes also have land grants this is not surprising as they are, despite their poor education, well represented in the ruling classes and have used other means to maintain their status (74). The pattern for craftsmen is probably the most uniform in all the four categories. Here the desire for education seems to be limited by pragmatism. No more than the absolute essential seems to be the pattern, though 5 per cent have had more than 13 years education (roughly equivalent to graduation). Whatever the quality of education it does develop

an individual in many ways. To the entrepreneurs
it may mean breaking from the schackles of the past
and surpassing their father's achievement.

Education and Occupational Mobility

How did their education effect the motivation of
people already in jobs? Let us consider the first
responses only of those entrepreneurs who changed
their occupations (Table 4.23). In four of the

Table 4.23: Effect of Education on Motivation (%)

Year of education	Job aversion	Low pay	Own work	Profit	Other
Less than 10 years	3	2	24	11	4
10+	5	6	30	5	11

Total response 10 sample: 112

five categories the more educated seemd to have a
preference for changing their coccupation, and did
so. The largest response came from people who
wanted to be their own master. Given the 'personal'
nature of administration it is not surprising that
individuals in an enterprise would want to leave it
at some stage, and they do so simply because in
such a personalised system an executive often has
to pay 'homage' and be available for odd jobs after
office hours. Given such a system the survival of
an executive is related to the work required to be
done by corporate management. Any inability to
carry out their requirements may result in a fall
from grace. There is a high turnover, even in
joint ventures, where the firm is not controlled by
expatriates. A variety of other reasons, e.g. a
legacy/or poor relations with the employer - lead
to people changing jobs. Low pay and an aversion
to an existing job came next. As the inflation
rate increases the problem of low pay is likely
to gain prominence, as it is becoming very difficult
for salaried executives to maintain a reasonable
standard of living.
    The profit motive seems to be least important
for educated entrepreneurs going into industry.
The relatively less educated gave an 11 per cent
response compared with the 5 per cent more educated.
The Papanek thesis (75) that Pakistan's

industrialists' response was motivated by a desire for profits is no longer correct. Pride in their performance and in their attitude to work had taken its place. Profit was seen for what it could achieve as a means and not as an end in itself.

There is little doubt that education helps in occupational mobility, although there may be attendant circumstances, such as the pay restrictions on civil servants and private employees. The trader's response, irrespective of their level of education, is remarkably stable, and is evidence that the best response to shortage in the entrepreneurial area may continue to come from this source (76).

The Experience Obtained by Entrepreneurs

Three kinds of experience seem to be relevant to the entrepreneur, technical, managerial and marketing expertise. With demand increasing and with market imperfect, entrepreneurs are normally not concerned with maximising returns. If that were so, there would be an attempt at improved management practises, and organisations would tend towards complexity. The indigenous corporate sector is not affected by such factors at present as the entrepreneurs' minds are not orientated towards these concepts. The large corporate sector is different. There is a managerial aspect, though this is modified to local requirements. Ownership is not very wide spread and there has not been one instance where the management has changed due to pressures by shareholders. In fact, even financial statements have a time lag of over eighteen months. The experience which is most relevant in the context of Pakistan and other Ldc's concerns technical knowledge. In order to succeed in the entrepreneurial field, factors of production should be co-ordinated, being either bought or hired. Where machines are bought, companies have their own factors of production and the cost of entry is limited. A minimum of technology can start an individual in the indigenous sector. Owens and Nandy found:

The crucial point is that cost of entry is very low economically. However, it is meaningless to see it in strictly economic terms. Talent, experience, social linkages, and daring are more critical to success than a specific cash outlay and this has opened up the engineering industry to groups other than the economically dominant segments of the society.

124

The Origins and Occupations of Entrepreneurs

A similar experience is reported for the Philipines by Carroll (77) and by Berna for Madras State (78). In Pakistan indigenous entrepreneurs started in a small way and, contrary to Berna and Owen and Nandy, not only in the engineering industry. In societies where mass consumption is not the order of the day, where productivity does not matter, where government control is all-pervasive, inefficiencies and diseconomies of scale persist and thrive. Even under improved market conditions, economies of scale in the garment and textile industries no longer exist (79). In Pakistan, because of the absence of economies of scale and limitations imposed by narrow markets, the nature of the firm tends to be simple rather than complex (Table 4.24).

Table 4.24: Kind of Firm and Experience

Kind of firm	No	%	0	1-5	6-10	11-15	16-20	21+
Proprietory	22	11	8	5	5	2	–	2
Partnership	69	35	28	12	13	7	6	3
Private limited company	85	43	34	17	13	12	4	6
Public limited company	19	10	8	4	4	1	1	1
Co-operative	1	1	1	–	–	–	–	–
Total	196	100	79	38	34	22	11	12

In the table, firms with proprietors and partners constitute 46 per cent of the total while private limited companies were created only for tax response. All firms in these three categories function as a proprietory concern. In fact, even the public limited companies, which are run by leading families, have a very strong centralised family management. As a result, the market for managers has also remained at a very rudimentary level. Roughly 40 per cent of the sample were without experience though they may have had some education and training. The number of public limited companies in the sample was nineteen

(10 per cent) but, even at this stage of their development, enterprises tended to be very strictly supervised and all important positions within the organisation were held by entrepreneurs or their immediately family. Entrepreneurs' experience did not seem to have any overriding effect on the kind of organisation of the firm. The pattern of industrialisation does not conform to the acceptable hypothesis that inexperienced entrepreneurs would enter an industry which had a relatively simple manufacturing process. The industrial pattern indicates a surprising spread of relatively inexperienced entrepreneurs. This could be only because of either relative ease of entry or because the profit potential and individual ability was easy to perceive. Of the 40 per cent who were without any experience the dispersal is indicated in Table 4.25.

We see that industries of all categories have found entrepreneurial talent. As we go higher up the experience, the various categories continue to diminish. Thus in the 1-5-year segment there are fourteen categories of industries, in the 6-10-year category, thirteen industries, in the 11-15-year category, twelve industries and in 16+ category six industries. The entrepreneur with greater experience and technical expertise tends to remain in the industry with which he is familiar. The policy implications of such a finding are very far-reaching so far as production technology is concerned. For high-technology industries the entrepreneurs who are locked into a particular industry would be the most likely entrants. The inexperienced would be involved in a rather wider spread of industries, and their strength would lie in a perception of a market gap. The industrialisation process would therefore be built on the relative strengths of human beings, i.e. a shift away from both products and technology. As industrialisation would seem to be dependent on these factors, an assessment of the internal strengths of entrepreneurs would become an important requirement.

Equilibrium theory holds good for relatively smaller industries. Wherever large profits are made new entrepreneurs can enter with or without government permission. If they have permission and are registered, they are relatively fortunate, for then they are entitled to or can manage an import license for the import of raw material. If they are unregistered, they must buy raw materials from

The Origins and Occupations of Entrepreneurs

Table 4.25: Industrial Spread of Entrepreneurs
with No Experience

S.no.	Industry	No.	%
1	Textile	16	20
2	Footwear and leather	2	3
3	Hosiery and garments	1	1
4	Furniture	5	6
5	Glass products	5	6
6	Chemical products	2	3
7	Steel rerolling	4	5
8	Metal machinery	8	10
9	Electric fans	1	1
10	Car equipment	2	3
11	Surgical instruments	2	3
12	Sports goods	4	5
13	Ceramics	1	1
14	Cutlery products	3	4
15	Pharmaceuticals	2	3
16	Agricultural implements	6	8
17	Cycle parts	4	5
18	Marble products	1	1
19	Commodity process	2	3
20	Miscellaneous	8	10 (likely to comprise more than one category)
	Total	79	100a

Note: a. Does not add up to 100

other sources, obtain an import license from
another industrialist by paying a substantial
premium (these licences are transferable) or do
the best they can. However, there is a very
significant point of differentiation from
equilibrium theory: despite ease of entry, the
prices of the products remain unaffected and the
difference in the amount of profit depends on the
nature of the firm. Theoretically, the
'underprivileged' firm should not exist, but this
does not happen. The privileged company survies,
with large profits, while the underprivileged firms
exist at the subsistence level.

The Origins and Occupations of Entrepreneurs

Environmental Oppurtunities
If the relatively inexperienced entrepreneurs finds
it easier to enter industry and then survives,
there may be other explanations in the economic
environment worth mentioning at this stage. The
sample indicates a continuous increase in
entrepreneurs in industry from 1930 to 1980
(Table 4.26).

Table 4.26: Industry Investment

Year	No	%
1930-9	3	2
1940-9	10	5
1950-9	47	25
1960-9	53	28
1970-9	75	40
1980	2	1
	190	100a

Missing no: 6

Note: a. Does not add to 100.

     The trend for the ten-year periods is on the
increase, with the periods 1950-9, 1960-9 and
1970-9 showing particularly encouraging signs.
Some of this acceleration may well be due to a
momentum initiated by general entrepreneurial
behaviour. However, the three periods need to be
explained specifically in terms of opportunities.
The 1950-9 period was remembered by entrepreneurs
as a period of encouragement by the government.
Anyone who applied for permission received it
immediately. In fact, the Director of Industries
(80), while on tour of the provinces, would give
orders on the spot, and administration was
completed later. There were no cost benefit
analyses, and paperwork was reduced. Authority
was decentralised. For those reluctant to promote
themselves the director carried out the work
himself and found pragmatic solutions. This was
also the period when the country had to prove
itself. The period 1960-9 was the Ayub era, decade
of the large corporate sector, a period in which
foreign aid was at its greatest and a time of
robber barons and high profiteering. The era

1970-9, according to these earlier barons, should
have been 'desert time' for Pakistan. On the
contrary, it was a period of response from the
indigenous sector. The public sector also
developed but at the expense of the large private
sector and not the small or medium private sector.
This was also the period when bureaucratic
constraints were reduced because of the
appearance of public representatives. Most of the
factors highlighted were non-economic ones. So far
as economic factors were concerned, the loss of
East Pakistan was serious, as it was a significant
captive market. The market had shrunk. Raw
materials for import substitution industries were
not available because of the disruption due to
war in 1970-1. The large entrepreneurs, the
Dawoods, the Adamjees, the Isphanis and others
lost all their assets and no compensation was paid
to them. However, whereas others would have
faltered, the family and community strengths kept
them afloat.

These three decades were ones in which
inexperienced entrepreneurs were able to invest
in ever-increasing numbers (average, 30 per cent).
Opportunities were seen by experienced entrepreneurs and seized. Uncertainty and instability,
whether internal or geopolitical, did not effect
entrepreneurial decision-making, and flexibility
was shown when the economic environment became
repressive.

The economists' contention that a shortage of
capital is not as important as absorptive capacity
needs further examination. We have seen no lack
of skill in Pakistan (in terms of production
functions) and for inexperienced entrepreneurs lack
of knowledge does not seem to have been a crucial
factor. Despite obviously poor managerial and/or
organisational ability, there is a degree of
'gut managerism'.

Location Policy Based on Experience
A different location policy was also adopted by
experienced and inexperienced entrepreneurs. The
inexperienced entrepreneur was 'footloose', and
tended to set up industry wherever he could,
though a substantial number of them had established
companies in their home towns. The ratio of
experienced entrepreneurs to locations is not
altogether surprising when one considers the mass
exodus from India in 1947. The majority of

refugees envisaged another era of hardship. Even
if profits were perceived elsewhere, the nature of
the social relationships and the derivation of
strength from one's community and existing
environment was such that movement was discouraged.

Size
Analysis of companies by size shows a preponderance
of industries in the small sector, which are
followed by the large and medium sectors (Table
4.27).

Table 4.27: Size of Firm and Experience of
Entrepreneurs (%)

Years of experience	Small	Medium	Large
0	19	8	18
1-10	18	9	9
11+	13	7	4

The result, surprisingly, is that inexperienced
entrepreneurs seemed to have a response in the large
sector similar to that in the small sector and
twice that in the medium sector. The large sector
seems to be favoured by entrepreneurs who can
co-ordinate and hire the factors of production.
Experienced entrepreneurs in the large sector have
reached that stage through growth. The medium-
sized industries remain at around 8 per cent,
whether experienced or inexperienced entrepreneurs
are involved. In the case of those who have grown
to this level and have a large amount of experience,
they may have no further desire for growth. One
reason for this attitude was given by a Memon
entrepreneur who said that he had nothing to live
for, as his two sons had died and the only redeeming
feature of his life was his daughter and her
husband, who lived and worked with him. Despite
extensive experience, knowledge and skills that
could threaten entrepreneurs in other sectors,
there was often no desire to grow any further.
Personal reasons of this kind may explain the
number of stagnant firms.

Training
Four kinds of training inputs were distinguishable
in the development of an entrepreneur. We
therefore propose to study entrepreneurs in four

distinct technical categories. Again, the
managerial and marketing aspects were specifically
excluded. Attention was therefore given
exclusively to the production function, which is
vital to the development of a country.

Apprenticeship

Contrary to general assumptions, the apprenticeship
system develops out of the prevailing extended
community relationships. For instance, it is
impossible for high-status castes to seek to
improve their skills at a craftsman's unit.
Similarly, extended family influence is very
influencial in developing a career. The apprentice
sytem operates at no cost to entrepreneurs. To
them it is beneficial in the short and medium terms,
although not necessarily in the long term, because
they may be developing a potential competitor.

Which entrepreneurs are likely to have the
largest number of apprentices? This depends upon
the credibility and reputation of the entrepreneurs.
The apprenticeship system follows two distinct
industrial patterns (as well as following social
patterns). The large sector operates differently
to the small sector, has its own, more personal,
methods. The period and type of training also
differ. In both sectors education is never a
criterion. In the large sector the individual
comes at the age of eighteen, moves through the
various learning stages and goes from unskilled to
semi-skilled and skilled stages in a distinct
pattern. The manpower development agencies
initiated by the government in many urban centres
operate in a similar way. Since the 1960s the
Small Industries Corporation has also opened up
training centres, but the intake is limited to ten
students per year and the course is of two years'
duration. So even if the students do qualify at
a rate of ten per year, the output is far too
insignificant for industry's requirements. The
formal and informal systems interact. In the course
of an extended stay in the industry the trained
employee becomes an informal tutor to his staff (81).

Apprentices are evenly spread in our sample
but they are more prominent in the electric fan,
ceramics and agricultural implements industries.
In the informal sector, for example, ceramics
industry, entire families form part of the labour
force. This industry is extremely labour-intensive
and a firm usually consists of either an extended
family or two or three nuclear families. Increased

labour is recruited from any family members remaining. The unit, however, rarely increases capacity, so these extra labour requirements are only theoretical. When a unit has to expand, it subdivides, with the remaining members of the original family providing the labour force. This works to everyone's advantage. Most of the entrepreneurs interviewed indicated no labour problems, though some of them were worried by the high labour turnover caused by higher pay abroad. But was there, in fact, any input of a technical nature in the entrepreneurs studied? The details of the various kinds of training as well as the entrepreneurial response to training and the size of firms founded are given in Table 4.28.

Table 4.28: Training and Size of Firms (%)

Kind of Training	Small	Medium	Large
Apprentice	5	1	2
Polytechnic	3	1	1
Self	2	–	1
Technical	7	8	11
None	34	14	12

Very few apprentices formed large concerns. They started in a small way and over a period of time moved to medium-range industries, but the fact of their survival by sales is unquestionable. Of the 5 per cent in the small sector (by size of employment) only 2 per cent remained in the progressive sector (i.e. sales of between Rs 50,0001 - 2,500,000) and if we take the mid-point figure of sales as the industrial average, the net sales would be in the margin of Rs 13,000 per month. If an industry operated at a conservative 20 per cent profit margin, the net return would be equivalent to the salary of the highest paid civil servant. These returns enable the entrepreneurs in this category to achieve social mobility and ensure a position in society. Other industries have a much larger return. In the ceramics industry, for instance, the total requirements at the lower end of the industry is less than Rs 1,000 per month. Premises can be rented or leased in small urban towns at minimal cost. Raw materials are normally available from nearby river beds and only a minimal

working capital is required. In fact, a loan of
Rs 2,000 in 1965(82) enabled an entrepreneur to
survive the difficult war period. Similarly, in
the electric fan industry entrepreneurs can start
at any level. If components are to be built the
cost of entry is very low, and since demand is
seasonal the large manufacturer is predisposed
towards subcontracting certain components to new
entrepreneurs.

The movement from small, through medium, to
large depends on the entrepreneurs. One of them
who started with Rs 500 in 1946 today has one of
his sons as a member of the provincial cabinet in
the Punjab (83).This is a new role as far as
entrepreneurs are concerned. Although the role of
initial training is important, what is really
required thereafter is a knowledge of the market
and an awareness of opportunities. Those who were
aware of the commercial, fiscal and industrial
policies and took advantage of them broke all kinds
of shackles. But, contrary to what others have
found,(84) all entrepreneurs did not begin their
industrial life as apprentices. The period of
acceptance of the formal apprentice system did not
begin until 1960-9. During this period, thirteen
new technical centres were proposed, adding to the
original five, with a total yearly facility for
3,750 students. So the industrial policies of the
1960s were linked to training facilities, and were
important in that they supplied the economy with
entrepreneurs.

Polytechnics
Of the 5 per cent who came from this category, 3 per
cent went into the small sector. Entry into polytechnics is conditional on a schooling of at least
ten years. The recent trend has been for small
industrialists to learn as much as possible about
the theory of metals and alloys. The growing
complexity of products made them appreciate the
importance of alloys. Nearly all the respondents
went into metal-based industries, i.e. agricultural
implements, metal machinery and electric fans.

The polytechnics came into existence in the
decade 1960-9. Initially, entrants were those who
aspired to enter technical universities and, having
failed to do so, saw this as a compromise solution.
It soon became apparent that the objectives of
polytechnics were different to those of technical
universities. Latterly, polytechnic training is
sought for the 'practical son', who, after

supplementing his studies with on-job training for
a number of years, become entrepreneurs. These are
usually to be found in the small sector.

The Self-taught.
The self-taught learn a skill in their spare time,
usually informally from a master craftsman or
entrepreneur. A number of factors distinguish this
category. Normally, they are in the poverty trap
of the Third World. The first stage of their
upward struggle is to find a way to break old
shackles, usually at the cost of a severe strain to
health. Over a period of seven to ten years these
people work hard at unsocial hours for their master
craftsmen. Usually acceptance by the master
craftsman is only obtained after much persuasion and
effort. The self-apprenticed normally begin in a
workshop. Of the 3 per cent in our sample, 2 per
cent started in the small employee-scale and stayed
in the small sales-scale. One entrepreneur
progressed to the large sector, but it took him a
lifetime, and his break came when his pride was
hurt, otherwise he would have had to play second
fiddle to Memon industrialists. Today he has
Japanese industrialists flying in to see him.(85)
This, then, was the only area in which the
entrepreneur stayed at the subsistence level. As
suppliers of entrepreneurs, this is the area where
probably, despite the level of existence, unfettered
ambition exists. This might sound paradoxical but
it is borne out by initiation into household
industries and then into the small sector. In a
marketplace, where there is a demand for cheap
services, these entrepreneurs fulfil a need.
Unquestionably this is the area of neglect so far
as major government policies are concerned.

Technical Education
This was the most prized of all the levels of
imparting technical knowledge. A significant
number of entrepreneurs had been to technical
university or had been educated abroad. Given the
number of engineers who qualify each year, the
number going into industry is insignificant. The
reason, accepted by planners, is that 'there is an
emphasis on acquiring degrees and diplomas in order
to secure white collar jobs' (86).Another reason
is the mix of technologies taught in technical
colleges, 'which were not responsive to local
requirements and requirements of employers' (87).
The problem is also deep-rooted. White collar jobs

have high status. Factory jobs are not well paid
or status-orientated, neither is there any security
attached to such work.

A shift in the government's attitude would be
helpful in increasing the supply of entrepreneurs,
but this is unlikely in the short term. In any
case, in Pakistan the universities do not work
closely with industry. Engineering graduates have
a world market and Pakistan suffers when these
trained people emigrate to other countries. (The
movement is roughly of the order of 12.5 per cent
per year). However, some engineers do find
resources to start an industry. Of the entrepreneurs interviewed, 7 per cent were in small sector,
8 per cent were in the medium sector and 11 per cent
in the large sector.

The period in which they started these
industries were, again, the three important decades
of 1950-9, 1960-9, 1970-9. Whether the increasing
momentum will be kept up by those professionals and
whether they, in turn, will supply the necessary
number of entrepreneurs is yet to be seen. The
higher pay abroad, especially in other less
developed countries, may certainly be attractive,
but entrepreneurs interviewed in this category
stated that in their class all professional
migration is of a temporary nature. Once enough
capital is saved these temporary emigrants will
return to set up their own industries (88).

Modernising Effects of Technical Education. The
response to opportunities would naturally have an
effect on the traditional functional castes (Table
4.29). Surprisingly, the response from agriculturalists with a technical university education
is at par with the that of the traders, indicating
that the agricultural sector is likely to interact
with the urban sector in general and with the
educational sector in particular.

Agriculturalists have always valued education,
but there were indications that they now value
technical education, due to their growing appreciation of the complexities of modern life. In
addition to being affected by the modernisation
process, they are a mass of heterogenous individuals
with no collective bargaining position, and a
negative result of various government policies on
land acquisition for development purposes has
resulted in a spate of evictions. The helpless
agriculturalist is unable to withstand such policies
and these encroachments have pushed him into new

135

Table 4.29: Caste and Technical Education (%)

No.	Caste	Apprentice	Polytechnic	Self	Technical	None
1	Agriculturist	2	2	–	7	16
2	Trader	2	–	–	7	13
3	Status	2	–	1	3	16
4	Immigrant	1	2	–	3	9
5	Craftsman	1	1	2	2	

Note: Numbers do not add to 100 because of rounding.

activities. The result has been that a number of
aggrieved agriculturalists have moved into
agricultural-based industry.

The trader see the related problems differently.
No longer is he the uneducated mercantilist of
another era, making his bid in situations favourable
to him. General education has given way to a
specific technical education. There is, in the
trader, a perceived causality between input and
action. They have moved away from the first
principles of profit-maximisation: challenges are
what they are looking for. We have already
mentioned entrepreneurs studying metallurgy prior to
going into the steel industry. Similarly, others
have obtained specialised expertise in chemicals
and pharmaceuticals.

The craftsmen are lowest in the scale of
elitist technical education. They seem to be locked
into their existing profession, satisfied with
day-to-day operations. Their limited or non-
existent understanding of market forces and of
technological developments in industry may be their
biggest stumbling block. Their strength lies in
their ability to imitate, though modern technological advances are beyond their comprehension. The
craftsmen, though they live and work close to
training centres, do not communicate with these
centres.

All these categories have one thing in common
to the factors of production, a complementary
entrepreneurship (89).The factors of production
can be substituted only to the extent of the
entrepreneurs' knowledge. In the case of the small
sector, capital-intensity, even for the most
critical process, may be replaced by labour-intensity.
As enterprise growth is towards the larger sectors,
some of the important production processes can be
identified, leading to substitution of labour for
capital-intensive processes. The effect on products
of such a substitution is an improvement in quality
and a comparative advantage in world and local
markets. In the large sector, the replacement of
labour by capital is not due to the desire for a
better product, though that may be a minor objective,
but is caused by the emigration of skilled labour
to the world labour markets.

The Nature of Training

The training process, in the universities, technical
colleges, polytechnics or privately run institutions
suffers from one major deficiency, notably relating

the training to actual industrial requirements. The
major obstacke here is, of course, the views of the
policy-making agencies on the 'dynamic nature' that
training curricula need to have, i.e. an understanding not only of modern processes and the
possibilities of simplifying them, but also an
awareness of the development of raw materials and
of technological advancement, for all sectors in
industry. In short, the efforts of the 1960s
require to be upgraded to the realities of 1980.
The lesser but equally important deficiency
is in the methods of assessing efficiency. The
marginal efficiency concept is non-existent. A
considerable public outcry has been made about
productivity but there is no in-service training in
enterprises neither is there any consistent
upgrading of skills or tools. As production
processes become increasingly linked to automated
planning and manufacture, Pakistan may find this
technological gap increasingly difficult to bridge.
The entrepreneurs questioned on this issue agreed
that after their initial technical training, further
knowledge has only been obtained through informal
methods, e.g. visits to principals, and tours and
informal discussions with technical experts abroad.

The Interface Between Training, Education
and Experience.
The entrepreneurs interviewed all had some gaps in
their entrepreneurial armour. If training,
education and experience are three factors of
significance, how have the entrepreneurs covered
their shortcomings (Table 4.30)? Forty per cent
entrepreneurs had no experience, 27 per cent of
these had no technical education as against 13 per
cent who had, and there were none with no education,
i.e. 40 per cent of these entrepreneurs had
education at some level or the other. In the second
category of 1-5 years of experience, training was
equally divided between the trained and untrained,
with each having 10 per cent, whereas the educated
were way ahead with 19 per cent, and only 1 per cent
were uneducated. In the 6-10 years' experience
category (and, in fact, in all the remaining
categories), two relationships were obvious, i.e.
the more experienced (above six years) varied
inversely with those who were technically trained.
In other words, the more experienced one was, the
less the chances of or requirement for training.
There was thus a degree of substitution of skills
(Table 4.30). The same could not be said about

138

Table 4.30: Experience, Training and Education Compared

S.no.	Experience Years	%	Training		Education	
			Technical	None	Educated	Non-educated
1	0	40	13	27	40	0
2	1-5	19	10	10	19	1
3	6-10	17	8	10	17	1
4	11-15	11	3	9	10	1
5	16-20	6	4	2	6	-
6	21+	6	3	4	5	1

Note: Figures do not add to 100 because of rounding.

education. Education for entrepreneurs continued to be a requirement (Table 4.31).

Table 4.31: Experience and Education (%)

Experience	Education		
	0	10-	10+
0	-	14	26
1-5	1	6	13
6-10	1	8	9
11-15	1	4	7
16-20	-	3	3
21+	1	3	3

Table 4.31 shows the quantitative content of education though not necessarily the qualitative content. The variation of quality in education has already been referred to. The entrepreneurs with no experience were divided into three categories, i.e. nil years, less than ten years and more than ten years. It was found that there was no entrepreneur in the nil-nil category. Fourteen per cent of the entrepreneurs with nil experience had less than ten years of education while 26 per cent had more than ten years. As the level of experience increased, there was relative reduction in levels of education. It can safely be assumed that experience is, at the higher levels, inversely related to the number of years spent in education. At the highest level of experience, i.e. 21+, both categories (less than ten years of education and more than ten years of education) drop to 3 per cent. The decrease from 14 per cent in the nil-experience category to 3 per cent in the 21+ experience category was significant, and indicates that, at some level of education, the entrepreneurs may have felt that being educated served a purpose up to a point, and thereafter it had no role and was mere waste of time.

In fact, education of one kind or another was considered more important initially by 27 per cent of the sample. Two control factors were kept constant, i.e. experience was considered nil and training was considered non-essential. Table 4.32 shows this nil-nil experience and training category. Two levels of education were relevant, i.e. the ten-year level,(90) when mathematical comprehension is developed, and the graduate level, when articulacy and more general abilities develop.

Table 4.32: Relevance of Education

Education (years)	%	Experience = 0 Training = None
1-5	2	
6-10	9	
11-12	6	
13-14	10	
15-16	2	

Notes

1. 1971 Census of Pakistan.

2. The major tribes are the Marris, the Bugtis, the Mengals, the Achakzais, etc.

3. The inhabitants of Baluchistan are called Baluchis.

4. Special Report to the Cabinet, 1974, carried out by the Cabinet Division, Government of Pakistan.

5. G.F. Papanek, Pakistan's Development. Social goals and Private Incentives, Harvard University Press, Combridge, Mass., 1967.

6. The bulk of the Army is Punjabi.

7. Pakistan has had three land reforms and more are likely to come.

8. The Sunni Law of Inheritance ensures divisions between sons but the Shia Law is more complicated and different. For details, see Asaf A.A. Fayzee, Outline of Muhammadan Law, 3rd edn, Oxford University Press, London, 1964.

9. The Punjab Tenancy Act 1889.

10. Traditionally the tenant was responsible for purchase of seed, fertiliser, water flow and cultivation. At harvest time he received 5% of the produce. Unless harvest failure could be attributed to a natural disaster, the landlord had the right to dispense with the tenant's services.

11. Papanek, 'Gentlemen at Work' in Pakistan's Development.

12. Ibid.

13. Papanek's observation is modified to that extent; see ibid., pp.77-9.

14. G.F. Papanek, 'The Development of Entrepreneurship', in Entrepreneurship and Economic Development, The Free Press, New York, 1971.

15. Papanek's use of the term 'education' was probably in the more general sense.

16. Adda literal meaning 'place' but with time has come to be known as the area where the mechanically orientated entrepreneurs are generally found. Each town has a few such areas which have sprung up.

17. Hanna and G.F. Papanek, 'Pakistan's Industrialists': Papanek, Pakistan's Development.

18. Hanna Papanek 'Pakistan's New Industrialists and Businessmen. Focus on the Memons'.

19. Y.A. Sayigh, Entrepreneurs of Lebanon. The Role of the Business Leader in a Developing Country, Harvard University Press, Cambridge, Mass, 1962.

20. Alec P. Alexander, Greek Industrialists: An Economic and Social Analysis', Athens Centre for Planning and Economic Research, 1964, pp.44-51 passim.

21. J.J. Berna, Industrial Entrepreneurship in Madras State, Asia Publishing House, London, 1960, pp.44-82 passim.

22. K.L. Sharma and H. Singh, Entrepreneurial, Growth and Development Programme in North India, Abinar Publications, New Delhi, 1980, pp.74-8 passim.

23. R.L. Owens and A. Nandy, The New Vaisyas, Entrepreneurial Opportunity and Response in an Indian City, Carolina Academic Press, North Carolina, 1978.

24. Gujranwala, situated 40 miles from Lahore, has assumed significance in small scale textile industry, light engineering, electric motors and in a variety of small manufacturing activities.

25. Gujrat, situated a further 30 miles from Gujranwala, specialises in ceramics, light engineering, electric fans and motors and leather and shoes.

26. The two major institutions, i.e. The Industrial Development Bank of Pakistan and the Pakistan Industrial Credit and Investment Corporation, had local industrialists on their board of directors. The chairmanship is rotated between senior industrialists.

27. M. Nazir Ali, 'Mobilisation of Resources', Pakistan Economist, 19 April 1980. Mr. Nazir Ali is Secretary of the Karachi Chamber of Commerce and is member of some subcommittees. So it is not a lone voice but a collective demand.

28. H. Papanek, 'Entrepreneurs in East Pakistan, in Bengal - Change and Continuity'.

29. Thirty per cent of the Hindus continued living in Bengal. In the Punjab the migration was total. In Sind, some landowning families remained.

30. The writer discovered this to be so while serving in East Pakistan between 1968 and 1971.

31. Under the best possible conditions, the journey between Pabna and Dacca, a distance of 98 miles, would take 6 hours by road,with five ferries to be used. By railway the journey would take 28 hours and one would alight 20 miles away. The flight time is 45 minutes to Pabna, but the airport is 20 miles away.

32. The parity principle, in fact, is a social concept and operates in the family and society by conventions and customs. It simply means that no-one in the family shall have preferential treatment.

33. G.F. Papanek, Hanna Papanek and Nafziger make this point.

34. H.G. Johnson, 'Pakistan - A case of frustrated take off'.

35. T.A. Timberg, 'The Origins of Marwari Industrialists'.

36. G.F. Papanek, 'Pakistan's Development'.

37. The Ahsan Group, with a major industry, Khyber insurance and the 'The Sun' newspaper simultaneously published in two towns, Lahore and Karachi.

38. The General Habibullah Group, in textiles and the Ghandara Industries (motor assembly).

39. G.F. Papanek, 'Pakistan's Development'.

40. Notably Ralph Braibanti and Muneer Ahmed Ironically, Muneer Ahmed did not suffer from the bureaucratic procedure of the civil service but from that now being faced by the country, the resurgence of Islamic thought. He has since lost his job in the Punjab University.

41. The writer himself has undergone approximately eighteen transfers in fifteen years.

42. The administrative reforms changed the pattern of recruitment and training. Henceforth the Finance Service (Treasury in UK) and the generalists, i.e. the Pakistani civil service, were to undergo the same kind of training. No differentiation were made in the training required for various government positions.

43. The word 'political' is used in the widest possible sense to devote those at the pinnacle, politicians, the military or civil servants.

44. 'Crossroads' normally emerged with

made by deliberative inputs.

frustrations while in service. A conscious decision made by deliberative inputs.

45. 'Challenge' came as a reaction. The response arose as a result of a decision elsewhere, i.e. when the authorities used civil servants as scapegoats.

46. 'The professionals' include doctors, lawyers, engineers, professors, etc.

47. This period saw the secession of East Pakistan following the civil war, the major industry being defence. The 1976-7 uprising led to many problems concerning law and order.

48. R.G. Fox, 'Pariah Capitalism and Traditional Indian Merchants, Past and Present, in Milton Singer (ed.), Entrepreneurship Modernisation of Occupational Cultures in South Asia, Duke University Press, Durham, 1973.

49. For details on the managing agency system in the sub-continent see R.K. Hazari, The Structure of the Corporate Private Sector, Asia Publishing House, Bombay, 1966, and R. Amjad 'Private Industrial Investment in Pakistan', unpublished PhD Thesis, Cambridge University.

50. For details see ibid.

51. The Pakistan Economist, 12-18 July, 1980, no. 28, p.5.

52. The irony is that this will not help those agencies following the concept of the managing agency system, i.e. providing expert management to subsidiaries (presuming that there is dearth of managerial talent).

53. The Pakistan Economist, 12-18 July 1980, no. 28, p.10.

54. Papanek 'The Development of Entrepreneurship, in P. Kilby (ed.) 'Entrepreneurship and Economic Development'. The Free Press, New York, 1971.

55. One frequently sees top management doing personal chores for the 'owners' and family.

56. Mines. 'Tamil Muslim Merchants in India's Industrial Development', pp.52-3.

57. Berna, Industrial Entrepreneurship in Madras State.

58. F. Redlich, as quoted in Mines, 'Tamil Muslim Merchants'.

59. 'Settled' is a term used for those areas where the tribal or Jirga form of government has been replaced by the writ of the federal government.

60. H. Papanek, 'Pakistan's New Industrialists and Businessmen: 'Focus on the Memons', Progress in Pakistan's Development gives graphic account of the

ability and work ethics of these groups, although
as H. Papanek has pointed out, E.E.Hagen and others
considered this as an immigrant group trying to
recapture its earlier position of eminence.

61. Sanctions were in three categories,
generally (1) unit with 12,500 spindles, (2) unit
with 25,000 spindles and (3) composite.

62. These were two textile units installed by
entrepreneurs originally in opposition to the
government of the day who later joined that
government.

63. Papanek, Pakistan's Development.

64. Different schools abound for Shias, Sunnis,
the Wahabis, Deobandis, etc. but the teaching is
similar.

65. This has now changed, and all government
policies include Islamic or religious teachings.

66. This transpired during interviews with
entrepreneurs.

67. B.S. Turner, Weber and Islam, London,
Routledge and Kegan Paul, 1974 (quoting Ziya
Gokalp, p.164).

68. Initially started by missionaries.

69. Growth of 'Babus' or 'Sahibs'. A Babu or
a Sahib is a respectable gentleman. The words have
connotations of superiority.

70. Personal interviews with entrepreneurs.

71. As Director, Finance and Marketing, Punjab
Flour Milling Corporation, it was the author's
duty to sit with the Accountants who had prepared
the financial statements for a committee chaired
by a senior official of the federal government.
The bonds thus given were redeemable in 1990. The
interest they bore was $7\frac{1}{2}\%$.

72. For details of Punjabi castes see
Chapter 5.

73. The Rajputs and the Qureshis are warriors
and the descendants of the tribe of the Holy
Prophet, Quresh.

74. The surrogates of the warrior class and
the elite class have followed similar trends and
acquired urban and rural land, much as the earlier
castes had done. They have always stayed close to
the power centre and therefore hope to acquire
productive assets at less than market prices.

75. Papanek, 'Social Goals and Private
Incentives'.

76. Ibid., p.48.

77. J.J.Carroll, The Filipino Manufacturing
Entrepreneur, p.155.

78. Berna, 'Industrial Entrepreneurship in

Madras State', p.93.

79. Uri Pierre (Development with Dependence, Praeger, New York, 1976) makes these points in great detail.

80. The same director then laid the institutional framework for the Atomic Energy Commission. He was eased out of his job for alleged misdemeanours because he quoted examples of 'good work' in Israel. He is now a director with the World Bank.

81. Literally Ustaad but it is deeper than the usual teacher-student relationship. It is a life-long veneration for the tutor by the student.

82. The war with India lasted for fifteen days. The state of tension was defused by the Tashkent Declaration some time later.

83. The Daily Jang. 19 April 1981.

84. A. Callaway, 'Nigeria's, Indigenous Education: The Apprentice System', as quoted in Nafziger, African Capitalism.

85. Besides a host of other idiosyncracies, such as watching incoming businessmen through a glass door which only allows him to see; providing religious publications to all who come and see him; having a harem, probably the only one in Pakistan.

86. The Fifth Five-Year Plan, 1978-83. Part II. Islamabad, Planning Commission, Government of Pakistan, 1978, p.319.

87. Ibid, p.319.

88. Interview with an entrepreneur.

89. Nafziger, African Capitalism, p.169, makes a similar point.

90. Roughly equivalent to 'O' level in the UK.

Chapter Five

THE DEVELOPMENT OF AN ENTREPRENEUR

Empirical studies on entrepreneurship in less
developed countries suffer from a variety of
shortcomings. The findings differ on variations in
culture as well as on attributes and attitudes.
The relevance of education seems to find favour
with most of the analysts. Papanek, in the case of
Pakistan, despite rapid growth in the large sector
found the entrepreneur to be 'with no significant
formal education',(1) while Carroll,(2) in the case
of the Philippines and Alexander(3) for Greece and
Sayigh(4) for Lebanon have found entrepreneurs to
be better educated than the rest of the population
and that this was a basis for firm success. In
Pakistan, in addition to formal education, a
significant amount of informal education is always
provided. This may take the form of simply
inculcating values and attitudes which are helpful
later on in the pursuit of one's vocation. This
has been difficult for analysts to quantify.
     The informal sector normally starts with the
extended or joint family system, but other societal
factors, e.g. caste, community,(5) play a significant
part in inculcating attitudes and values.

Extended and Joint Families
Analysts considered the extended family to be a
barrier to economic development in general and to
entrepreneurial activity in particular. The
evidence available in Pakistan is contrary to
general findings elsewhere. In the present instance,
the effects of the informal sector will be
considered with reference to (1)development of work
ethics, (2)as a financial intermediary, (3)as a
risk-minimiser and (4)as a decision-maker.

Development of Work Ethics. The influence of Islam
in the development of work ethics is powerful, and
its present resurgence in Pakistan is merely the
reflection of the will of the masses. The first act
of parents, no matter to which segment of the
society they belong, is to instill into their
children appropriate religious principles. This
may take one of two forms, i.e. it may precede
formal Western-style education (in which case only
in the last couple of years is it allowed to take
place simultaneously with formal schooling) or it
may be carried out in parallel with formal schooling.
In both cases, but much more so in the latter,
leisure time is either completely eliminated or is
drastically reduced. Parents are proud when their
children finish reading the Holy Quran and the
culmination is when children become Hafiz-I-Quran,
i.e. they have learnt it by heart. The lower the
age level at which this is achieved, the greater
the accolade from society. What is more relevant
is that this religious exercise inculcates a work
habit and an ability to deal with difficult
situations. It also develops an understanding of
the articles of faith and the tenets of Islam.
This may have considerably changed where a modernisation process has taken place, e.g. in urban
towns where 'status-achievers' exist. Islamic
ideology is all-powerful in small towns and in the
countryside. The teaching is ingrained and shows
itself in the form of saying prayers five times a
day. Therefore by the time children are ten to
twelve years old, the ability to perform certain
actions at set times is firmly inculcated.

      This formal religious teaching is further
supplemented when the child-apprentice starts
working with the craftsman (Mistri) (6). This
normally takes place at a very early age, and one
can see apprentices working with Ustaads (7). In
order to be accepted and to learn the trade, the
apprentice works literally from sunrise to sunset
with no remuneration, except possibly a share in
the Ustaad's meals. From apprentices they become
helpers, when they receive some pay and are able to
do relatively small mechanical jobs independently
of any supervision. Table 5.1 indicates that in
towns with population of over a million, informally
developed apprentices are 16,14,10 per cent of the
skilled labour force in the factory. In districts towns this
varies between 8 - 17 per cent and in small rural
towns this varies between 4 and 29 per cent. The
significant variation within the small towns is a

Table 5.1: Foremen, Supervisors, Helpers and Apprentices in the Small Textile Units in the Punjab (selected towns).

S.no.	City/town	No. of units	Foreman	Skilled workers	Helpers	Apprentices	% 6+7 of 5
(1)	(2)	(3)	(4)	(5)	(6)	(7)	
1	Gujrat(b)	6	3	24	4	-	17
2	Jalalpur(c) Jattan	784	777	300	55	1	4
3	Lahore(a)	72	89	233	30	8	16
4	Kasur(b)	598	725	1,133	89	-	8
5	Raja Jhang(c)	130	173	214	49	12	29
6	Kamalia(c)	400	469	713	52	3	8
7	Faisalabad(a)	5,187	4,881	1,143	928	171	10
8	Multan(a)	715	961	781	109	3	14

Notes: a. Towns with population of over 1 million. b. District towns. c. Small rural towns.

Source: Basic Statistics on Small Textile Units in Punjab 1978-9.

a reflection of the fragmented markets. Where small towns are close to large towns the number of apprentices is higher. An apprenticeship of this kind has definite advantages over the apprenticeship development schemes of the government: (1)there are no barriers to entry, i.e. no formal education, no minimum age and no regional recruitment quotas, (2)the industrial apprenticeship tends to be more appropriate and realistic and (3)it ensures a job, because the foreman or skilled worker knows the abilities of apprentices at first-hand.

This apparent flexibility is of considerable importance. It instils the habit of long working hours into a skilled worker and his apprentices and it develops, based on that working system, certain values, unquantifiable but of great importance. To this class of people, ingrained as they are with Islamic religious values, duality in thought and action is not possible. In the case of certain Communities, H. Papanek(8) found this duality in religious terms. In their case, a much wider interpretation of life is shown, as can be seen in their founding of charitable institutions. Allied to their faith is the system of Zakat, whereby a certain percentage of their income is set aside for the poor. The community Papanek studied did this, and thus came to terms with their faith. A different nature of work ethics was developed by this and other such communities. Nothing was given to their children by right: they had to prove their worth. The offspring of the Memons studied, had to excel in the theoretical aspects of, for example, metallurgy and business studies before they assumed leading positions in the organisation. Traditional and conservative as these Memons are, excellence is justly rewarded within the inner family circle as well as in the larger community. Those who had been formally educated had to go through a gradual process of training, beginning with being, for example, a messenger boy (9). Promotion followed job-proficiency. Promotion in executive positions only came with the ability to do better in examinations than others. The ground rules show a growing awareness of merit, and the dilution of communal preferences and connections.

The influence of the family in ensuring religious education and in enabling their children to acquire skills led to a reduction in leisure hours. Similarly, such an individual may also be helped by the dowry which his wife brings in marriage, which would set him up as an entrepreneur. The fatalistic outlook of Muslims ensures rationality in failure and success. In Pakistan, at least, the joint family system seems to have provided important links, where work ethics and a system of values are positively related to hard work.

In the joint family system a father's occupation might well determine the basis for that of his heir. The degree of independence developed by children in the West is not available to Pakistan's youth. For one thing, there is no such concept as coming of age or of having to fend for onself. The relationship with the family is continuous. As there is virtually no social security arrangements, the family provides the necessary support.

The industrialist father did believe in giving his son education. Although the quality of this education may have differed, it provided a basis for meeting basic requirements. Only 1 per cent of the sample had not been given any education and 4 per cent had been taught only at primary level, i.e. less than five years. The category which could manage their own accounts, for example, were those with up to ten years of education (equivalent to UK 'O' levels) and they comprised 31 per cent of this sample, while 21 per cent had been educated to secondary level (A levels) and the graduate and post-graduates provided the remaining 43 per cent, which is a substantial improvement on previous recorded figures for Pakistani entrepreneurs.

Although every father would expect his son to manage his own industry, the experience that was provided varied. Experience was considered valid only if it was obtained on the shop floor. Thus a corollary to Table 5.2 needs to be taken into consideration. Very few sons would dare to cross swords with their fathers, for to do so might mean complete ostracism not only by the immediate family but from the joint family, and in some cases the community itself. Table 5.2 indicates the level of experience obtained, with 27 per cent having no technical experience whatsoever (although we shall see whether they have any training or technical education), while 26 per cent have shop-floor experience. The greater preponderance of such experience is in the small sector (less than 50 employees) where approximately 16 per cent of the total obtained work experience. The remaining 47 per cent had more than 10 years' experience, and these were to be found mostly in the small and medium categories.

Table 5.2: Level of Experience

Size by employment	Experience					
	0	1-5	6-10	11-15	16-20	21+
0-10	3	4	3	-	-	2
11-15	6	8	8	5	3	2
51-100	4	1	1	-	-	1
101-200	2	1	3	2	-	1
201-1000	4	2	2	1	-	1
1,001-5,000	2	3	-	-	1	-
5,000+	-	1	-	-	-	-
Total	21(79)	20(38)	17(33)	8(22)	4(11)	7(12)
	27(41)	26(20)	22(17)	10(11)	5(6)	9(6)%

Note: Number of fathers in parenthesis.

The Development of an Entrepreneur

When this is compared with the occupation of
the fathers of the entrepreneurs for the total
sample it is immediately apparent that there is a
significant reduction in the level of inexperienced
entrepreneurs in industry. This number in
percentage terms decreased in the case of father
and son from 41 per cent to 27 per cent.
 The other two inputs, i.e. the education of the
entire entrepreneurial sample, indicate the great
wish in every category to provide sons with some
education. Only 30 per cent had no education and
another 7 per cent had received primary education,
but there is an unmistakable trend towards further
education. Four categories were identified as
relevant for training: apprentice, polytechnic,
self-trained, and technical. Seven per cent of
the sample had undergone apprentice training, 5 per
cent received polytechnic education, another 3 per
cent were self-apprenticed (which really meant that
they had undertaken, in an informal way, some
alternative form of training and another 25 per
cent had received formal graduate training, at
reputable Western universities. These people were
the elite and some of them would have found leading
positions anywhere in the West. The highest category
again was the non-technical,i.e. 60 percent (Table
5.3). The variables need to be crosstabulated to
determine whether uneducated were also inexperienced. The results are given in Tables 5.4
and 5.5, and indicate that entry into industry is
always a well-calculated move in which there is
a systematic elimination of risk as far as technical
matters are concerned. In the category of no
education, all entrepreneurs had some amount of
experience,ranging from one to twenty-one years. The
relatively more educated had no experience at all,
Column 1 of Table 5.4 shows that 40 per cent of
educated entrepreneurs had no experience and another
26 per cent had more than ten years education.
Doubts must be expressed regarding the category
which has had only primary education, i.e. less
than five years, although the number is not significant. The category of 6-10 years of education is
the most difficult to explain. Generally, these
were people who had been closely supervised by
their relatives. Table 5.5 indicates that this
category again has a high 20 per cent with no significant technical training. It is unlikely that
the 6-10 years education category is the same as
those with no technical training. The sample shows
a very high degree of entrepreneurs with a formal

Table 5.3: Father's Occupation and Training of Entrepreneurs

Father's occupation	Training				
	Apprentice	Polytechnic	Self	Technical	None
Agriculturalist	1	3	–	4	15
Civil servant	1	2	–	8	11
Private employment	–	–	–	1	3
Trade	3	–	1	7	28
Industrialist	9	4	4	26	55
Professional	–	–	–	3	5
Others	–	1	–	–	–
	14	10	5	49	117
	7%	5%	3%	25%	60%

Table 5.4: Education and Experience of Entrepreneur

Education	Experience					
	0	1-5	6-10	11-15	16-20	21+
0	—	1	1	2	—	2
1-5	2	2	1	3	2	4
6-10	26	9	14	4	3	1
11-12	15	5	7	2	3	2
13-14	30	11	10	6	—	2
15-16	6	10	1	5	3	1
	79	38	34	22	11	12
	40%	19%	17%	11%	6%	6%

Table 5.5: Education and Training of Entrepreneurs

Education	Training				
	Apprentice	Polytechnic	Self	Technical	None
0	2	1	1	–	2
1–5	1	1	1	–	11
6–10	7	5	1	4	40
11–12	2	–	1	10	21
13–14	–	1	–	23	35
15–16	2	2	1	12	9
	14	10	5	49	118
	7%	5%	3%	25%	60%

technical education (25 per cent), with only 5 per
cent representation for the polytechnics. Nafziger
(10), amongst others, compared the literacy of the
population with the number of entrepreneurs (given
an average education). He came to the conclusion
that education is positively correlated with the
quantity of entrepreneurs when those in firms with
no more than eight employees are considered. No
such correlation can be explicity stated for
Pakistan.

Those with less education, i.e. less than 10
years, are to be found in the highest size by sales
category. The explanation for this lies in the
informal development of abilities and work ethics.
Roughly 30 per cent of the sample are in leading
positions and of these, 9 per cent had an education
of less than 5 years. The attitudes thus developed
play a pivotal role in conjunction with market
forces. Growing demand is linked not only with
the disposable income of an individual but also
with the Jones purchaser effect. In a society
where status is now becoming dependent on the
possession of consumer goods, the race for
acquisition is on. Increased earnings and the
accumulation of wealth by the workforce, which
frequently returns to its homeland from Europe, the
Middle East and Australia, ensure the sustenance
and growth of markets and new consumption patterns.

The effects on work ethics of education,
experience and training could only be conducive to
entrepreneurial growth. It has been more than
obvious that, whatever form education takes, be it
formal, technical training or experience in the
workplace, great emphasis is placed on results.
The family, and especially the elders, ensure a
'meaningful' existence for their children. The
joint family system brings benefits with it which
may be difficult to understand in any other
cultural context.

As a Financial Intermediary
The financial systems developed in the early 1950s
suffered from societal deficiencies. A World Bank
group studying the experience of the Punjab Small
Industries Corporation came to the conclusion that
2 per cent of the entrepreneurs were financed by
credit institutions. This means primarily those
industries located on industrial estates. The
financial institutions which provide industrial
credit are (1) the Pakistan Industrial Credit and
Finance Corporation (PICIC), (2) the Industrial

Development Bank of Pakistan (IDBP), (3)the Small
Business Finance Corporation (SBFC), (4)the Equity
Participation Fund (EPF), (5)the Investment
Corporation of Pakistan (ICP) and (6)the National
Investment Trust (NIT).

Of these, SBFC and EPF were set up specifically
for small industries. The minimum loan criteria
for PICIC prevents any small or medium size industry
from applying for loans from it, while the IDBP has
responsibility for all categories of industries.
The ICP and NIT underwrite loan debentures as well
as provide equity participation for the large
corporate sector.

IDBP is the only financial institution which
plays a part in the large, medium and small sectors.
An examination of its role may indicate the pattern
of advances and loans as well as any bias that may
be apparent in its policies. In 1973-4 (Table 5.6)
only nine loan applications were admitted and
Rs 6 million were disbursed, with an average of
Rs.67 million (Rs 4.75 = S1)(11) per admitted
application. If we compare this with the 1977-8
figures we see sixteen applications admitted for
Rs 12 million or Rs 0.75 million per admitted
application (Rs 9.90 = $1)(12). Even in money
terms, the applications admitted would hardly be
sufficient. However, more significant figures for
the same years, updated to 1979-80 and including
the five other banks scheduled to provide loans,
illustrates the dilemma of small industries. These
figures are for the Punjab only (Table.5.7).

In 1972-4 only 33 per cent of total applicants
were satisfied, in 1975-6 only 50 per cent, in
1976-7 only 25 per cent, and in 1979-80 only 48 per
cent. (This refers only to applications processed
by the financial institutions).

Time and again these financial institutions
failed to live up to their stated objectives. Even
institutions exclusively created for the benefit of
small industries failed to provide help, basically
because of the political influence used for the
sanctioning of loans. This can be seen from the
SBFC loan operations (Table 5.8).

The SBFC never evolved any criterion to
implement its objectives and, as a result, most of
its loans were used for other than the stated plans.
The average loan in each category was insignificant
except short-term consumption. Probably the loan
was made for political graft: it is unimaginable
how such laudable objectives as 'harnessing
technical knowhow and skill of those who have the

Table 5.6: Loans Approved by the IDBP for the Large and Small Sectors (Rs million)

	1973-4		1974-5		1975-6		1976-7		1977-8		Cumulative since inception	
	No.	Amt	No.	Amt	No.	Amt	No.	Amt	No.	Amt	No.	Amt
Large sector	134	369	162	266	148	346	71	121	86	193	2,165	2,574
Small sector	9	6	10	10	56	13	19	7	16	12	954	113
Row 2 as % of Row 1	7	2	6	4	38	4	26	6	196	6	44	4
Average loan per unit in small sector		0.67		1		0.23		0.36		0.75		0.118

Note: All figures are rounded.
Source: Annual Reports IDBP 1975-6, 1976-7, 1977-8.

Table 5.7: Statement showing Annual Progress of the Corporation in the Development of Small Industries with Financial Assistance through IDBP and Five Nationalised Banks up to July 1980 (for the Punjab only).

Financial year	Projects sponsored by IDBP and nationalised banks.	Amount of loan (Rs million)	Proposals sanctioned by bank.	Amount of loan sanctioned/disbursed.	
1972-3-4	72	9.5	26	1.766	(0.067)
1974-5	46	7.99	32	4.37	(0.136)
1975-6	42	7.343	21	2.73	(0.13)
1976-7	28	6.55	7	0.795	(0.113)
1977-8	32	4.75	16	2.16	(0.135)
1978-9	33	7.08	17	2.37	(0.139)
1979-80	27	6.1	13	2.29	(0.176)

Note: Figures in parenthesis : average amount per sanction/disbursement.

Source: Punjab Small Industries Corporation.

Table 5.8: Loaning Operation Small Business Finance Corporation (Rs million)

S.no.	Category	Sanctions		Disbursements	
		No.	Amount	No.	Amount
1	Shopkeepers	4,342	34.3	3,603	28.7 (0.008)
2	Small transporters	308	4.0	232	3.3 (0.014)
3	Small-scale industry/cottage/ artisans	854	8.6	459	4.8 (0.010)
4	Professionals	128	0.9	107	0.6 (0.005)
5	New entrants	226	1.5	228	0.9 (0.004)
6	Importers and exporters	51	0.6	41	0.5 (0.012)

Note: Figure in parenthesis indicate average amount per sanction.

Source: Government-sponsored Corporation 1974-5. This Corporation came into existence in 1972 by an act of parliament.

necessary talent' could be achieved by a one-off
loan amounting probably to Rs 8000 (or $800) in the
shopkeepers category, Rs 14,000 for small transporters, Rs 10,000 (S1,000) for small-scale
industries and Rs 4,000 for new entrants (13).

The EPF had no organisation of its own but its
funds were placed at the disposal of the IDBP. The
stated objectives were (1) to encourage small and
medium-size entrepreneurs who were handicapped in
raising resources from capital markets and (2) to
provide equity support to enhance risk-bearing
ability and creditworthiness. Its performance was
equally disappointing. The equity participation was
hardly worth while or effective. Only in one
sector, wool spinning, was there any effective
participation.

Given this inadequacy of the financial
institutions how did small industry manage its
requirements? Table 5.9 and 5.10 are two examples
of sectoral growth in the small industries, i.e.
light engineering and small textile units.

The vigorous growth of units in these two
sectors illustrates what has been happening in the
small sector. Tables 5.9 and 5.10 demonstrate the
inadequacy of financial institutions so far as
these sectors are concerned. Having seen these
deficiencies, one is bound to seek other answers
to the question of how such exceptional growth rates
can be maintained. The explanation lies in the
extended family system, in the well-knit fabric of
family life, which enables entrepreneurs to live
frugally and well within their means, and which
gives them advantages which ensure their subsequent
success. Besides financial inputs, the family's
total commitment ensures a vigorous approach to
achieving objectives.

A common basis for analysing the extended
family system in a given economic framework is to
blame the underdevelopment of countries on obvious
shortcomings. For instance, the extended family is
considered to be a burden, in as much as it
militates against accumulation of capital (14). The
other elements are not considered, for example, in
the absence of any joint income, expenditure would
have to be incurred by either the state in some
form of social security payment, assuming that these
people cannot support themselves. In such a case
social security taxation would be higher than
existing expenditure on survival, in as much as
nucleus family's fixed costs (housing) and variable
costs (food and clothing) would have to be provided.

Table 5.9: Annual Installation in Light Engineering Sector

S. No.	Name of industry (col.1)	1970 (2)	1971 (3)	1972 (4)	1973 (5)	1974 (6)	1975 (7)	1976 (8)	Increase(%) col.(8)over col.(2)
1	Agricultural implements	150	170	197	222	247	272	306	104
2	Industrial plant and Machine Tools	151	169	206	261	311	360	426	182
3	Cycle and car parts	132	146	163	196	228	256	296	124
4	Weights and measures	20	21	22	27	33	37	52	160
5	Sewing machines	37	42	44	59	70	92	119	222
6	Light engineering service units	979	1,203	1,454	1,817	2,201	2,552	3,144	221
7	Fabricated structure and metal finishing	558	666	784	912	1,204	1,392	1,646	195
8	Standard metal articles	40	47	54	62	65	69	80	100
9	Hardware	75	87	113	142	172	190	235	213
10	Wire drawing	12	14	18	20	24	28	34	183
11	Wire netting	10	12	18	22	24	25	27	170
12	Electrical goods industry	106	129	150	174	218	284	351	231
13	Cutlery and surgical	187	210	244	293	359	442	595	219
14	Brass, copper and aluminium wires	102	120	137	156	193	241	332	226

Source: Basic Statistics on Small Light Engineering Industry in Punjab, Punjab Small Industries Corporation, Lahore.

Table 5.10: Annual Installation in Small Textile Units

S. No. (co.1)	Name of industry (co.1)	1970 (2)	1971 (3)	1972 (4)	1973 (5)	1974 (6)	1975 (7)	1976 (8)	Increase(%) col.(8)over col.(2)
1	Canvas	173	203	229	226	315	353	402	132
2	Cotton cloth	3,111	4,089	5,041	6,133	7,199	8,067	9,016	190
3	Silk cloth	878	1,152	1,532	1,941	2,270	2,794	3,482	297
4	Towel	25	29	35	44	54	60	81	224
5	Readymade garments	4	8	12	19	23	27	30	650
6	Hosiery	70	82	110	136	153	173	205	193
7	Sizing yarn	25	27	34	37	44	61	82	228
8	Printing textiles	27	38	51	64	70	75	87	222
9	Narrow fabrics	110	130	157	182	219	235	260	136
10	Dyeing and calendering	37	51	60	70	80	98	125	238
11	Specialised textiles	296	384	477	638	770	903	1,087	267

Source: Basic Statistics on Small Textile Units in Punjab, Punjab Small Industries Corporation 1978-9.

A system would have to develop some kind of work ethic, otherwise apathy towards working for a living would set in. There is, in an extended family system, a continual moral commitment towards the family. Besides the work ethic developed during this period, normally through the 'informal' system, everything is taught by example. Family relationships in Pakistan are important in helping entrepreneurs through their difficult initial efforts.

Similarly, marriage could be so arranged as to reinforce economic opportunities. Deficiencies in capital or links with the bureaucracy or with political elites are helped by marriage arrangements. Useful though these could be, it would be extremely difficult to measure the costs and benefits of providing this kind of security. For instance, Wolf writes: 'The joint or extended family system provides another example of the institutions deterring economic growth' (15). Owens, on the other hand, suggests that India provides examples of the extended family being helpful in an entrepreneur's development and growth (as well as sometimes being a hinderance). Owens finds the role of the head of the family as crucial:

It is in his interest (entrepreneur's) to provide generously for the education of members of the commensal(16) family and later, on the basis of trust and obligation built up in this and other ways, to bring them into his firm as partners. ...If such firms are regarded as one of the most dynamic expressions of industrialisation, then they also most dramatically belie the general expectation that industrialisation is inimical to the joint family system (17).

The debate on whether the extended family is inimical to industrialisation will continue, and will depend on the particular social milieu.

An indication of the impact of the extended family on Pakistan has already been given, based on the survey of small firms. To suggest that its influence on a small firm is limited would be to understate the case. In Pakistan, the extended family system has effectively modified the corporate sector to conform to its requirements. Family directorships and interlocking directorships(18) explain the overriding influence of links within a family as well as those with another family. There has, of course, been a two-way relationship, and the process of change has, for example, affected the extended Memon and Habib families. To say that

these families have only come to terms with the
economic aspect of life is to ignore their influence
and impact on the political as well as religious
aspects of contemporary life in Pakistan.

In the sample of 196 firms, 11 per cent were
proprietorary concerns, 35 per cent were partner-
ships, 43 per cent were private limited companies,
10 per cent were public companies and 1 per cent
were co-operatives. The sector which had a mix of
all kinds of organisations was the textile industry.
In the partnership firms, roughly 89 per cent of the
partners were relatives, 10 per cent friends and
1 per cent acquaintances. The overriding dependence
on members of the family cannot be disregarded.

The transition from a partnership to a private
limited company normally occurred on the basis of
tax advantages. The majority of entrepreneurs,
however, indicated that the movement from proprie-
torship to partnership was based on acquiring
capital, or technological expertise or managerial
help (for example, accountants) to recover debts.
In the technical field such trust meant that one of
the partners was in a position, for example, to
travel outside the country or to contact officials
for action on important issues affecting the firm.
The inclusion of a partner from amongst the family
members meant a spread in the sphere of influence.
On the other hand, responsibilities and obligations
to the family normally increased with the growth of
the firm.

Approximately 97 per cent of the directors
were relatives and only 3 per cent were friends,
indicating the great reliance on the extended family
when the firm became a private limited company.

Since the stakes were always high and the
risk involved almost all the savings of everyone
in the family, success had to be ensured. But the
more important factor is the loss of face, the
shame that comes with failure, and the almost in-
variable self-ostracism that follows. Failure can
seldom be attributed to impersonal reasons; to the
fatalist that might seem an act of God, but to the
majority it indicates a failure in terms of inputs.
The 3 per cent who were friends would be very
different. The tradition regarding the social
creation of brotherhood is still prevalent. The
bonds thus developed are bonds superior to those of blood-
brothers. Thus a publicly acclaimed brother who
goes into partnership or becomes director in a
private limited company enjoys a life-long relationship, and is almost invariably given preferenve over

one's own kith and kin. The basis of such social brotherhood is developed over a long period of time. In the corporate sector all the representatives on the board of directors, except those from financial institutions (normally two directors in lieu of equity participation), are relatives, again indicating that ordinary shareholders do not have any representation in the management of the corporate sector nor can they upset the constitution of the board of directors. In the history of corporate management in Pakistan there has never been any major takeover bid. In fact, the minority shareholders accept whatever decisions are taken by the board of directors.

Non-repatriable Investment
In Pakistan, the firm, irrespective of size, is heavily family-orientated. A more significant aspect of family orientation and mutual help may be gathered from the Non-Repatriable Investment (NRI) policies offered by the government. Under the NRI scheme Pakistanis abroad can send machinery into the country according to Pakistan's natural resources. Compared with private foreign investment there is no foreign exchange repatriation of profits. The impact of these policies has been significant, and Pakistanis working in the Middle East and in the UK and other countries who have developed an expertise are forming an important source of supply of entrepreneurs. While they continue to work abroad their relatives manage the affairs of the industries. Thus, despite two decades of living far apart, family ties have not been broken. The provisional figures for sanctions and investment up to July 1980 are shown in Table 5.11.
    The promise held out by the non-repatriable investment sector is very encouraging as well as important. Here were a number of individuals who had endured extreme hardship, had lived frugally and saved and had now invested in industry. The experience and the skill that these emigrants have acquired over the years could be utilised even more if administrative procedures were streamlined (19). Table 5.11 provides evidence of delay, red tape and other administrative bottlenecks. The inability to counter these delays resulted in less investment. The point worth noting, though, is that foreign-earned incomes have filtered back to Pakistan, not only through financial institutions but through the more traditional family structures.

Table 5.11: NRI Sanctions and Investments 1975-6 to
1978-9. (Rs million)

Year	Sanctions			Investment		
	No.	Total	Ext.	No.	Total	Ext
1975-6	187	69.5	50.2	117	33	30.3
2976-7	179	58.9	48.6	83	24.6	24.5
1977-8	335	240.8	174.2	167	53.5	52.4
1978-9	376	445.5	306.7	184	126.6	94.7
Total	1,077	814.7	579.7	551	237.7	201.9

Source: Internal Review Report, Ministry of
Industries, Government of Pakistan, Islamabad.

Sources of Finance
If the extended family system has been criticised it
is because of the evidence provided by certain
empirical studies:
    It seems clear that family obligations require
substantial amounts of current consumption expenditure, some of which might otherwise be saved and
reinvested ... The number of dependents is
positively correlated with income (20).
The matter, in the context of Pakistan, is not as
simple. Given the articles of faith in Islam, this
would be an essential element in the armoury of
every entrepreneur. The concept of zakat(21) is
fundamental. Although this is being formalised
at present, the informal method of implementation
has ensured that the less wealthy relatives improved
their chances in this world. It was diametrically
opposed to Goldsmiths' 'poor relation who had
outstayed his welcome'. Materialism was not an end
in itself but a means for social improvement. So
where there was a need, the 'poor relative' was
taken within the fold. Did this impede reinvestment
of profits? There are no means of comparing the
consumption expenditure of the large corporate
sector, the other sectors and the consumption
pattern of the population in general. However, it
may be asserted that the consumption pattern in the
industrial sector, though far in excess of any norm,
could hardly be called conspicuous except in a few
limited cases. So far as capital utilisation and
absorption capacity was concerned, entrepreneurs
knew where to obtain credit either in the formal
or informal sectors. Moreover, they had the ability

to tighten their belts in adverse circumstances.
The desire for additional capital does not
necessarily represent an effective demand for it,
as Schatz discovered in Nigeria (22).

To some entrepreneurs in Pakistan an interest-
bearing loan was against the tenets of Islam. Usury
is to be abhorred and there was a considerable
amount of moral indignation. This came to be
accepted in the Pakistani context simply by rationa-
lising between private and public morality (23).
Though there were dogmatic entrepreneurs with a
doctrinaire approach who refused to deal in any kind
of usury, there were others who explained away such
conflict with Islamic thought by other equally
important concepts.

Entrepreneurs were extensively questioned on
their financial resources to determine what their
own resources were and what contributions friends
and relatives made to their resources at the
earliest stages, i.e. when there were maximum risk
and uncertainty and when loans might be refused.
The results in Table 5.12 indicates that 39 per cent
relied on financial help from friends and relatives,
finances which were available to them because of
the extended family system. These savings would
normally be outside the organised, formal sector.
Sixty-one per cent of the sample did not accept any
help initially but did seek working capital
arrangements as and when the need arose. It was
also abundantly clear that roughly the same number
did not seek any finances from investment agencies
or banks, i.e. they generated their own resources
and reinvested their profits. Significantly, the
textile, steel rerolling, metal machinery, electric
fans, agricultural implements industries were
prominent in this category. In some of these
sectors, especially textile, agricultural implements
and metal machinery economies of scale are
unimportant (24). In each industry the firm was
established at the smallest level, so that costs
were kept in check: some industries may even have
been initiated with technologically obsolete
machinery. In such cases, the skill of the artisan
was more important. Others, where the industry
was started by the entrepreneur's own resources,
were the relatively labour-intensive industries,
i.e. furniture-making, sports goods manufacture,
leather tanning and leather goods.

The degree of family or friends' resources in
the firm vary considerably (Table 5.12). Eight per
cent supplied upto 25 per cent of the initial

169

Table 5.12: Industry and Capital from Informal Sources

Industry	Resources from friends and relatives in total capital employed (%)					
	0	1–25	26–50	51–75	76–95	96–100
Textile	22	6	3	5	1	–
Footwear and leather	3	–	1	1	–	–
Hosiery and garments	2	–	–	1	–	–
Furniture	4	2	2	–	–	–
Glass products	4	1	1	–	–	–
Chemical products	4	1	2	1	–	–
Steel rerolling	6	2	4	–	2	–
Metal machinery	18	–	5	3	2	–
Electric fans	18	1	1	1	1	–
Car equipment	4	–	–	–	1	1
Surgical instruments	2	–	–	–	–	–
Sports goods	4	–	1	1	1	–
Ceramics	2	–	1	2	–	–
Cutlery products	3	–	1	–	2	–
Pharmaceuticals	2	–	1	1	–	–
Agricultural implements	7	–	6	–	1	–
Cycles and parts	1	–	–	–	2	–
Marble products	1	1	–	–	–	–
Commodity prices	3	–	–	–	–	–
Miscellaneous	8	2	2	–	–	–
	118	16	31	16	12	1
	59	8	15	8	6	1%

Missing observations: 2

capital and another 16 per cent up to 50 per cent of
the capital, which indicates that 24 per cent relied
on personal savings to a great extent. How does one
explain 15 per cent of the entrepreneurs obtaining
more than 50 per cent financial aid? Clearly,
these are cases of total family support and proves
the strength of the extended family. Of these
approximately 7 per cent were provided with between
76-100 per cent of resources. How does this, then,
compare with empirical studies which support the
hypothesis that the extended family is an impediment
to growth and development? The evidence is
overwhelming in asserting that it is not so, at
least, not in the case of Pakistan. In fact, the
extended family system, irrespective of sector, has
been able to influence modern institutions and bring
about modifications. Whether these modifications
should be incorporated into the system is again a
matter of detail.

Table 5.12 does indicate, for certain
categories, a degree of capital-intensive investment
and high capital gearing. In such cases might it
not be argued that the extended family was not in
operation? On the contrary, the extended family
was operating at full strength. The non-quanti-
fiable aspects were, in fact, more important, and
will continue to be so, unless government
intereference is drastically reduced. The majority
of the entrepreneurs now maintain offices in or near
Islamabad, as well as guest houses, to maintain contact with
government. The role of the government is a reality
and, sooner or later, entrepreneurs will have to
come to terms with it. Even the least important
officials in the bureaucratic hierarchy can create
substantial delays and have a nuisance value.

So far as enterprises are concerned, positions
of trust, where money is involved, are given to
relatives or trusted loyalists. In Pakistan, in
short, the extended family is very much a reality.
There are no half-way measures, no contradictions
which some writers have found. A strict economic
criterion is, in any case, impossible to apply at
this stage of development. The entrepreneurs, for
all their help from their respective families, in
turn receive substantial support from the system.

The Extended Family as a Risk-Minimiser
The extended family provdes strength in another way.
H. Papanek's study of the Memons(25) demonstrates how
the large industrial houses are based on the extended
ramily. Amjad and White also show the spread of

investment. In a traditional economic sense this is rational decision-making, given a free and vigorous market economy. However, where barriers to entry of various kinds, political, economic and administrative exist, where is the need for such action. One explanation is the competition within these large companies (26). To remain leaders, they need to continue to increase their assets. Second to meet the increasing needs of the extended family and the community expansion could lead to more jobs and a stronger economic base. With an increase in assets came an increase in pressure, which, if it could not be completely removed, had to be neutralised.

But first what kind of pressures were to be minimised at the micro level? These could be generated internally within the firm in connection with the accounts, management decisions or industrial relations (27). Where trust is limited and personal and where institutions are virtually non-existent it would be ideal to have members of one's own family in important positions. The more important the position, the closer the relationship: the two are directly proportional. In the event of a shortage of suitable candidates for the job, the longest-serving loyalist would be trained for this crucial position.

Where family ties were either demolished(28) or weakened, a process of modernisation had set in. This could be seen from the marriage pattern, where siblings married women outside their caste or communities. The result of all this led to a division of family assets. The process of modernisation inevitably led to reduction in concentration and power.

Where modernisation has not been so drastic, where marriages have followed traditional lines and accepted customs,(29) there has been no such dilution of holdings. Family members continue to fill the critical posts. There is, of course, another distinction from the previous large company in as much as the Karta Dharta still exists, and is supreme.

In the tribal belt where industries have been set up the entire labour force is taken from the owner's tribe. The advantages of this system are immense, as the social utility of this type of patronage is based on a morality of mutual help. The entrepreneurs do something for their tribe and in return the tribe provides work over and above that required. Industrial relations problems, if

they ever occur, are tackled outside the factory,
in the village. The village elders (Mashar(30)) are
brought into action. In the Pathan culture the
elders do not take kindly to their wards not
performing according to ethical standards. Thus
during the most turbulent times these units have
had no human problems and, through the success of
one unit, two others in the large sector have been
set up. Thus labour problems are diffused through
the social sanctions system existing in an area.

The Extended Family as a Decision-Maker

Whilst there are advantages in the extended family
system, there are also certain constraints,
particularly in the area of decision-making. Seldom
is a decision made which is not in keeping with the
expressed wishes of the senior member of the
family(31) or the Karta Dharta. This is in keeping
with economic rationalisation. The position of
Karta Dharta generally devolves on someone with an
excellent track record, not merely because he is
old (32). A similar situation develops at the family
level. In families where education, travel and
training abroad have been provided their advice is
normally taken. The important fact is that the
joint or extended family takes a mutual decision
at critical junctures in the firm's life. In that
sense, even in the large corporate sector which has
a formalised authority, the informal inputs into
decision-making can be seen. Hanna Papanek's
version is still in keeping with the times, when
she stated:

H.K. was still alive at the time of Partition,
though very old and set in his ways. But his voice
continued to be crucial in personal and business
decisions in the whole big family. It became
difficult to reach an agreement among the many sons
over the steps the family should take under the new
circumstances of Pakistan and without H.K's decisive
leadership, they could not make up their minds to
invest in a large industrial venture (33).
The pattern, however, varies with the traditions of
an area, a community or a caste. In the case of
the Chinioti sheikhs(34) one of the male members
stayed in his home village while the others
travelled as far as Calcutta (practically crossing
the subcontinent) to set up joint leather-tanning
ventures. The male members were to take turns at
looking after the wives and children of brothers,
uncles, etc. Rotation used to be every six months.
In fact, even when they emigrated to cities, all

these people lived together and shared the same
office, and, while decisions were being formulated,
obtained the views of the Karta Dharta, no matter
where he was.   Decisions in absentia are never taken.
The development of such bonds ensured a credibility
and a consistency of action. With success, as in
the case of the large houses, came pride and self-
confidence. The natural corollary to a joint family
extension was not heard of. Two separate joint
families have never merged their resources for a
joint industrial purpose. The trust within a joint
family does not necessarily extend to another
family, unless, of course, avowed brotherhood has
been established (35). Some of the houses(36)
ensured that the basis for collective decision-
making was maintained. Their ingenious plan to
counter the nationalisation policy of the 1970s was
simply to take steps to create separate business
entities, no holding company, no subsidiaries each
independent of the other. However, it was
compulsory for all the leading managers of the
concerns to meet at one place for lunch every day, a
two-hour informal session in which problems were
discussed and settled. So even in the most modern
sector one finds that the family influence on
decision-making is predominant.

The Caste System

The caste system is usually synonymous with the
Indian subcontinent and is attributed to the Hindu
way of life, of some form of hierarchial ordering,
or a differentiating treatment of people in the
system. The implication of the caste system on the
Muslims in India was different. With Muslims there
was no specific order of status attached to the
caste and subcastes. It was simply a way of
ordering the division of labour. In its simplistic
form, the agriculturalist needed to be differentiated from the milkman, from the artisan and from
the blacksmith and, since the economy was not
monetised, goods came to be exchanged on the basis
of barter. This is practised even today. The modern
system is exclusive to urban and to rural areas
close to towns. It is still the practice to locate
village artisans and to have work done for so many
'handfuls of grain'(37). Papanek's hesitancy to use
'caste' for the 'Memons' was based on firm grounds,
as all Memons were not necessarily in an
occupational specialisation': they were to be found
in other vocations as well. The Memons as a caste
are not linked with the other social caste orderings

in Pakistan. A distinctive feature of Islam in the
sub-continent, though, is the existence of caste
divisions (38).This distinctive feature appeared
partially as a result of economic and occupational
specialisation which became hereditary and took
on a permanent or semi-permanent nature. The other
reasons were, of course, the continuous process of
absorption into the culture and the fact that
Muslim missionaries helped to convert Hindus to
Islam. These converts continued with their castes
(39) even when the original connections were removed.
     The reason for considering caste in the
present context is simply to determine how much
influence the caste background may have in the
development of entrepreneurs. As a source of
informal learning, its significance cannot be
denied. In the extended family system we have seen
the strength of the head of the family. But what
makes the analysis much more complex is the
heterogeneity of Pakistan's population. The North-
West Frontier Province, with its tribal links and
serai owners(40) may have gone into trading. The
link was established through the immigrant
community in the UK. Since verbal pledges are very
important amongst the Pathans of the North-West
Frontier Province, credit and trade links were
established between Pathans in the province and
abroad. The result was a market area, in the
wilderness, where any luxury item from the UK was
made available at prices lower than those at normal
retail outlets. Even delivery of bulky modern
durable consumer goods is undertaken for a token
fee. They have, in a sense moved from a form of
hotel-keeping to trading, but have yet to go into
manufacturing, probably because the needs of
nomadic tribes given to animal-laden goods and no
permanent abode is one of subsistence (41). The
only demand for such tribes was to safeguard
community pastural land, for which weapons were
needed and these were provided locally. The link
of the craftsman gun manufacturers of the North-
West Frontier Province with the traders is too
tennous to be stated firmly, but certainly, as a
response to demand, gun manufacturing was established, and despite government. restrictions, it has
thrived (42).Technical knowledge is based on first
principles: there are no foundries, no technology,
no training in metallurgy, nothing but the ability
to 'feel' a metal, to determine how well it is
'tempered'. It is an extremely useful example of
appropriate technology. On the other hand,

Baluchistan, with a similar tribal situation, is bereft of both trade and serai living. In rural Sind, the Waderas (43) and the Haris (44) enjoy a different kind of living. In the metropolitan city of Karachi, the attitudes of its conglomeration of immigrants are different, materialism and financial motives abound. The Punjab, again, is different in the sense that the major impact of the caste system is felt here. Links established would therefore indicate the nature of informal training attributable to societal factors.

Caste and Industry. To determine movement into industry, entrepreneurs' caste was determined and is shown in Table 5.13. In all, fourteen castes and sub-castes of the Punjab were identified in the sample. Of the castes represented, 20 per cent were

Table 5.13: Castes of Punjabis in Industry

Caste	No	%
Sheikh	39	20
Arain	20	10
Jat	12	6
Malik	8	4
Rajput	29	15
Gujjar	2	1
Moghul	19	10
Qureshi	10	5
Rehmani	3	2
Khawaja	24	12
Khokhar	5	3
Kakazai	1	negligible
Blacksmith	1	negligible
Immigrants	2	1
Memons/Bohras	21	11
Total	196	100

traders (sheikhs), 23 per cent were agricultural castes (Arains, Maliks, Khokhars and Kakazais), 13 per cent were craftsmen (Gujjar, Moghuls and Rehmanis and blacksmiths), 20 per cent were status castes (Rajputs and Qureshis) and 24 per cent were immigrant castes (Khawajas, Bohras, Memons and other immigrants, though, strictly speaking, the Bohras and the Memons were not castes).

The Development of an Entrepreneur

Caste Characteristics (45)

Trading Castes (Sheikhs). Traditionally the
Sheikhs were small traders, merchants rather than
mercantile traders. In so far as they were
merchants the sheikhs (46) catered for the immediate
needs of the community, and therefore a time of
high profits was linked with scarce supply
conditions. As a result, stocks during these
conditions are normally high, and selective selling
is carried out (47). The buyers are carefully
selected and must eithr be members of a current
power group, or a regular purchaser of goods. These
windfall profits, through frugal living, are saved
for productive use.

There are two sub-castes to the sheikhs and,
in addition to these traders there are the
Qanungo sheikhs (48). The attributes of the trader
sheikhs have been given in detail by Papanek,
Timberg, Spodek, Nafziger and others. Evidence
as to their main characteristics, however, differs
but the fact that they are a source of supply for
entrepreneurs cannot be denied. Rather than
consider normal attributes and the ability of the
trader/merchant to save or invest, let us consider
the strengths and skills which these castes
possessed.

Bargaining. Invariably the traders/merchants
ensure imperfect or limited markets, and as a
result the bargaining factor is paramount. It is
almost as if the merchant/traders live by their
wits. They must have the ability to not only assess
demand and price differentials but also to quantify
purchasing trends. Strong buying and selling
attributes require a near-perfect knowledge of
price and quantity, and information on market trends
can be obtained from all kinds of diverse sources.

Credit. A trader's success is also dependent upon
establishing credit lines, both formal and
informal. Immediate credit is necessary if an
order is to be fulfilled at very short notice.
This manipulation of credit enables the merchant/
trader to acquire capital resources from formal as
as well as informal sources. Hoselitz (49)
distinguishes between the different fields of the
credit operator and the credit operator turned
entrepreneur by analysing the commitment of assets
in the production process. The two are worlds
apart and there has to be another factor, perhaps

a threat (50) or need for status for such a conversion to take place. However, he places this in its proper perspective when he states: 'The supply of capital is an indispensable feature of economic development. However, the importance of accumulating large quantities of capital is sometimes overstressed' (51).

Markets and Raw Materials. By virtue of their trading activities, the traders/merchants develop a good idea of market size and in the process, consumer preferences. This is especially so if the goods are import substitution products and satisfy local consumer demand. Those who managed to enter industry in Pakistan's initial stage of modernisation and who catered for basic needs were assured of rich takings (52). The early corporate entrepreneurs made a further distinction to save themselves from adverse publicity by limiting their efforts to sectors other than commodities. As early as 1947 (53) these traders were aware that government intervention could not be avoided when (1) health was to be safeguarded or (2) essentials supplied during periods of scarcity and famine. Under these conditions the government of the day would intervene with industrial operations. The corporate entrepreneurs understood this only too well, and, as they desired a minimum of government intervention, they avoided industries that would be affected.

How were raw materials? If production was based on local raw materials, the government was asked to create zones (54). This, of course, was in extreme cases. In the case of steel, for example, even the small artisan managed to have his source of raw materials. Where family members were part of the management team foreign travel ensured access to overseas markets for raw materials. In any case, traders have developed over a number of years a systematic knowledge of critical inputs and of minimising factors that might hinder the production process.

The Industrial Pattern. If the factors listed above were important, what was the pattern of movement into industry? Did the profiles of sheikh entrepreneurs conform to the factors which were stated to be their strengths (Table 5.14)? The trading class has a significant spread and is represented in thirteen of the twenty industrial sectors, indicating that trade does form a basis

The. Development of an Entrepreneur

Table 5.14:   Industrial Pattern, Sheikhs

No	Sector	No of entrants	%
1	Textile	12	41
2	Footwear and leather	3	10
3	Hosiery and garments	-	-
4	Furniture	3	10
5	Glass products	1	3
6	Chemical products	3	10
7	Steel rerolling	2	7
8	Metal machinery	5	17
9	Electric fans	2	7
10	Car equipment	1	3
11	Surgical instruments	-	-
12	Sports goods	-	-
13	Ceramics	-	-
14	Cutlery products	-	-
15	Pharmaceuticals	2	7
16	Agricultural imports	1	3
17	Cycles and parts	1	3
18	Marble products	-	-
19	Commodity processing	-	-
20	Miscellaneous	3	10
	Total	39	100a

Note: a. Does not add to 100, rounding error.

for an entrepreneur's development. Had it not been
so, the range of industrial activity would not have
been so diverse. Although the sample showed the
largest number of traders to be in the textile
sector, the most significant fact is that 27 per
cent are also in areas of technology, indicating
that they have been able to co-ordinate factors of
production and acquire relevant technical expertise.

Agricultural Castes. A number of castes or
quasi-castes are predominantly agriculturalists,
though with significant differences. For instance,
the Jat, the Waraich and the Khokhar differ from
other agricultural castes in that they have crossed
religious boundaries. The Jats are converts from
Hinduism. Normally Rajputs would be equated with
the warrior class. The point of difference from
the other agricultural quasi-castes lies in their
own view of themselves. For example, the Awans

and the Maliks consider themselves as descendants
of one of the caliphs and therefore attribute
status to themselves. The Kakazais, on the other
hand, although agriculturalists, declare themselves
to be non-agriculturalists (55). In fact, the
Kakazais were mobile traders living along the main
highway (56), trading in cross-sections of the
market and benefitting from price differentials in
different markets. As a result, the Kakazais are
probably the only pure caste in the provinces with
regard to trading.

The Arains, on the other hand, were the crop
growers around large towns and cities. Because of
its perishable nature their produce was taken to
town and sold daily. The interaction with the
city market traders was constant and on a day-to-day
basis.

Table 5.15 indicates the industrial pattern
of the agricultural castes. From the industrial
pattern it is obvious that some of the agriculturalists ventured into areas which normally were
the strongholds of the artisans and craftsmen (57),
i.e. electric fans, metal machinery and car
equipment. The Arains, who comprise approximately
43 per cent of the agriculturalists' sample, were
forced out of their normal vocation. Their land,
situated close to cities, had been indiscriminately
acquired for urban growth and housing societies
were thus provided with land at below market prices.
However, despite hardship, these agriculturists have
responded to negative factors arbitrarily created
by the government. The small amount of capital
provided as compensation was used, not for short-
term consumption, but for long-term survival. This
was due to their work ethics in particular as well
as their willingness to work long hours. A
distinction needs to be made between the work
ethics of the feudal absentee landlords and the
agriculturalist tenants. The landlords have
suffered from successive land reforms and, in order
to maintain their status, they entered the
corporate sector, where they had many connections.
The tenants had handled mechanical agricultural
implements, and so had a propensity towards
acquiring a skill. The response of the two was
therefore distinctly different and in keeping with
their status. Survival was dependent upon extreme
hard work. The normal preference of the
agriculturalist was for agricultural implements.
Although there were only 7 per cent of agriculturalists in the sample, the response in this

180

Table 5.15: Industrial Pattern of Agricultural Castes

	Textile	Footwear and leather	Hosiery and garments	Furniture	Glass products	Chemical products	Steel rerolling	Metal machinery	Electric fans	Car equipment	Surgical instruments	Sports goods	Ceramics	Cutlery products	Pharmaceuticals	Agricultural implements	Cycle and parts	Marble products	Commodity processing	Miscellaneous	Total
Arain	4	-	-	1	1	-	2	1	-	2	1	1	-	-	1	3	1	-	1	1	20
Jat	1	-	1	-	-	-	-	2	6	-	1	1	-	-	-	-	-	-	-	-	12
Malik	1	-	-	-	-	-	1	1	3	-	-	-	-	-	1	-	-	-	-	1	8
Khokhar	1	-	-	1	-	-	-	2	1	-	-	-	-	-	-	-	-	-	-	-	5
Kakazai	-	-	-	-	-	-	-	-	-	-	-	-	-	-	-	-	-	-	-	1	1
Total	7	-	1	2	1	-	3	6	10	2	2	2	-	-	2	3	1	-	1	3	46
	16	-	2	4	2	-	7	13	22	4	4	4	-	-	4	7	2	-	2	7	100a

Note: a. Rounding error. Of the total sample, 23% of entrepreneurs were from the agricultural castes.

181

sector was positive and is a likely source for
supply of entrepreneurs.

The Effect of Mechanisation.   The Green Revolution.
came to Pakistan in the late 1960s, and the
consequence of industrial links with the revolution
was to raise technological levels.   The farmers,
despite their illiteracy, could only use this
technology if they knew how to do so in the absence
of technical knowledge.   Therefore villagers
travelled to small workshops in towns to learn about
maintenance of initially simple and subsequently
very complex machinery.   With 1.57 million farmers
in the category of less than twelve acres (58),
and with increasing mechanisation, there was an
entrepreneurial response.   For example, in one
small town near Sialkot (59) there were as many as
196 entrepreneurs in the middle and small category
(Table 5.16).

Table 5.16:   Metal Working Shops in Daska

Type of firm	No
1 Diesel engines	105
2 Associated with diesel engines	11
3 Associated with agriculture	10
4 Centrifugal pumps	20
5 Machine shops	21
6 Metal working shops	29
	196

Source: E.H. Smith and T. Durrani, 'A Survey
of The Diesel Engine Industry of Daska, Sialkot
District April 1969'.   Paper No. 20, Government
of Pakistan, Planning and Development Department,
Lahore.

The hypothetical capacity worked out by Smith
and Durrani for these firms was 1,600 diesel engines
per year (60), the population of the town in 1968
was 25,000.   With this kind of response in largely
rural areas it was not surprising that agriculturalists turned towards entrepreneurial activities
and, since the population was mainly involved in
agricultural activities, the probability of the

response emerging in that population could never be
entirely ruled out. As well as positive factors, a
number of negative aspects reinforce the supply of
entrepreneurs. Landowners are very proud people
and, when they change their profession to a position
which is subservient, their pride is effected.
Therefore when their expertise is sufficiently
developed, other inputs are ensured in order to
regain their earlier independence.

The Artisan Castes. Nyerere's Ujamaa was a
practical concept in the sub-continent. Where
infractural facilities are limited, where more
than seven hundred dialects of four languages are
known, where physical barriers make movement
difficult, the centre of economic activity was the
village. Every village had land (61) set aside for
carpenters, blacksmiths, potters and Gujjars (62).
This provided a permanent basis for settlement and
therefore services were provided for the population.
Entertainment was also provided by Marasis (63).
However, in time and as their prosperity increased
these castes modified their entire social development. The Lohar (blacksmith) sought more respect
and became a Moghul, whose ancestry could be traced
to the armies of the Moghul emperors who ruled
India for three hundred years before being displaced
by British. The potter became a Rehmani (a
provider of succour) while the Gujjars remained in
the agricultural sector, without any ambitions.
Table 5.17 indicates the industrial pattern of these
craftsmen entrepreneurs.

In occupational terms the Moghuls seemed to go
into different product lines and were the most
flexible. Initially they provided spare machine
parts for established enterprises, but over a
period of time, they developed an ability to maintain and purchase machinery, ultimately entering
the industrial sector themselves.

Status Castes. In this category two unrelated but
nevertheless significantly important castes, the
Qureshis and the Rajputs will be considered. The
Qureshis, or the Malwaneys (64), have a high status.
They are descendents from the Quresh tribe of
Arabia and therefore established their links with
the tribe of the Holy Prophet Mohammad. The
Qureshis influenced the development of ethics and
were responsible for the spread of Islam. The
decline in their influence may be attributed to the
growth of the modern educational system. Their own

Table 5.17: Pattern of Craftsman Entrepreneurs

No	Sector	Gujjar	Moghul	Rehmani	Total	%
1	Textile	1	1	-	2	8
2	Footwear and leather	-	-	-	-	-
3	Hosiery and garments	-	-	-	-	-
4	Furniture	-	1	-	1	4
5	Glass products	-	1	-	1	4
6	Chemical products	-	-	1	1	4
7	Steel rerolling	-	2	-	2	8
8	Metal machinery	-	6	-	6	24
9	Electric fans	-	2	-	2	8
10	Car equipment	-	-	-	-	-
11	Surgical instruments	-	1	-	1	4
12	Sports goods	-	1	-	1	4
13	Ceramics	-	1	2	3	12
14	Cutlery products	-	1	-	1	4
15	Pharmaceuticals	-	-	-	-	-
16	Agricultural implements	1	2	-	3	12
17	Cycles and parts	-	-	-	-	-
18	Marble products	-	1	-	1	4
19	Commodity processing	-	-	-	-	-
20	Miscellaneous	-	-	-	-	-
	Total	2	20	3	25	100

response so far as their children were concerned was to obtain the maximum benefits from this system and they are now probably the best educated caste in the country. The Rajput were warriors, settled mostly in the Potwar (65) area, which still provides the army's entire sepoy strength and some of its commissioned ranks. These soldiers sought duty away from the family, and their salary plus earnings from the land were barely sufficient to exist. When life became difficult, they emigrated. Since their wives and children were used to not having them at home for eleven months of the year, they accepted this emigration. The majority settled in the UK, and others went to the Middle East. Their living conditions in the new countries reflected their previously low level of subsistence, and considerable amount of saving was possible. On their return, their first response was to improve their living conditions through new housing and increased consumption. The second effective change was to seek another profession. This, of necessity,

was based on the nature of their experience obtained
abroad.

Table 5.18 shows the details of the pattern of
industrialisation for these castes. In the
subcontinent, Berna(66) found that in his sample of
indigenous industrialists in the light engineering
sector, Brahmins and Naidus (warrior caste) figured
prominently. The industries finding favour with
the entrepreneurs were textiles and agricultural
implements and, surprisingly, the ferrous and
ferrous alloy industries.

Immigrant Castes. Strictly speaking, the Kashmiris
(67) are recent entrants to Pakistan. Traditionally,
the Kashmiris in the present geographic area of
Pakistan were known as labourers and weavers of
very fine shawls (68). They have not been
classified as 'community' because they did not
maintain their traditions and occupational
specialisation as rigidly as the Memons and the
Bohras. These occupational specialisations are two
extremes, but this would be typical for Kashmir(69),
where, despite an 80 per cent Muslim population,
the ruler was a Hindu. Important positions were
given to people considered to be loyal to the
ruler. This led to the complete absence of Muslims
from any position of authority.

Table 5.18 indicates the industrial pattern of
the Kashmiris. When they first came to Pakistan,
these craftsmen were penniless, and were employed
for example, as darners by dry cleaning shops. All
that was required was a small corner of the shop,
with the Kashmiri with his darning needle sitting
on the ground covered by a piece of old cloth. In
time, these darners of woollen and expensive clothes
became in great demand. Such was their expertise
at strengthening and improving the machine weave
that exorbitant sums of money would be spent in the
repair of priceless woollen articles. They were
excellent bargainers because of their ability to
determine tourists' purchasing power. They have
spread their entrepreneurial talents evenly across
the categories listed at Table 5.18, usually by
adapting to the requirements of the local population.
For instance, if they settled in Sialkot (known for
its manufacture of sport goods, cutlery and surgical
instruments), they undertook the making of those
items. If they settled in Gujrat, they went into
the metal industry. In fact, they settled in towns
which were close to the Indian-held Kashmir border
(Sialkot, Gujranwala, Gujrat) hoping for an early

Table 5.18: Immigrant and Status Castes, Pattern of Industry.

No.	Sector	Kashmiris (1)	Qureshi (2)	Rajput (3)	Total 4(2+3)	Total (%)
1	Textile	4	4	2	6	15
2	Footwear and leather	1	1	-	1	3
3	Hosiery and garments	-	-	2	2	5
4	Furniture	1	1	-	1	3
5	Glass products	1	1	-	1	3
6	Chemical products	-	1	1	2	5
7	Steel rerolling	2	-	4	4	10
8	Metal machinery	3	1	3	4	10
9	Electric fans	2	2	2	4	10
10	Car equipment	-	-	3	3	8
11	Surgical instruments	-	-	-	-	-
12	Sports goods	-	-	-	-	-
13	Ceramics	2	-	-	-	-
14	Cutlery products	3	-	2	2	5
15	Pharmaceuticals	-	-	-	-	-
16	Agricultural implements	1	-	6	6	15
17	Cycles and parts	2	-	-	-	-
18	Marble products	-	-	1	1	3
19	Commodity processing	-	-	1	1	3
20	Miscellaneous	-	-	1	1	3
	Total	24	10	29	39	100a

Note: a. Rounding error. Col(1), immigrants castes; col (2) and (3), status castes.

solution to the political problem which would enable them to return home.

The influence of the caste in supplying entrepreneurs is undeniable, the Moghuls predominent in ferrous industries and the agriculturalists in the commodity and agricultural implements sector, areas which are familiar to them. The Rehmanis did the same in the ceramics industry. The predisposition to entrepreneurial behaviour is enhanced by the familiarity of the object to be manufactured.

The Development of an Entrepreneur

In some cases, decisions by others have stirred the
would-be entrepreneur into positive action.
Survival has been uppermost in the minds of all
these entrepreneurs.
     Not all the castes are discussed here, neither
is this a detailed study of their socio-economic
characteristics. We have attempted only to
ascertain the impact of caste on the supply of
entrepreneurs. If the probability for an entrepreneurial predisposition is enhanced it should be
important for areas where caste systems prevail.
More research in this direction is required,
although amongst the Muslims there is a negative
attitude towards the caste system and its
implications as it is related to the Hindu way of
life.

Entrepreneurial Performance and Caste
Table 5.19 and 5.20 indicate the comparison of size
by employment and sales as an indication of the
ability of entrepreneurs from various castes. Such

Table 5.19: Comparison of Firms by Employment for ·
the Various Occupational Castes (%)

Occupational specialisation	Small(a)	Medium(b)	Large(c)
1 Traders/merchants	46	10	44
2 Agriculture	52	20	28
3 Craftsman	56	32	12
4 Status	59	28	13
5 Immigrants	50	35	15

Note: Size by employment   a. 0-50 employees
                            b. 51-200 employees
                            c. 200+ employees

a comparison, besides indicating a better utilisation of resources, also shows the ability and
merket knowledge of the various castes. In small
firms a high turnover is almost universal in all
the castes, with or without occupational specialisation. In fact, the least variation can be seen
in the trader/merchant category, indicating either
a more narrow perception of opportunities or a
more conservative approach. The size by sales
figures also show that there is an insatiable
demand for products. Pakistan may well be

187

The Development of an Entrepreneur

Table 5.20: Comparison of Firms by Sales for the Various Occupational Castes (%)

Occupational specialisation	Small(d)	Medium(e)	Large(f)
1 Traders/merchants	18	3	79
2 Agricultural	–	7	93
3 Craftsman	8	8	84
4 Status	3	3	94
5 Immigrants	–	8	92

Note: Size by sale   d = Less than 50,000 rupees
                     e = 51,000-2,500,000 rupees
                     f = more than 2,500,000 rupees

approaching the period in her development when narrowness of markets is no longer an explanation for a lack of industrialisation. The most significant move is that of the agriculturalists, who despite 52 per cent having less than fifty workers, have no firm in the small-scale category. The craftsmen tend to remain evenly balanced, and seem to be entrepreneurs whose growth is gradual over a period of time. The size by sales is also predominant in the immigrants, in whose case the shift is indicative of their resourcefulness and market strength. Not surprisingly, these are in the higher selling category as their perception of insecurity, despite the passage of time, is different from that of the general entrepreneur as they came to Pakistan under very difficult circumstances, and these circumstances continue to prevail. Their marketing methods are different and their profit margins are much tighter as a result of the market channels that they use. Because of the large influx of refugees, the majority of them became hawkers and are used as cheap outlets by the manufacturers. Their success is noticeable by the absence of vehicular traffic in such market areas. To be successful, these hawkers have to undercut the retail shopkeeper, and this is done very effectively. Invariably the first step for a refugee is to move into the hawker trade and to be involved in a degree of selling 'piracy'.

Community Influence
The word 'community'(70) is used in its widest possible sense, devoting a group within which

intermarriage habitually takes place. An attempt
has been made to classify the main communities in
the sample, and two are identified by areas, i.e.
the Punjabis and the Pathans and their characteristics are analysed at pages 199-209. Over the last
thirty years there has been consensus on many
economic and social grounds but political and
religious conflicts still exist. For our purposes,
the various Punjabi castes intermarry, and the
barriers have been broken. The Pathans are
organised as tribes and still believe in tribal
affiliations. The more adventurous have travelled
and set up industries, despite severe hardships,
and have thus broken away from the old Pathan
traditions in some ways. Their economic attitudes,
whatever their internal tribal conflicts, are
similar. An important point of conflict is in
determining who is a Pathan. Invariably whatever
Pathan one is talking to is a true Pathan, the
others are pretenders. The Pathan's method of
operation is different and, although generalisation
may be unacceptable on the basis of sample
limitations, important points can be seen. The two
other specific communities, i.e. the Memons and the
Bohras, are from former India. They were immigrants
but they have zealously guarded themselves against
acculturation. Despite merging with a large
heterogenous group and living permanently in a
metropolitan centre such as Karachi, there has not
been any dilution in community attitudes. The
Memons have been the subject of research, as have
also the Chinioti sheikhs from the Punjab. The
Bohras also ventured successfully into the
industrial field. The overriding influence on these
two communities came from two mercantile centres,
Bombay in India and Karachi in Pakistan. In fact,
for a time the two communities traded successfully
from both countries until the early 1950s, when
India introduced restrictive measures and forced
them to operate either from India or from Pakistan.
The 'others' category consists mainly of Kashmiris
and certain entrepreneurs who came in as immigrants.
The Kashmir area is a source of constant conflict
between India and Pakistan, and is a subject
frequently raised in the United Nations. The first
act of refugee Kashmiri Muslims was to find a
living. Having been successful in this, they turned
to industry. Seventy-one per cent of the 'others'
category belong to this community, but the common
strand would be insecurity and their responses
would be tempered by their comprehension of this.

The Development of an Entrepreneur

The Memons

Industrial Pattern. The Memons specialised in the
textile industry, and the 1970 assets figure showed
this community(71) to be leading all the others.
In fact, some of the Memons had been in industry as
far back as 1921-3(72), when they began manufacturing matches. The same Memon family, went into
the canvas shoes industry nine years later. The
Memons have been in the textile trade since 1901
but, although this seems to be their preference,
since Partition their response in the industrial
field was different and had nothing to do with
their occupational specialisation. Between 1943
and 1947 they undertook commodity-prpcessing, for
example, an oil mill in Calcutta in 1943, cotton
ginning in 1943, coconut oil crushing at Madras
in 1944 and a motor repair workshop in Calcutta in
1944: this from a family of six brothers. These
brothers came together in 1929, when their father
died after starting a trading shop in 1925. At
Partition, their liquid capital was Rs 50 million
and their first reaction was to set up offices in
Manchester and purchase machinery from Japan,
where some of the other Memons were already
operating trading offices(73). Their knowledge of
manufacturing thus extended to two leading textile
technological areas, Lancashire and Japan. Since
1947 the community diversified not only into
cotton, woollen and synthetic textiles but also
into the paper industry and recently in the
fertiliser industry. However, it would be
misleading to think of this community as being only
in the large sector. Their entrepreneurial strength
can be found not only in the chemical industry but
also in subcontracting the manufacture of perfume
for multinationals. A large part of the community
is in the specialised steel rerolling industry.

Unity. The Memons have been able to maintain their
extended family system as well as their community
life without any of the adverse effects of
modernisation found in close-knit cultures. The
six families in the sample have not separated: in
fact, one family has been united since 1929, a span
of fifty-one years. The eldest brother is still
the head and, when questioned stated:
    The cultural factors have been looked after,
and despite education abroad and business influence
they have been taught how to respect certain
intrinsic human values, i.e. they have been taught

190

to spend less on themselves and more on the firm;
that actions must be above board so that they are
visible to all, not only in the family but in the
community. This is our nation and therefore our
response should be for the needy, for the
poor (74).
Another community elder who had lost two sons and
had only one daughter explained his attitude
towards family unity in much the same way. The
pain of the death of his two children had left him
a broken man, but the community had helped him to
survive and prosper. One entrepreneur from this
community came from an industrial family which was
probably the first one to complete successfully with
a multinational. This family had lost 70 per cent
of its assets(75) and had again suffered set backs
during the 1972-7 period. Despite this, it had
diversified its industrial holdings not only by
product range but also by size. The emphasis was
no longer on the large modern sector but rather in
the small, capital-intensive sector.
     How do these families maintain this unity?
There have been some effects of modernisation in   ·
that there is a strict attitude to work and
achievement. Although loyalty is cherished, it is
not accepted if it is in conflict with honesty. A
further distinction is made between mistakes and
blunders. The new generation is effectively in
command, the earlier generation having faded away.
The demands of hard work and long working hours
are accepted by all. The Memons, either first or
second generation, take into account the welfare of
their workers, and have provided interest-free
loans for employees to purchase or build their own
homes. They have thus ensured the life-long
commitment of the workers(76).
     The unity of the Memons(77) is maintained in
the most simple way. The elders constitute the
panchayat, and matters of communal concern are
placed before this committee. Very few major
conflicts emerge unresolved, although one needs to
be mentioned(78). In this case the elders determined
the financial settlement for the work put in by a
family. This particular branch of the Memon family
was given the responsibility of running a textile
mill in a remote area in the Punjab. Differences
developed and the sons and the head of the family
were given a golden handshake, enough for them to
enter the corporate sector independently. Their
first attempts were unsuccessful, and the entrepreneurs admitted product-deficiency. They moved into

the motorcycle trade, became agents for a leading
Japanese firm and have now again ventured into
manufacturing. Despite hurt pride, each side
accepted the ruling of the panchayat elders. To
the author's knowledge this is the only case of
conflict in the entrepreneurial field.

Competitiveness. The Memons originated from
Kathiawar but traded in all the large industrial
and commercial centres. Thus the headquarters of
the Memons were situated in Bombay, Calcutta and
Rangoon. The nature of their commercial connections
meant continual contact with the leading Hindu
entrepreneurs and business castes. The Halai and
Kachi Memons were initially in the Kirana (grocery)
trade and subsequently in the cotton and rice trades.
The mercantile trading communities in India also
came from this area. Table 5.21(79) indicates the
occupational origins of these communities while
Table 5.22 shows their industrial assets.

Table 5.21: Mercantile Communities and Nature
of Trade

Community	Total	Port trade	Inland trade	Other
Marwari	11	6	5	-
Gujerati	13	7	4	2
Bengali	2	-	-	2
Other	11	2	3	6

Table 5.22: Trading Communities and Industrial
Assets(80)

Community	Assets (Rs billion)
Marwari	7.5
Gujerati	3.8
Bengali	1.5
Parsee	4.7
Punjabi	1.7
Other	0.4

The Memons had understood the meaning of
commercial power and industrial strength and the
status that these bring. The present generation of

elders had come into power in 1929. Their manufacturing origins were humble, and they had already
seen the power of the textile magnates. There were
thirty-seven textile mills in Ahmedabad alone, and
the Tatas towered above the others in the steel
industry. They had seen and absorbed these lessons.
They could not have competed with this world and
saw their chance elsewhere. In 1943 they started
organising religious based Chambers of Commerce,
one in Bombay and one in Calcutta. Hannah Papanek
confirms this:(81)

In the immediate circle around Jinnah, several
big businessmen and industrialists played important
roles, not only in helping to finance the Pakistan
Movement ... and ... these men were active in
setting up private firms which were to fulfil
important economic roles(82).
She goes on to say:

In terms strikingly reminiscent of resentment
against colonial rulers, many of them described how
they had been angered by statements that Muslims
were obviously not capable, in business and finance
or industrial management.

The emergence of industrial concentration and
economic power had its roots in these two decades
of contact with Hindu industrial entrepreneurs.
Unable to compete, they started off humbly, a match
factory here, a leather-tanning factory somewhere
else, all humble beginnings but successful enough
to counter criticism of Muslim incompetence in
financial matters.

The views of entrepreneurs on competition at
this stage of their development need to be qualified
because they have been so successful. Early entry
has ensured profits and control of financial
institutions has meant that they are also successful
in that area. Liberalisation of policies, however
small, is acceptable at this stage. Their economic
strength is of a different nature: these large
houses can overcome all internal competition, rather
than compete at an international level. They can
negotiate with the Islamic Development Bank and
with Communist China and they are at ease with
Western countries. The Memons' cumulative
experience exceeds that of any industrial house in
Pakistan.

Location Policy. The Memons may have originated
from commercial centres but their strength also
lies in creating an 'industrialising effect'(83).
More than any community, they foresaw the benefits

193

of a geographic dispersal of their industry. This came easily to them. They had endured greater personal hardships for fewer benefits(84). They had developed a pattern of mobility in that husbands had left their respective wives with the family while they travelled in their work. In East Pakistan they set up companies in Chittagong, Khulna and Dacca, in West Pakistan they dispersed to the Attock district, a thousand miles from their home base. The new location usually had no skilled labour force or infrastructure, only a potential for obtaining raw material from primary sources. Raw materials initially had to be transported a thousand miles. How could industry in such conditions be viable? They named the place Lawrencepur. Thirty years later this area of virgin land is now industrial area; in fact, it is now suffering from a shortage of labour. Similarly, they went to the Punjab, to the hinterland, away from the main highways. Besides helping the national economy this was desirable from their point of view in that labour was cheap and without the 'acquired culture' of the towns. One Memon family in 1970 had 40,000 workers and, in a span of twenty-five years, had not seen one strike. Today some of their most skilled labour has been lost to the international market. They now have 26,000 skilled workers and circumstances seemed to have forced them into more capital-intensive technology(85). Their success should not be belittled: the work was difficult, many decisions needed to be taken and industrial services were rare or non-existent. The indirect benefits in respect of the two areas may be gauged from Table 5.23.

The impact of industrialisation on the two districts in the table is very marked. What are the significant differences between them(86)? First, Vihari is in the prosperous cotton-growing area, where almost everyone is involved in agriculture, while the Attock district is arid and people are living at the subsistence level. The response of industrialists in the areas is different. In the newly sanctioned units(87) Vihari concentrates on cotton-ginning and Attock in textile spinning and weaving, sheet glass and specialised glass manufacturing. The response is encouraging, and entrepreneurs have capitalised on industrialisation by the Memon family. Therein lies the strength of this pioneer family.

Table 5.23: Comparison of Industrialisation, Attock and Vehari Districts

S. No.	Industrial category	No. of units	District	Employed	No.	District	Employment
1	Commodity processing	4	Attock	180	28	Vihari	821
2	Cotton spinning (since increased to 3)	2	Attock	2,973	1	Vihari	3,917
3	Woollen/worsted textile	3	Attock	3,701			
4	Construction material (sheet glass, RCC pipes, marble, etc.)	17	Attock	1,956			
5	Metals and allied products	4	Attock	376			
6	Petrochemicals	2	Attock	70			
	Total	32		9,256	29		4,738

Management Practices. The Memons' recruiting
methods are different from those of the rest of the
entrepreneurs and are a result of a complex
organisations that they have created. The latest
management practices are followed and some of the
Memon entrepreneurs are highly educated. In this
area the Memons show an increasing awareness of
the need for specialised education. Responding to
pressure from the younger generation, the senior
Memons have accepted the need for reorganisation
along corporate lines. Even in the remote areas
of Attock, senior management survives only by
having been trained, at the company's expense, in
the latest methods at business schools of the
West(88). However, despite having given way to
superior education, the elders have not lost their
position. While the younger generation are allowed
free expression, the realisation of their ideas is
based on the work experience of the elders.
     One such modification could be seen in the
workings of the managing agency system. This was
introduced to the subcontinent as a result of
British company law and was a direct response to
limited managerial manpower. The managing agents
were originally utilised by owners, who placed the
management of the firm in safe hands while
contributing share capital. Over time, these
managing agents acquired a reputation for restoring
the credibility of a previously unsuccessful
company. The Memons had been aware of these
practices before partition(89) and sought similar
positions, but they carried out some modifications.
First, they assumed control of the managing agency
themselves, in other words, for a commission they
became their own agents. However, the Memons,
developed in regional offices a core of highly
trained personnel who acted as consultants and
troubleshooters. This system also served as a
means of promotion. If a manager showed outstanding
ability he was noticed by headquarters. So although
the Memons believed in the managing agency system,
they modified it to their own requirements.
However, there is no evidence that they utilised it
for extensive control based on relatively minor
equity holdings.
     Another Memon system of recruitment, as in
Pakistan in general is to give priority to their own
community members. If the position to be filled is
an important one, a trustworthy member of the
community is generally trained. Confidential work
also falls on the members of the community as their

196

business decisions are closely guarded secrets.
In acquiring other services, legal, consultative,
the Memon will certainly look for the best in the
market place.

The Bohras

The Bohras and the Khojas came from Bombay and had
more or less the same informal experiences with the
Hindu trading communities as the Memons. Besides
the Memons, these were the two other communites who
influenced M.A. Jinnah, the founder of the nation.
In fact, it was one of the Khoja families that
provided the banking system for the new state in
1947.

Industrial Pattern. The Bohras also followed the
classical pattern of industrialisation by beginning
textiles but, after installing two units, one in
1947 and the other in 1952, they diversified into
industries requiring technical ability of a
different nature. In 1953 came synthetic leather,
woolen textiles in 1959, cement and chemicals in
1962 and specialised steel plant in 1967, with a car
assembly plant included in the unit. The most
remarkable achievement of these leading industrialists was to create an airline and a shipping
concern, the former becoming nationalised in 1956,
the latter in 1972. These two concerns are the only
instances where a joint venture of several important
families was formed. The Bohras were also active
outside their communities, and have given freely
to charitable trusts.
     The Khojas' industrial pattern was different.
They traded in anything. As markets were volatile
and uncertain, the entrepreneurs required considerable finance and credit facilities. The grandfather
of the present leading Khoja family was a penniless
orphan who started as an office boy in a trading
shop. He eventually became a partner and then the
sole owner of the shop. The main trade has been in
cottonseed oil and metals, and their international
experience has been mainly in Europe. They opened
offices in Geneva and Vienna (90) dealt in scrap
metal and copper and benefitted from the civil war.
They then realised the importance of banking and
insurance, and became initially a lending house and
then merchant bankers and insurers. Their entry
into industry came when the banking sector was
nationalised. Since then they have traded mostly
in commodity processing. They are now considering
further investment in capital-intensive technology.

Unity. All these communities are very strongly
knit, united by different kinds of bonds. In
adverse circumstances their reactions are different.
The Memons will not conflict with authority, the
Bohras will disappear, the Khojas will remain in
the background and each one will surive. All
three communities have a survival instinct. The
Memons have systematically decentralised power and
decision-making to well-qualified managers, the
Bohras have survived on their marketing strength
and on the knowledge that they bring to bear on all
their business transactions and the Khojas meet
informally at lunch every day where outstanding
issues are discussed. Despite the fact that the
Khojas were not so well established in industry,
they have now taken up investment systematically.
With their financial experience they have the acumen
to perceive gaps in the market.

One would imagine that a member of these
communities automatically goes to the top, but this
is not the case. Privileged community members are
required to prove their worth and start from the
very levels, as messenger boys, and go through a
'graded apprenticeship'. On the matter of formal
training, they have to compete with the brightest
in Pakistan. Failure could mean relegation to
secondary positions.

Location Policy (91). The Memons, as we have said,
are dispersed over a wide geographic area: not so
the Khojas and Bohras. The Bohras were all located
in the town of Karachi and suffered heavily through
enforced nationalisation. They gave all their
concerns family names and located these companies
opposite each other. They were thus very prominent
and, paradoxically, they more than the others came
to be looked upon as evil. They were even less
deft in handling industrial relations, which led to
political demands for nationalisation. The Khojas,
on the other hand, moved to the rural areas of
Sind: this is understandable as sugar-cane
processing requires the plant to be near raw
materials. (It would be interesting to see where
they locate other industries, whether they choose
other parts of Sind, or the Punjab, and, if so,
for what reasons).

Management Practices. Because of their prominence
the Bohras' firms are very tightly controlled. The
family firm, in the true sense, is in operation and
one does not find any decentralisation of authority

or qualified individuals in leading positions.
Now that only one member of the senior generation
survives, what is likely to become of this very
substantial industrial house? The probability is
that the family, with the help of the community,
will come through. Unlike the Memons, they used
the managing agency system for 'siphoning off'
profits and not for the building up of a technological or managerial base.

The Khojas, on the other hand, are not so
tightly knit. Recruitment follows two distinct
streams: that from the family or community stream
and that from outside. There are no favoured
positions. Since the Khojas are now entering
high-technology, capital-intensive industry (92)
it is interesting to see how they are going about
this. Figure 5.1 shows their basis for
information-gathering and technological determination. They are concerned with product choice,
and adapt their technology to this. They have
moved away from accepting whatever is offered.
The Khojas have established a basis for
decision-making and tend not to compromise on
(1) the quality of the product, (2) an elimination
of wastage, (3) automative cargo handling which
is not at the expense of labour and (4) a higher
productivity by developing skills and improving
tools and technology. Given this kind of thinking,
the Khojas will probably have to look to their
organisational structure and rationalise it in the
light of their technological requirements. On the
basis of their past performance there is no doubt
that their response to the challenge will be
positive.

The Pathans

The inhabitants of the North-West Frontier Province
are called Pathans. The sample of Pathan
entrepreneurs, although limited, provides an insight into entrepreneurial qualities which reflect
their community characteristics.

The Pathan entrepreneurs were rebels against
the system. One of them, despite the very best
education, rebelled against the patronage being
extended and ran away from home to become a textile
apprentice with a Memon entrepreneur. For two and
a half years he remained an apprentice for pocket
money and board and lodging, despite his background.
The search for a meaningful vocation continued and
for five years he was a survey inspector with a
clearing and forwarding company at Karachi port.

The Development of an Entrepreneur

Figure 5.1: A basis for choice

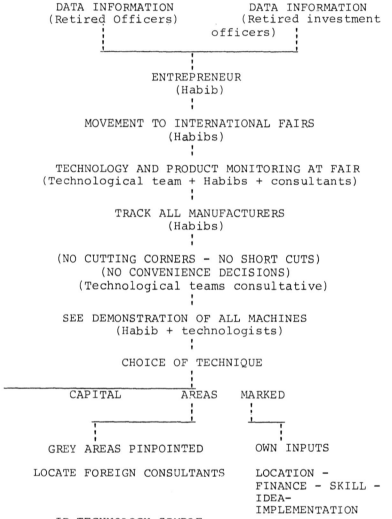

DATA INFORMATION   DATA INFORMATION
(Retired Officers)   (Retired investment
        officers)

ENTREPRENEUR
(Habib)

MOVEMENT TO INTERNATIONAL FAIRS
(Habibs)

TECHNOLOGY AND PRODUCT MONITORING AT FAIR
(Technological team + Habibs + consultants)

TRACK ALL MANUFACTURERS
(Habibs)

(NO CUTTING CORNERS - NO SHORT CUTS)
(NO CONVENIENCE DECISIONS)
(Technological teams consultative)

SEE DEMONSTRATION OF ALL MACHINES
(Habib + technologists)

CHOICE OF TECHNIQUE

CAPITAL   AREAS   MARKED

GREY AREAS PINPOINTED   OWN INPUTS

LOCATE FOREIGN CONSULTANTS   LOCATION -
             FINANCE - SKILL -
             IDEA-
             IMPLEMENTATION

IF TECHNOLOGY SIMPLE
WAYS OF ELIMINATING WASTE
i.e. BRICK INDUSTRY - BREAKAGE

ᐳASK CONSULTANTS TO ORGANISE RESEARCH
AND MODIFY THE PROCESS IF NECESSARY

The Development of an Entrepreneur

Another five years were spent in transportation,
this time as a partner. Eventually he bought out
the shares of the other partners and is now one of
Pakistan's largest transporters of machinery and
heavy equipment. This is very specialised work
because the road bridges are narrow and the road
surface at times non-existent. His move to
manufacturing came when he purchased a soap and
detergent factory.

The other entrepreneur was a 'rebel' from
within the system and set up his ice factory at the
most turbulent time in 1947. Without a single day
of production he had to abandon it and escape to
Pakistan as a refugee when the subcontinent was
partitioned. No compensation was ever paid.
Undeterred, he came to Jhelum, a small district
town in the Punjab a hundred miles from Lahore and
eighty miles from Islamabad, where he decided to
set up a glass factory. In between setting up
both factories he was involved in the timber trade.
Why did he change his vocation? Simply because the
timber trade had become dishonest, graft had become
the order of the day. To the question that he was
not qualified technically, the reply was typical
of a Pathan, nothing is impossible. Now that they
undertake specialised bottle-making, with
sophisticated screw tops and lift tops, where was
the technical guidance coming from? He had solved
the problems of two representatives of a leading
food-processing company despite the technicians
around him. His was a self-taught expertise and,
when a foreman came to him with technical problems
he suggested a number of alternative solutions.

Location Policy. North-West Frontier Provinces are
mainly rugged and mountainous. They are excellent
for growing sugar-cane, maize, tobacco and
beetroot. The crops on which industry is based
are sugar-cane, beetroot and tobacco. The entrepreneurial response from this area came from the
landlords and the elite, not from the traders or
mercantiles, although a trading class has developed
recently. Tobacco was sent to the multinationals,
and this, with pharmaceuticals, is one of Pakistan's
major products. In the North-West Provinces the
sugar industry is not seasonal, as in the rest of
the country, but, with modifications in machinery,
sugar would be extracted from beet. It is in this
area that the Pathan entrepreneur was traditionally
found and, since the industry could be regionally
dispersed, this was done so. Ironically, there

have been no industrialising effects as created by
the Memon and Bohra entrepreneurs elsewhere. The
two entrepreneurs in our empirical sample were
rebels, and any Pathan industrialist in the plains
is typical of our sample, a rebel against the
system in the North-West Province.

Competitiveness. Life for a Pathan entrepreneur is
one long struggle. While most wealthy families
would protect their offspring, the two entrepreneurs
in our sample moved away from the family. They
were thus able to assert their independence.
Commensurate with their rebellious personalities,
the industries they entered are very competitive.
In the detergent industry the entrepreneur was
competing at two levels, with an efficient
multinational and cheap indigenous products (93).
Despite these odds and the internal problems of the
acquired unit, the entrepreneur made the unit
viable by (1) paying off the liabilities of the
previous owner and (2) changing the pattern of the
labour force. This was done on the basis of
voluntary redundancies and recruitng skilled
hardworking personnel.
     What were the strengths of this entrepreneur?
He had risen to such an extent that he had been able
to sell shares to the industrialist (94) for whom
he had worked for two and a half years as an
apprentice. He was formulating a marketing
strategy, and was confident that the nature of
demand was such that it would continue to grow and,
provided that he maintained a high quality, as he
intended to, there would be no problem. Raw
materials would be imported for this.
     The other entrepreneur was at a disadvantage,
and always had been as far as the government was
concerned. The machinery he received was on
barter and tied aid from a socialist country. It
ran on expensive oil (there was no natural gas)
while his competitiors were able to use cheaper
fuel. Since the machinery had been bartered, spare
parts could not be supplied. How, then, did he
survive? First, he developed a friendship over the
years with a number of technicians who came
regularly as his guests and advised him. As an
entrepreneur utilising modern factory methods, he
mingled with his workforce. He remains a market
leader, despite competition from manufacturers of
synthetic containers, because he believes that the
presentation of a good product in a glass container
attracts the consumer to the shelf. In the

The Development of an Entrepreneur

Pakistani context he has been proved right.
Product-improvement has always been upermost in his
mind, and he does not divert complaints from his
valued customers onto technicians and subordinates
but deals with them himself, in a concise and
careful way.

Management Practices. The stakes for these two
entrepreneurs were very high. They had either to
succeed or be held up to ridicule. In such
societies everyone is known as 'someone's son' or
'someone's cousin', so the shame of failure is
shared by all. Despite the fact that they were
running modern factories, the level of organisation
was most rudimentary. They operated as family
firms, and there was no ostentatious spending and
no decentralisation of authority. While the
runaway entrepreneur was working for one of the
leading industrialists, the other was working with
his own sons.

The Punjabis
The borders of the Punjab are sealed with blood.
The break with India, so far as the Punjab is
concerned, was final and unequivocal, and there is
no going back for the six million who managed to
cross the border. All of them came penniless, with
only their clothes and suffering extreme hardships.
They were lucky if they did not lose a family
member to marauders. They came to their new
homeland with simply one objective, to make
something of their lives.

Industrial Pattern. The Punjabi industrial pattern
is totally different to the rest. There are no
limits to a Punjabi work schedule, and their
strength lies in their attitude to work. The
Chinniotti sheikhs (95) were the leaders in
industry, although small-scale industry was always
a characteristic of this province. Industries are
now being set up in every part of the Punjab.
    The province has accepted entrepreneur from
all categories. The large Punjabi houses were the
Chinniottis, the Saigols, the Syeds and the Sheikhs
of Multan. They may be important by virtue of
their size but they are not certainly the only
leading entrepreneurs in the Punjab. This is the
distinguishing feature between the Punjab and the
other provinces. Two of the larger groups, the
Chinniottis and the Saigols, had their entrepreneurial baptism in Calcutta and the presidency

towns. So the influence of the Marwari and other large Indian houses cannot be discounted. The Chinniottis' ingenuity in managing business and trade matters from a far away was exemplified by the way in which they managed their extended family. One of the male members would stay at home while the others deported for Calcutta and elsewhere. Family responsibility was joint, and each member had to stay six months with their families on a rotation basis. Since Chinniot was their family home, the Chinniotties made no permanent transfers. They considered housing as wasteful expenditure and, in fact, only started to invest in property in 1971-2, mainly because of the loss of assets in East Pakistan in 1972 and the nationalisation of 1973. The first action by industrialists in Calcutta was to move to East Pakistan. But they soon realised that economic power really lay in the classical format of starting with textiles, then moving into textile chemicals, then pesticides and then synthetic rayon, always maintaining advantage of entry and supplementing this by trading wherever possible. Thus the Saigols later became importers of cement wherever they had contacts. The Monnoos became traders of motor cars and Hitachi refrigeration equipment. The Crescent group of Sheikhs and the Syeds of Lahore had experience of the cotton trade in the Punjab. The industrial pattern was typical: yarn-manufacturing, trading in motor vehicles and a joint venture with Sweden in the paper and board industry. The sheikhs of the Crescent group were in the cotton-ginning industry and simply upgraded their skills to go into the textile industry.

The Monnoos are probably the most versatile of the large groups. They have certainly overtaken the Saigols, whose group lost its monolithic character with the death of its founder, Saeed Saigol. The Saigols have shown distinct features of modernisation. In fact, the family assets are distributed among the sons of the original entrepreneur.

The Monnoos started with a rubber factory in Calcutta in 1936, which was exchanged for an industrial unit in Naryanganj (a Dacca suburb in East Pakistan). In 1962 they moved to West Pakistan and their success story really starts there. Textile mills were installed, one after the other, until in 1972-3, they were confronted with the Economic Order and they decided to quit. It was a chance meeting with a Sufi which enabled them to grow once again (96). The mystic's advice on the

loss due to nationalisation was simply to consider
the factory as God's gift and organic in nature.
It had to die some day. Since death had occurred
prematurely, this had to be accepted, like the
premature death of a member of the family. This
advice worked. The Monnoos put all their
reservations on one side and redoubled their energy.
Seven textile mills were built between 1973 and
1976, at a time when all industrialists were wary of
investment. The sales figure in 1980 stood at
$12.5 million. The advice of the mystic, that
nothing in this world belongs to one, had paid off.

Lesser Chinniottis were also included in the
sample and they had the same strengths in common.
All could do mental calculations and all were aware
of their requirements. Even the lesser houses had
unobstensibly built five textile mills and were
looking for other opportunities.

Probably the entrepreneur typical of the
Punjab is one who started in 1948 with one
sock-making machine, operated it himself and sold
his wares on a cycle, and who, by dint of sheer
hard work became a leading textile industrialist.
From sock-maker in 1947 he wanted more rewarding
work and in 1951, went to Rochdale for a refresher
course for six months. On his return to Pakistan
he purchased reconditioned machinery, and from
employing 15-20 employees in 1948, making socks,
he now has a textile industry, a consultancy
service and an export house, and is considering
joint ventures in various industries.

For a province which had hardly any industry in
1948 the response in the sample was astonishing,
not only in the large corporate sector but also in
the small sector. The competitive spirit, for a
variety of reasons, had developed a kinetic force.
Again it would be misleading to think that assets
have increased only in the large sector. It is
common, even in the small sector, for a family to
increase its assets by increasing capacity by
building units elsewhere.

Pakistanis who emigrated to the Middle East,
the UK and Canada still maintain links with their
country. Their roots are not completely cut, and
they are the new source of supply of entrepreneurial
talent.

Location Policy. With the exception of the large
industrial houses, the majority of the Punjabis have
established their enterprises near their own home
towns. In fact, for those who started as craftsmen,

205

their homes were the first workplaces. Such
craftsmen entrepreneur do not travel. Those who
had worked under difficult conditions away from
home, living frugally wanted to return to show the
community that they had left in despair that they
had succeeded and could now attempt other things.
Working abroad had developed a variety of inner
strengths and abilities, notably (1) an ability to
work long hours, (2) the skill to work on different
machines, and (3) a cumulative experience which gave
an insight into modern production processes.
     In the large industrial houses of the
Chinniotti Sheikhs the pattern of industrialisation
was markedly different. They avoided existing
industrial locations and developed a very skilled
mobile workforce which was used in the new units as
and when these were established. Except for the
Lahore textile mills, which was their first venture,
they installed units in villages such as Chichoki
Mallian, where there would be very few houses.
They created seven such units in the large sector.
Although it may be too early to predict, this may
have an industrialisging effect as pronounced as
the Memons had in the Attock district.
     The Syeds have only one textile mill in a
depressed area, while their other concerns are
situated in major towns. Some of the other large
houses have followed the traditional pattern and
set up units where others have been before them,
taking advantage of market situations. This was
to their advantage, as they were in the cotton-
ginning industry in this area and a link was
established by entry into textile yarn and weaving.
The pioneer generation has now moved to, not
setting up original, new units but acquiring old,
run-down ones. The younger generation's methods
are slightly different but equally effective, again
having been educated in Western business shools.

Management Practices. Management practices,
understandably, are just as diverse. The large
industrial houses are very firmly controlled, with
all financial decisions taken by the owners and
only technical problems being decentralised. There
is, of course, a sound reason for the large houses
believing in this kind of organisation: it serves
as training ground for the younger generation. A
sound theoretical basis is supplemented by on-job
training.
     What are the responses of the small sector
entrepreneurs to management skills? The only

expertise they are assumed to have is rudimentary accounting: profit margins are not dependent on management. The organisation, if there is one, is on the factory promises. The concept of executive offices being separated from the production process is only found in some of the largest houses. Generally, the office consists of a single room, furnished in a most rudimentary way and overlooking the shopfloor. The owners' availability to the workforce gives an example of hard work and enables them to lead from the front. There is no question, in this sector, of a distant head office. If this were the case, the owners' prestige would diminish and in time they would be openly questioned and disobeyed by the workforce. The entrepreneurs realise this. If an owner's labour force must work from sunrise to sunset (and after), he must set a personal example.

The Punjabi entrepreneur does not like to be slighted, and occasionally one came across a decision to leave a job for this reason. Thus in the case of one totally illiterate entrepreneur the remark 'What do you know about scrap?' caused him to resign and start his own company. Since then, he has overtaken his previous employer who, surprisingly was a Memon. The dispersal by size (in number of employees) is equally varied, indicating no specific preferences. The Punjabi craftsmen entrepreneurs start with basic tools, and the initial, financial constraints are minimal. However, they do require a form of industrial patronage which would allow them to survive in the market place. Once that niche is created, the rest is up to them. They will undersell services to prove themselves. They have pride and patience. For them, no machine has outlived its utility; there is no such thing as technological obscelescence. A spare machine lying around can be made to work. One of the electric fan manufacturers saw a machine at a customs auction, purchased it, transported it 700 miles to Gujrat and then decided what to do with it. He made melamine and plastic wares.

Competitiveness. Punjabi entrepreneurs realise that competition is an important aspect of life, and one way to stay ahead of the pack is to ensure quality of product. The more successful of the craftsmen entrepreneur have practically no formal channels for marketing their products. So sales, or rather an increase in sales, is dependent on

credibility established the hard way. All products
which have skill factors involved display the
manufacturer's name, which then becomes the brand
name. Entrepreneurs do not travel with their wares,
using the services of salesmen to increase their
sales. The nature of the demand is such that
buyers will always go to a local retailer rather
than purchase a product from a multinational.
Consider the example of a sewing-machine manufacturer whose order-book is full for the foreseeable
future. Why is he selling when such multinationals
as Singer or Toyota are not doing so well? The
answer partly lies in the segmentation of the
market not only by income but also by status: the
elite versus the non-elite, the urban rich versus
the rural poor, and by a very important non-economic
factor, every girl of marriageable age must know
how to sew and cook. The nature of rural markets
and the absence of a market for readymade garments
ensures the viability of these enterprises. As
there is ease of entry and skills are available
in abundance, the entrepreneurs must maintain
product quality. Price wars do not take place
as profit margins are low.

However, competition does tend to become
unfair in the Punjab when government resources are
used. If, for instance, benefits were given to
some entrepreneurs to the disadvantage of another,
the profit margins of the beneficiary increase
substantially. For example, in the case of the
agricultural implements industry in Mian Channu, of
the thirty-two manufacturers only one has received
government aid, another has been trying unsuccess-
fully to register with the government for three
years and the other thirty accept their fate.

In the case of cheap consumer goods, outlet to
could be large traders, small merchants or pedlars
and hawkers, who operate at the lowest possible
profit margins, have flexible pricing and are
usually involved in lengthy bargaining. The large
trade outlets are for a fixed clientele. Their
profit margin is higher but the relatively small
bazaar merchant is generally threatened by pedlars
and hawkers.

Where the quality of the product is its
selling strength, the price can go up. The
Pakistani consumer now prefers expensive goods
in the hope of buying 'quality'. Although Pakistani
markets may be imperfect, there is no question
that they are narrow ones. In a country whose
'work bench' has extended abroad, assessment of

consumer purchases has changed considerably.
Although not exactly a consumer society, Pakistanis
still manage to spend a substantial part of their
ever-increasing disposable income on luxury goods.
Consumer durables can now be seen in the remotest
areas of the country. In any case, a country with
a population of 71 million could hardly be
considered to have narrow markets, and this has
meant an entrepreneurial response to meet increasing
demand.

Note

1. G.F. Papanek, Pakistan's Development.
Social Goals and Private Incentives, Harvard
University Press, Cambridge, Mass., 1967, p.47
2. J.J. Carroll, The Filipino Manufacturing
Entrepreneur: Agent and Product of Change, Cornell
University Press, Ithaca, 1965.
3. A.P. Alexander, Greek Industrialists,
Centre of Planning and Economic Research, 1964.
4. Y.A. Sayigh op.cit.
5. The exception is Hanna Papanek's excellent
study of the effects of modernisation on Memons.
6. Mistri, colloquial term for one who works
with machines.
7. Ustaad, literally means 'educator',
although it may be used in common usage as 'teacher'
Ustaad carries with it cannotations of extreme
respect and is generally a title for a person whose
skill and ability in the area is renowned.
8. H. Papanek, 'Pakistan's New Industrialists
and Businessmen', in Bengal Change and Continuity,
eds R.P. Beach and M.J.Beach, Asian Studies Centre,
Michigan State University, East Lansing.
9. This transpired during an interview with
one of the Habibs.
10. E.W. Nafziger, African Capitalism. A Case
Study in Nigerian Entrepreneurship, Hoover
Institution Press, Stanford, Cal., 1977, p.157.
11. The official exchange rate until mid 1973.
12. The official exchange rate since 1973. In
both cases, though, there would be a scarcity value
attached for conversion, which, during an acute
shortage, could almost be double the official rate.
13. The objectives of the corporation was to
harness the technical knowhow and skill of those
who had the necessary talent but insufficient
financial means to use it for personal as well as
social goals.
14. For details see Charles Wolf, Jr,

'Institutions and Economic Development', A.E.R., vol.XLV (December 1955), A. Papelasis, L. Mears and I. Adelman, Economic Development; Analysis and Case Studies, Harper, New York, 1961.

15. Wolf, 'Institutions and Economic Development'.

16. Commensal is the word as those members of a family who eat together (a hearth group).

17. R. Owens, 'Industrialisation and the Indian Joint Family', Ethnology, vol.X, April 1971.

18. For details see L.J. White, Industrial Concentration and Economic Power in Pakistan. Princeton University Press, Princeton, N.J., 1974, and R. Amjad, 'Private Industrial Investment in Pakistan', unpublished PhD thesis, Combridge University, 1976.

19. Interview with an entrepreneur. These problems originate not only at the Pakistani end but also at the embassy. For obtaining approval of the embassy, documents pertaining to the manufacturer have to be provided. The embassy then double-checks on the purchases. Why it should do so is a mystery.

20. J.R. Harris, 'Industrial Entrepreneurship in Nigeria', unpublished PhD dissertation, North-Western University, 1967, p.284.

21. Zakat, every individual has to contribute 2½% of his earnings towards the welfare of the poor.

22. S.P. Schatz, 'The Capital Shortage Illusion. Government Lending in Nigeria', Nigerian Journal.

23. Reforms in the banking system were recently announced. Concepts conflicting with Islamic ideology have been excluded in the new banking system. The earlier and the new system, however, are operative at the moment.

24. Pierre Uri, Development Without Dependence, Praeger, New York, 1976, p.148.

25. H. Papanek, 'Pakistan's New Industrialists and Businessmen. Focus on the Memons', in M.Singer ed., Entrepreneurship and Modernisation of Occupational Cultures in South Asia, Duke University Press, Durham, N.C., 1973.

26. The first six were Dawood, Saigol, Adamjee, Jalil (Amin), Sheikh, Fancy (from White, Industrial Concentration).

27. Examples will be provided from the contemporary scene., the veracity of which may be questionable. But we are merely asserting the performance of an act and the consequences that flow from it.

28. One way to consider this would be through marriage ties.

29. Papanek's 'Pakistan's New Industrialists' makes this point thoroughly and exceedingly well.

30. Mashar, an elder who creates harmony, for it is he who fulfils the requirements of industry and recruits on their behalf. The entrepreneurs recruit staff not as labourers but as Khattaks. Since the position of industrial relations officer would be very important, he is usually a trusted and close relative.

31. R. Owens uses the word Karta in 'Industrialisation and the Indian Joint Family'. Actually the words Karta Dharta, means 'all in all'. The word is significant in as much as it signifies the all-pervasive impact and character of the head of the family.

32. The example of the present Agha Khan illustrates the point neatly. Instead of the eldest son becoming the spiritual leader of the Ismailis, the responsibility devolved on the grandson.

33. Papanek, 'Pakistan's New Industrialists', p.76.

34. Interview with a leading Chinioti sheikh.

35. One of the most successful firms in the large sector has three such people, not related to each other. They live together, take joint decisions and, in one case, one of the members of this triumvirate ostracised his own son and family for speaking disrespectfully to one of the avowed brothers.

36. I was a witness to such a lunch 'proceedings'. It was here that I was able to assess the impact of the elders.

37. 'Handful' being the measure.

38. M.N. Srinivas, 'Comments on H.Papanek's "Pakistans New Industrialists and Businessmen"' in Singer (ed.) makes a similar point.

39. Caste indications were given in terms of either a prefix or a suffix appearing with the name.

40. Serai, resting places for the wealthy in the North-West Frontier Province. These serais were huge constructions in remote areas providing resting places for the caraven, both its people and the beasts of burden.

41. They move with the snowline and have no idea of international boundaries.

42. As demand has been considerable because of the Afghan War.

43. Waderas, feudal landlords.

44. Haris, tenants at will.

45. The basis for this is an informal interview with an elder based in Birmingham.

46. Mostly grocery trade (Kirana merchants).

47. As a matter of favour.

48. Qanungo, literally law-knowing. The Qanungo sheikhs were interpreters of rules and laws.

49. B. Hoselitz, 'The Entrepreneurial Element in Economic Development in Ward, The Challenge of Development, Aldine Publishing, Chicago, 1967.

50. G.F. Papanek make this point as push and pull factors in Pakistan's Development.

51. B.F. Hoselitz, quoted in M. Mines, 'Tamil Muslim Merchants in India's Industrial Development', p.52.

52. Interview with an entrepreneur.

53. Pakistan was a net exporter of commodities until 1956.

54. The raw material from these zones was ensured by law for the enterprise. The prices were usually fixed by the government. The zones and permanent purchase, though are usually in the commodities sector.

55. As a result they became eligible for service in the Indian Army.

56. These are found along the Grand Trunk Road which runs from Khyber to Calcutta, a distance of roughly 4,000 miles.

57. J.J. Berna, 'Industrial Entrepreneurship in Madras State': R.L. Owens and A. Nandy, The New Vaisyas Carolina Academic Press, Durham, N.C., 1978: and Sharma and Singh, Entrepreneurial Growth and Development Programmes in North India, Abinar Publications, New Delhi, 1980.

58. From Economic Survey 1979-80, Finance Division, Government of Pakistan. The figures are for 1972. After this date two more land reforms have taken place besides further fragmentation of holdings by inheritance.

59. A small suburban town 60 miles from Lahore.

60. The missing error is estimated by the Authors at 5-10%.

61. Usually two acres, enough for part-subsistence. The remaining income was to come from barter for services rendered.

62. Gujjars normally came to small towns but maintained links with the rural sector, where they acted as indigenous vets.

63. Caste specifically for occasions. The village Marasi lives by his wits.

64. Literally plural of <u>Maulvis</u>, priests, or theologians.

65. Potwar Plateau, from Campbellpur to Jhelum (a length of roughly 130 miles) in the Punjab. The capital Islamabad is also situated in this region.

66. Berna, 'Industrial Entrepreneurship in Madras State'.

67. After annexation of part of Kashmir to India.

68. Shawls, stoles, wrap-arounds, very fine woollen cloth woven at home and very intricately worked.

69. Partition, curiously, was to be on the basis of division of area by majority of population. Certain disputed areas were not finally settled. The two outstanding were Kashmir and Mysore. In Mysore the situation was reversed. The ruler was Muslim but the population was predominantly Hindu. One State was annexed while the other is in dispute.

70. The author knows of no authentic study along caste' and community lines in the social sciences in recent times. Research on Pakistan on the basis of primary data has been very limited.

71. For details see 'Industrial Concentration and Economic Power', and Amjad, 'Private Industrial Investment'. White lists assets of just one Dawood family at Rs 557.8 million for the year 1968. They have since lost some of these assets.

72. Based on interviews.

73. In fact, one of them studied in Kobe, Japan, and was apprenticed in Japanese factories between 1931 and 1934.

74. Interview with an elder community member.

75. White, 'Industrial Concentration and Economic Power', p.61 gives indications of these assets prior to the separation of Bangladesh as Rs 437.6 million. The 70% figure was given by the entrepreneur interviewed.

76. There are no building societies and no formal institutions for providing basic housing facilities.

77. The writer does not differentiate between Kachi Memons and Halai Memons simply because the factors being assessed are common.

78. One of the entrepreneurs interviewed.

79. T.A. Timberg 'The Origins of Marwari Industrialists', in Singer (ed.) p.152.

80. Ibid.

81. H. Papanek, 'Pakistan's Big Businessmen. Muslim Separatism, Entrepreneurship and Partial Modernisation' in <u>Economic Development and Cultural</u>

Change, vol.21, no.21, no.1 Oct. 1972.
82. Ibid., p.9.
83. The district now has fifty-one industrial units in the large modern sector.
84. H. Papanek makes a similar point in her Pakistan's New Industrialists'.
85. Interview with a leading Memon entrepreneur. The financial assistance for the project came from the Islamic Development Bank.
86. A district is an administrative unit. Attock is 4,148 square miles, while Vihari is 1,685, the population is 1.1 million and 1.2 million, respectively.
87. Nine units in the large corporate sector have been sanctioned for Attock and thirty-one for Vihari district.
88. Harvard, London and North-Western being some of the schools utilised for this purpose.
89. Timberg 'The Origins of Marwari Industrialists', accounts for the reason for the managing agency system.
90. Where their banking houses still survive. Apparently the European section was different and when nationalisation of the banking system took place they were successful in a court action.
91. Based on interviews.
92. Interview with a Khoja entrepreneur.
93. At the most indigenous the only requirements are pans and chemicals. One such person was interviewed. He was totally illiterate but had conducted over 1,700 experiments to try to improve the quality of detergents.
94. This was the Memon family with assets in 1970 of $558 million.
95. Chinniot today is a small urban township. In the 1930s and 1940s it was a small village. Today, as then, it is known for its wood carving and craftsmanship. Intricate wood-carved trollies, doors and windows attract tourists. From Lahore, the provincial capital, it is 130 miles.
96. Chinniot is located in the Jhang District, where the various sects of Islam have a strong hold. Sufism and mysticism is also accepted.

CONCLUSIONS

In the years since independence in 1947 Pakistan has
achieved considerable growth and development in the
industrial field. This was made possible by the
interaction of incentive policies, the response to
these policies by entrepreneurs and the technological means utilised. The entrepreneur's role has
been central to the development process, and was
influenced on the one hand by the informal sector
and on the other, by the formal sector. The interaction of the values and attitudes characteristics
of each sector accordingly moulded entrepreneurs.
Their contribution to the economy in terms of
value-added, though a useful measure for quantitative analysis, is too simplified to be of any
consequence in determining quality. The variables
are so complicated in the context of countries such
as Pakistan that recourse needs to be made to other
factors, which are unquantifiable. The initial
step, therefore, is to identify such factors and,
having done so, to determine a measure for these
variables. The identification of these variables
is unique to a particular social cultural milieu,
and therefore may not be universal. Not only would
these factors differ but also when there is an
apparent similarity the strengths of the variables
may differ.
     Since the central purpose of this book was to
encampass the modern corporate sector as well as
the most indigenous one, entrepreneurs' perceptions
not only of government incentives but also of
technology and technological information would be
significantly different. The modern corporate
entrepreneur would, for instance, be at ease at
any government level and may even influence
government policies, whilst the small entrepreneur
may try to avoid the most unimportant government

215

official. While the former may even refuse to be administered, the latter may be over-administered. The gap between these entrepreneurs is so large that, in arriving at any conclusions, it needs to be firmly kept in mind. In fact, any government policy becomes discriminatory. Policies devised for the smaller entrepreneurs could be used to the advantage of the corporate entrepreneurs, whose sphere of influence is so extensive that they are in a position to influence policies.

The impact of the corporate entrepreneurs was such that the development strategies that were followed left much to be desired as far as the utilisation of scarce resources was concerned, with inefficient allocation and utilisation of these resources.

Capital-versus-Labour-Intensive Industries
In following a strategy of growth through the modern corporate sector the country's planners did not relate the economic conditions prevailing in the country with the technological means by which industrialisation was to take place. Pakistan despite its massive emigration of labour, continues to be a labour-surplus economy, endowed with a large work-force and scarce capital. Any strategy followed would have to be a mix in which these factors of production are used to maximise utilisation of both labour and of capital. The management of this capital would be a determining factor, though not necessarily the only factor under consideration. A balance between capital and labour and the stage of development of a particular sector would determine the ultimate mix.

By providing cheap capital to a limited number of entrepreneurs, by overvaluing foreign exchange and by the very nature of government aid, Pakistan has committed itself to industrialisation in the large corporate sector. The basis for such policies not only distorted the market prices of the factors of production but also created considerable strains on the economy. The reinvestment of profits, for which these policies were suggested, was never sustained, and the marginal propensity to save, decreed by economists as a necessary condition for a continuous vigorous environment, were not fulfilled. The 'advanced technological leap' also was not comparable with that of more advanced economies, and therefore did not create conditions in which the technological base could be continually improved by research.

216

Conclusions

The nature of aid provided also limited the
development of any significant technical expertise,
linked as it was to the capital goods industries
of the donor countries.
    The shortcomings, however, must be analysed
in terms of employment opportunities. Of the three
different aspects of employment, income, production
and recognition, income in a surplus economy is
significant, as it eventually raises issues
relating to income distribution. Again the
production factor and the quality of the product
may be determined by the technological process.
When this happens, the options are limited. Again
because of the nature and development of markets
and the paucity of management it may be worthwhile
to reconsider scale factors, and to determine the
optimal size of the enterprise.
    Any decision involving a mix of the above
variables needs to consider the product, the
technologies available, the modifications possible
in the technological process, the linkage effect,
the present demand and the future growth of demand.

Public versus Private Sectors
The question as to who should own the means of
production can only be answered by a detailed
examination of the performance of the public and
private sectors. Pakistan in the 1950s and 1960s
followed a strategy of promotional public
enterprises. In the 1970s the pendulum had swung
to the other extreme. Since 1978 the ratio of the
public to the private sector, in terms of investment, has moved from 0.13 to 2.42, a nineteen-fold
increase. The controversy as to what should be a
basis for an industrialisation effort will never
be conclusively settled. Inefficiencies in the
public sector will attract criticism while the
lack of control on the private sector and the
difficulty of administering them adequately will
encourage governments to operate in the public
sector. The decisions will alternate, and will
depend largely on the aspirations of those who
are at the helm of affairs and how they perceive
both sectors. Efficiency in the private sector,
dependent as it is on market functioning, is
practically non-existent, while the public sector
suffers from classic management inefficiencies.

Capital Goods, Consumer Goods and Appropriate Technology
Pakistan since 1972 has moved from consumer goods
(import substitution) to an emphasis on the capital

217

goods industry. The choice between the two is not
in terms of one or the other, for between these two
sectors is the humbler entrepreneur, utilising local
technology and effectively undercutting modern
corporate entrepreneurs. When used intelligently,
the technological modifications to such production
process are not critical to product quality.

Location

Location of industry assumes special significance
for Pakistan given the heterogenous nature of its
inhabitants. Earlier industrial policies not only
aggravated income distribution but was also
responsible for a transfer of resources from the
predominantly rural agricultural sector to the
urban industrial sector. The impact of these
policies created an adverse income affect and
resulted in rural-urban migration. Planners had
to contend with another dilemma on how resources
were to be distributed in the provinces and the
criteria to be followed. Should such division be
on economic grounds or were egalitarian issues to
be considered? Therefore to the normal economic
rationality was added what appeared to be chaos
and irrationality. Some of the problems initially
encountered were the entrepreneurs' inability
to manage from a distance, the nature of isolated
communities and the diverse languages (Pakistan
at the moment has four regional languages,
countless dialects, a national language which
does not belong to any region and an official
language, English).

The normal conditions regarding location of
industry do not apply to Pakistan. No longer is
it advantageous for industry to be located in
urban areas, despite availability of inputs, access
to administration and markets. Entrepreneurs have
found that in Pakistan a rural location has distinct
advantages. Not only is it favoured by the
government because of the obvious income and
employment opportunities but also because the work
ethics of the newly employed are valuable. There
is evidence in Pakistan to show that firms
initially located in non-economic areas are not
only doing well compared with those in economic
areas but that they are also cost competitive in
world markets. The requirement of rural industry
is in terms of the integration of fragmented
markets. Although government policies have
provided tax holidays and other advantages, much
more needs to be done if only to provide a basis

for integrating these markets.

Import Substitution
This strategy requires constant review if it is not
to suffer from saturation of markets. The loss of
the East Pakistan market in 1972 meant that industries created by this strategy either had to find
export markets or go into liquidation. At some
stage in Pakistan's development the emphasis should
have shifted to export-orientated industries,(1)
as was possible in areas where Pakistan had a
comparative advantage. This may only have been
possible through well-conceived competitive
policies and increased efficiency. Pakistan's
policy-makers, in fact, were hostages to the
industrialists in these areas of comparative
advantage, and subsidies and incentives allowed the
inefficient to exist, structural imbalances were
not corrected and the failure of management
continued to be attributed to the nature of
government policies. The inability of the
government to counter the industrialists is a
classic example of policies favouring elites in
such less developed countries.

Industrial Concentration
Evidence was provided to indicate that this was a
universal phenomenon. While in some countries
the social conscience of the entrepreneur was
exemplary, in others it left much to be desired,
and Pakistan falls into the latter category.
Clearly, policies were not devised where the
entrepreneur with a socially developed consciousness
was favoured: rather, government policies were such
that no conscious effort was made towards identifying these entrepreneurs. The result was a
distorted entrepreneurial field, leading to
economic power in the hands of a few.

The Role of Government
Given Pakistan's circumstances, the management of
scarce resources devolved on the government.
With savings stagnating at 10 per cent and with
foreign exchange always in short supply(2) the
government's task was anything but easy. The
demand for both local and foreign capital far
exceeded the supply. Given these conditions, the
administration was forced to allocating these
scarce resources as best it could. Initially, the
matter was not as complicated but, with requirements becoming increasingly complex, it was

difficult to evolve a fair criterion. This led not only to preferential treatment for some but to the encouragement of uncrupulous elements, on both sides.

The government also took upon itself the role of entrepreneur, and initiated projects in areas where the private sector had not ventured. As long as these projects supplied internal markets there seemed to be no problem, but not only was there mismanagement in later years but also gross inefficiencies. Wherever these public sector industries provided intermediate goods to other industries, the ultimate consumer suffered from continually increasing prices.

Occupational Options

These tended to vary because of continuous political and economic uncertainty, and migrants initially sought occupational options which would reduce insecurity. In that sense, occupational mobility, irrespective of caste, was noticeable. Later, as insecurity increased there was a consequent reduction in the number of options for later generations. Some of these went into agro-based industry, those who could obtain the necessary factors of industry went into the modern corporate sector while the smaller entrepreneur proceeded in gradual steps. Two of the groups who reduced their insecurity by diversifying their occupations were the agriculturalists and the civil servants. Surprisingly, these two groups were powerful, and the threat to their prestige was responsible for the shift in occupational options either for themselves or their heirs.

Earlier research indicated the prevalence of traders among industrial entrepreneurs. The response from the mercantile traders as well as from the merchant traders is valid in the case of Pakistan. The heirs of industrialists increased their entrepreneurial effort not through increase in the size of the original unit but by establishing independent ones. Given the nature of the inheritance laws this also minimised any future conflict over ownership of the enterprise. Other factors such as the threat of nationalisation and keeping organisations to a manageable size were also discussed.

Credit Resources

The financial resources available to entrepreneurs depended largely upon their occupational origins.

Conclusions

To the mercantile trader, their availability
presented no problem. The bazaar merchants, on the
other hand, depended significantly on informal
means of credit and for supplementing their own
resources. The agriculturalists bridged their
requirements either by a sale of assets or by
pledging these assets and undertaking loans, not
at preferential but at commercial rates of interest.
The peasant agriculturists, especially those who
manufactured agricultural implements, started small
servicing workshops and graduated into manufacturing
units, using their own financial resources. The
civil servants relied on their experience and
connections with former colleagues to obtain credit
at considerably reduced rates of interest. In
short, an entrepreneur's previous occupation was
vital in determining the source of capital, and
the amount available was determined by the nature
of established contacts. The smaller craftsman
entrepreneur had rarely any such advantages.

Motives

The entrepreneurs' motives were obtained from two
levels, i.e. those who had shown occupational
mobility and those that had entered industry
directly. There has been disagreement amongst
economists as well as between sociologists,
psychologists and anthropologists on the motive
that played a prominent part in determining the
move into uncertain ventures. Papanek has stated
the importance of financial motives but this no
longer seemed to be the case. The highest response
(50 per cent) was given for a desire for independence, and financial motives were a poor second
(16 per cent).

For entrepreneurs who entered industry directly
the maximum response was elicited by patriotism and
by a need for independence. Patriotism was a
direct result of partition and the mass migration
from India to Pakistan. The need for independence
was reinforced by a desire on the part of entrepreneurs not to be subservient to any one, to be one's
own boss.

Even in the large corporate sector the second
generation seemed to have shifted their motivational basis towards pride in one's work and to be
outstanding in a particular industrial sector.
This motive is important in societies in which
authority is absolute and in which institutions
which might reduce this power do not exist.

Conclusions

Education

Earlier research in Pakistan indicated that the
entrepreneurs' level of formal education was not
important: they had developed their abilities
through an informal process. Nearly all the early
entrepreneurs were from mercantile communities,
and their strengths lay in bargaining skills and
access to credit facilities. Since those early
days, the Pakistani entrepreneur is more aware of
the need for formal education, and the sons of
those early mercantile entrepreneurs have undergone
specialised education in Western business schools.
The advantages that accrue from education were
obvious to the entrepreneurs and it was apparent to
them that an appreciation of complex technology was
in direct proportion to the number of years of
formal education.

Even the economic entrepreneurs understood
the advantages that formal education provides:
their problem had been not in assessing market
opportunities but in an inability to articulate
their needs to those in authority. Although
education in Pakistan towns compares favourably with
education in developed countries, that in small
district towns and rural areas seems to have not
only limited facilities but also a poor qualitative content.

So far as quantity of education was concerned,
two levels were identified and it seemed that
those with up to ten years of education had
sufficient numeracy to manage their affairs in a
reasonable way and to make progress, while those
who had more than ten years' education were able
to manage their resources very well. These
entrepreneurs may have started their enterprises
at a low level but they had progressed to the
highest one. In terms of profitability, however,
the maximum amount was indicated in increasing
numbers by those who had spent more years in
education. There also seemed to be a larger
number of poor performers in this category. So
education may have been a necessary ingredient in
the supply of entrepreneurs.

Experience

A number of economic entrepreneurs started small
workshops and over the years, with diligence and
hard work, became manufacturers. In using
experience as reference this only applied to
technical, production-orientated entrepreneurs.
Pakistan has always provided opportunities for the
skilled due to the nature of its import-substitution

222

policies. Since an unforeseen result of import
substitution was a strain on the balance of
payments resulting in strict control of imports and
spare parts for machinery a situation has been
created for the skilled to provide repair services
for the modern sector. This is why some of
experienced entrepreneurs, in time, entered complex
manufacturing industries. As their strength lay
in production processes they were not only efficient
but also cost-effective. Others progressed in the
system through sub-contracting during expansionary
period for a larger enterprise. Experience was
relevant in as much as the first move was towards
entering a familiar industrial sector, and it was
only after a period of time that diversification
into other sectors was considered.

Occupational Mobility

This changed since partition and reflects the
altered environment circumstances. The time-
honoured professions, i.e. the civil service and
the military, no longer hold their attraction. As
a result of the three attempts at land reforms, the
earlier traditional feudal structure has also been
threatened. These negative forces in the country
meant that the best young men were looking for
satisfying careers elsewhere. To the occupations
which have traditionally supplied entrepreneurs,
i.e. mercantile traders and merchants, were added
relatively new occupations, i.e. civil servants
and those in the private sector. The traditional
feudal employees have regained their earlier
dominant position by and successfully becoming
entrepreneurs in the large corporate sector.
Although the professionals (e.g. engineers) were
also represented as supplying a modest number of
entrepreneurs, their contribution was not
significant. This may be because of their ability
to find lucrative jobs in more developed economies.

Informal Development

Recourse must be made to the culture in which the
entrepreneur exists. Only too often one finds that
this aspect has been completely ignored, either
because of lack of knowledge of the culture or
because this aspect was never considered important.
Aid-giving countries in particular have tried to
transplant their own institutions without first
assessing their chances of success. These
institutions have therefore been accessible only to
an insignificant minority while to the majority of

223

entrepreneurs these Western transplants have been
more of a hindrance.

In studying the entrepreneur the impact of
the joint family system in some categories has
indicated an overall positive effect. The rules
governing entrepreneurs were informal and varied,
depending on the traditions and values of the
particular community, caste or family. The effects
of modernisation were also apparent, especially
where the informal sector came in continuous contact
with the modern formal sector. As a rule, it may
be stated that when entrepreneurs needed anything,
the traditional, informal agencies supplied it.

The recent incomes of families living abroad
(in the UK, Canada and the Middle East) have been
channelled through non-repatriable investment (NRI).
This system allows for incentives and has a distinct
advantage over the repatriable scheme in that
earnings are not allowed to be transferred out of
the country. The links to NRI follow from the
informal sector, for while some members of the
extended family continue to earn abroad, others
would be involved in its actual implementation.
A balance needs to be made of factors impeding and
encouraging investment. The removal of such
impediments may be an essential requirement for
having a continous and increasing supply of
entrepreneurs.

Recommendations

The problem of implementing these recommendation
still remains. Mention has already been made of
the ineptness of the administration first, to
articulate policies in the formal sector and second,
to persuade entrepreneurs to accept these policies.
The informal sector is not within the jurisdiction of
the authorities. In any case, due to the dynamic
nature of technology, officials can only have a
certain amount of technical information at any point
in time. An efficient administration, in addition
to an ability to respond, maintain a basis for
continuously updating technical information through
a well-planned information system. The time span
for planning and maintenance of such a system is
considerable.

To plan a technological framework which
balances a mix of capital and factors of production
requires, at the very least, a knowledge of and an
ability to trade off competing requirements,
initially for these two variables and subsequently
for other factors. This might well prove to be

impossible. To date, experience has been that, depending on the cateogry of entrepreneur, a project's feasibility will be 'created' and a distorted weighting will be provided for the variables. Far too often, projects have been sanctioned which have required balancing, modernisation or replacement (BMR). As BMR policies carry a preferential import duty this suits the entrepreneurs with connections even more. Recently some entrepreneurs have used the non-repatriable investment scheme (NRI) for the same purpose. Project-evaluation has been unsuccessful in some projects, despite the levels at which they were studied.

It may be easier to strike a new balance between the public and the private sectors, though this is not as simple as it seems. Despite the fact that government has redemarcated the lines between the two sectors, the private sector has continuously criticised the public sector, notably on the allocation of scarce resources such foreign exchange and equity. The private sector is aware that its share of the cake will be considerably reduced unless steps are taken to reduce government's investment in the public sector.

Having followed an industrial policy based on import substitution, what should be the direction in the short as well as in the long terms? Should the trend be towards export-orientated policies and, above all, how should industry be made competitive and efficient? Surprisingly, in certain sectors where there is minimal government intervention, entrepreneurs are appearing who are both competitive and efficient. Some of them have entered the non-quota markets and therefore it may be possible to study the attributes of these entrepreneurs and to try to compare them to those in other countries.

In order that the entire country, or as much of it as possible, should have the benefits of development particular attention needs to be made to the location of industry, failing which income gaps will continue to widen. Pakistan has already suffered from policies which seemed to indicate economic preference for the areas now comprising Pakistan. The important point is not whether economic resources were managed in a way beneficial to certain areas but whether once such a 'feeling' developed it may be impossible to controvert this with facts. Evidence has already been provided to show that an underdeveloped location need not be

necessarily a disadvantage in the performance of
the enterprise. In fact the labour force more than
compensates for shortcomings in the location.

Economic Concentration and Power

The country has already suffered as a result of
creating powerful monopoly groups in the manufacturing and financial sectors. The strength of such
minority groups were first noticed because they
increased regional disparities. A degree of
industrial concentration is apparent in all
developing economies, and powerful groups elsewhere
have contributed significantly to Pakistan's
development. It is not only in relative terms
that the concentration of power seem excessive but
also in economic terms. The methods of acquiring
these assets also leave much to be desired. The
social cost of such acqusitions are reflected in
a lower marginal propensity to save and to
reinvest, despite the fact that preferential
policies were devised for entrepreneurs. Pakistan
can now turn this to its advantage and a sensitive
balance can be struck by encouraging industrial
houses to go into sectors where private capital
and entrepreneurial effort are not forthcoming.
The caveats mentioned earlier, however, remain. It
is necessary to introduce more conscious decision-
making rather than a clever manipulation of the
system. Certainly some of the experiences of
various industrial inputs and their bargaining
power, could be utilised more productively.
However, linked with this is the question of equity
and welfare in society. Eventually a balance
between an economic versus non-economic basis
for decisions must be obtained.

The Role of Government

In their desire for industrialisation and economic
development governments have announced their
intentions with a considerable amount of rhetoric,
though their actions have not matched their words.
As one economic failure followed another, there has
tended to be an increase in government intervention
in the economy. The plea, invariably, was for
corrective action but in so doing the government
has taken great responsibilities upon itself,
responsibilities which, in time, have become
increasingly complex. No effort was made to
create institutions to understand the nature of the
problems or to improve organisational skills.
Governments have considered themselves to be adequately

equipped to solve problems whereas in fact they
have been delegated to an ineffective and untrained
administration. Poor communication channels,
absence of criteria for allocating scarce resources,
expedient decisions, turning a blind eye and even
helping the powerful to bend the rules and
regulations are some of the weaknesses here.
Efforts must therefore be made to supplement
government policies, and this can only be done
by formulating decisions that can be implemented,
by acquiring professional expertise and by improving
its own human resource base. The other aspect of
the administration is that it needs not only to be
responsive but to be able to engineer social
changes, so that all areas of society can move
towards acceptable standards of living. Thus it
needs to be sensitive to the requirements of
entrepreneurs in all sectors.

Industrial Efficiency

The purpose of stimulating the economic environment
by providing incentives is to energise areas in the
industrial sector that are lagging. Policies need
to be initially tailored so that once the objective
for which they have been designed is achieved, they
can be modified systematically to make these
sectors competitive internally and, over a period
of time, internationally. If such policies are not
continuously introduced and overall policy not
reviewed, fiscal incentives, and tariff protection
will continue to increase and import licensing will
become available only to a limited number of
entrepreneurs, even in the large corporate sector.
All this points towards inefficiency in resource
allocation and poor resource management.

Financial Institutions

Pakistan's financial institutions were developed in
the 1960s and are located in the large towns and
cities. It is obvious that these institutions
bypass the majority of the entrepreneurs. Limited
as they are, their resources are usually tied to
a few large industrial houses. The majority of
economic and progressive entrepreneurs have
therefore developed their own indigenous sources
of finance. Despite the limitation of these
resources, these entrepreneurs have managed to
grow. Although guidance has been given by the
government from time to time, this has been of
limited help. What is really required is the
creation of institutions which, over a period of

time, develop links with the informal sector,
draw savings from it and reinvest these savings in
the formal sector. The financial institutions
should be organised to meet the needs of these
entrepreneurs. If a complicated organisation is
provided, entrepreneurs will not come forward, as
cross-cultural factors tend to be very inhibiting.

Complementing Industrial Strengths

A basis for industrial extension services has been
established throughout the country. For instance,
there are the Pak-Swedish Technical Extension
services, in which each estate has a centre in a
particular industrial area, e.g. Gujranwala has a
Metal Industry Development Centre on a small
industries site and Gujrat has a Ceramics Institute.
However, these institutes do not provide any
industrial services. There is no point in providing
extension services which work below the levels of
existing technology (as has happened at Gujranwala),
or where the high-temperature furnace is so
expensive that entrepreneurs cannot afford to use
it. This is, understandably, a very difficult
area but its success could enable entrepreneurs to
develop further their technology. Similar steps
are required in respect of management and marketing
methods.

A Probability Pool of Entrepreneurs

As they are at the centre of decision-making,
emphasis must be on the quality of entrepreneurs.
In the case of existing entrepreneurs a 'probability
pool', based on specific criteria of enterprise
performance may be kept and continuously updated.
This pool may be developed after consideration has
been made of certain unquantifiable factors, e.g.
work ethics, knowledge and reputation.

For new entrants a basis for basing a judgement on human factors may be developed. Motives,
education, occupational mobility within the family,
experience and other similar informal factors such
as caste, community and the extended-family need
to be considered. It may be possible to incorporate
this factors into project feasibility reports.
This could be a list of existing entrepreneurs in
the economic, progressive and political categories
who, on the basis of established criteria, have
shown promise of better thing . For instance, it
may be possible to identify the metal-machinery
manufacturers and to systematically develop their
technical knowledge. The progressive enterpreneur

with strengths in production areas may be encouraged
to concentrate on new markets and to compete
internationally. But it is essentially with the
corporate entrepreneurs that the administration
will have to come to terms. As a group corporate
entrepreneurs have become very powerful and have
developed strong links within the most influential
groups in the country, and the majority of them do
tend to influence policies in a way that is
counterproductive to the rest of the economy. So
far as new entrepreneurs are concerned, the
barriers to entry need to be minimised, if not
eliminated.

Feasibility of Implementing Recommendations
Is Pakistan capable of implementing any of these
recommendations or to incorporate the conclusions
within their economic planning framework? This
will depend on the stability within the country and
the long-term horizons of the entrepreneurs. Under
conditions of extreme political uncertainty and
unstable world markets the time scale is considerably shortened.

Decision-making in Pakistan tends to
reinforce the existing economic and political
power blocs. This is now undergoing change and,
despite the earlier tendency of collusion between
the modern sector and the administration, small
manufacturers' associations are bringing pressure
on the government to devise policies for their
sector. The identification of the small sectors
contribution to export earnings and the World
Bank's attempts to encourage manufacturing in this
sector has improved the chances of appropriate
government policies.

Such pool of potential entrepreneurs will be
dependent on the development of an objective
criterion. So far, in Pakistan entrepreneurs
have not been subjected to value judgements.
Although such a procedure is subject to considerable
trial and error, it needs to be implemented if
only to train and promote those who have worked
hard, and whose success has not been appreciated
because of their low status in society. The
probability of this being carried out with any
degree of success is linked to the creation of
responsive financial institutions. Once these
are located in the smaller towns, the increased
interaction between the formal and informal
sectors is likely to lead to a growth in industrial
activity. These financial institutions could, in

229

time, also act as technology information centres.

The manufacturing sector operates at many levels, from the indigenous to the modern, and it may be difficult to devise policies which provide equal opportunities for all. The chances of improving industrial efficiency in the modern corporate sector are dependent on the competition that their products will have in the marketplace. In the case of Pakistan, the modern corporate sector has been challenged by the products manufactured by the indigenous one. This market-orientated competition has forced the modern sector to improve its cost-effectiveness and productivity.

The organisational structure for extension work already exists and only requires reactivation. This would be possible only by acquiring technically qualified personnel, and steps have already been taken in this matter. Other activities such as extension services for management and marketing need to be undertaken, but this process takes a considerable amount of time.

It may be difficult to check the high concentration of industrial assets, as this will have a negative effect on the industrial sector. However, in the Pakistan context such entrepreneurs should be directed into other industrial sectors. Given the earlier experience of Pakistani entrepreneurs and their ability to take advantage of early entry into industry there is no reason why the lead in this matter will not be taken by some of them.

Notes

1. The distinction between export substitution and export-orientation is given on page 36-7.
2. As in the case of Japan.

--:o:--

BIBLIOGRAPHY

Ahmed, A.K.   'Export Bonus Schemes',
                           Pakistan Development Review,
                           Spring, 1966

Ahmed, N.   Peasant Struggle in a Feudal
                           Setting, Geneva, International
                           Labour Office, 1980

Akeredolu - Ale,E.O.   'Nigerian Entrepreneurs in
                           the Lagos State', unpublished
                           PhD thesis, University of
                           London, 1974

Alexander, A.P.   Greek Industrialists,Centre
                           of Planning and Economic
                           Research, Athens, 1964

Ali, M.N.   Mobilisation of Resources in
                           Pakistan, Pakistan Economist,
                           April 1980

Amjad, R.   Private Industrial Investment
                           in Pakistan, unpublished
                           PhD thesis, Cambridge
                           University, 1976

Azhar, B.A. and   The Effect of Tax Holiday on
Sharif, S.M.   Investment Decisions, Pakistan
                           Development Review. Winter
                           1974

Bardhan, P.   External Economies, Economic
                           Development and the Theory
                           of Protection, Oxford
                           Economic Papers, 1964

Daumol, W.J.   Entrepreneurship in Economic
                           Theory, American Economic
                           Review, May 1968

Bibliography

Beech, R.P.,and Beech, M.J.,	Bengal Change & Continuity, Michigan State University, East Lansing, 1969
Berna, J.J.,	Industrial Entrepreneurship in Madras State, Asia Publishing House, Bombay, 1970
Bhagwati, J.N.,and Krueger, A.O,	Exchange Control, Liberalisation and Economic Development, World Development 1973
Brimmer, D.,	The Setting of Entrepreneurship in India, Quarterly Journal of Economics, 1955
Bruton, H.,	Import Substitution Strategy, Pakistan Development Review Summer 1970
Calkins, R.A.,	Technology, Innovations and Economic Development, unpublished PhD, dissertation, Duke University, Durham N.C. 1970
Carroll, J.J.,	The Fillipino Manufacturing Entrepreneur. Agent and Product of Change, Cornell University Press, Ithaca, 1965
Cauthorn, R.C.,	'Contributions to a Theory of Entrepreneurship', unpublished PhD dissertation, Tulane University, 1963
Chamber of Commerce and Industries,	Industrial Development and Productivity, Proceedings of Conference, 11-13 August, 1977
Chambers of Commerce and Industries (Karachi)	Annual Reports (1970-1978)
(Lahore)	Annual Reports (1972-1977)
Cody, J., Hughes, H., and Wall, D.(eds),	Policies for Industrial Progress in Developing Countries, Oxford University Press, London, 1980

232

Bibliography

Fritschler, A.L.,	'Industrialists in the Government Process in Pakistan, unpublished PhD thesis, Syracuse University, 1965
Garlick, P.C.,	'The Ghanaian Entrepreneur, unpublished PhD thesis, London University 1962. The African Traders and Economic Development in Ghana, Clarendon Press, Oxford, 1971
Geiger, T., and Armstrong, W.,	The Development of African Private Enterprise, National Planning Association, Washington, D.C., 1964
Ghouse, A.M.(ed.),	Studies in Economic Development with Respect to Pakistan, Ferozsons, Lahore, 1962
Gledhill, A.,	Pakistan, Stevens, London, 1957
Grechkel, F.E.,	'Import Substitution in Underdeveloped Nations and Regions. The Mexican Experience', unpublished PhD thesis, Indiana University, 1969
Griffin, K., and Khan A.R. (eds.),	Growth and Inequality in Pakistan, Macmillan, London, 1972
Hart, K.,	'Entrepreneurs and Migrants. A Study of Modernisation among the Frafras of Ghana', unpublished PhD thesis, Cambridge University, 1969
Harris, J.R.,	'Industrial Entrepreneurship in Nigeria', unpublished PhD thesis, North-Western University, 1967
Hawrylyshyn, O.,	'Capital Intensity Biases in Development Country Technology Choice, Journal of Development Economics, September, 1978

Bibliography

Hazelhurst, L.W.,   'Entrepreneurship and the Merchant Castes in a Punjabi City', unpublished PhD thesis University of California, 1966

Helleiner, G.K.,   'Manufacturing for Exports, Multinational Firms and Economic Development', World Development, July 1973

Hernandez, N.,   'The Entrepreneurial Role of the Government in Economic Development in Puerto Rico'., unpublished PhD thesis, Rutgers University, 1965

Hoselitz, B.F.,   Sociological Aspects of Economic Growth, The Free Press, Glencoe, 1960

Institute of Economic Affairs, London,   'The Prime Mover of Progress', Institute of Economic Affairs, London, 1980

Iqbal, Z.,   'The Comparative Advantage of Developing Countries in the Manufacturing Industries and the Effects of Generalised Tariff Preferences', unpublished PhD dissertation, Michigan State University, 1977

Islam, N.,   'Tariff Protection Comparative Costs and Industrialisation in Karachi, Pakistan, Pakistan Institute of Development Economics, 1967

Japan, Ministry of International Trade and Industry   White Paper on Small and Medium Enterprises, 1976

James, J.,   'Appropriate Technologies and Inappropriate Policy Instruments', Economic Development and Cultural Change, vol.II, 1980

Kahf, M.,   The Islamic Economy, Muslim Students Association, Plainfields, 1980

234

Bibliography

Kennedy, P.T.,   The Ghanaian Businessmen.
                      Weltforum-Verlag, Munich,
                      1980

Khan, M.Z.,   'The System of Export
                      Incentives in the Manufactur-
                      ing Sector of Pakistan',
                      unpublished PhD dissertation,
                      Johns Hopkins University,
                      1979

Kilby, P.,   African Enterprise. The
                      Nigerian Bread Industry,
                      Hoover Institution Press,
                      Stanford, cal., 1965
                        Entrepreneurship and
                      Economic Development, The
                      Free Press, New York, 1971

King, B.B.,   'Obstacles to Entrepreneur-
                      ship in India. The case of
                      Bengal', Paper presented to
                      the Congress of Orientalists,
                      University of Michigan, 1967

Knight, F.,   Risk, Uncertainty and Profit,
                      Houghton Mifflin, Boston.
                      Reprint; Harper Torch
                      Editions, 1965

Krueger, A.O.,   The Benefits and Costs of
                      Import Substitution in India.
                      A Micro-economic Study,
                      University of Minnesota Press,
                      Minneapolis, 1975

Landsberg, M.,   'Export-Led Industrialisation
                      in the Third World; Review
                      of Radical Economics, Winter
                      1979

Lamb, H.B.,   'The Rise of Indian Business
                      Communities', June 1955

Lee, H.S.,   'The Entrepreneurial
                      Activities of the Government
                      in the Economic Development
                      of Puerto Rico', unpublished
                      PhD dissertation, University
                      of Wisconsin, 1965

Lee, K.J.,   'Technology Transfer and
                      Development Strategies. The
                      Role of Large Firms in Korea',
                      unpublished PhD dissertation,

235

Bibliography

	University of Hawaii, 1977
Leibenstein, H.,	'Entrepreneurship and Economic Development', <u>American Economic Review</u>, May 1968
Lewis, S.R. Jr, and Guisinger, S.,	'Measuring Protection in a Developing Economy. The Case of Pakistan', <u>Journal of Political Economy</u>, 1968
Lewis, S.R. Jr,	<u>Economic Policy and Industrial Growth in Pakistan</u>, Allen & Unwin, London 1969 <u>Domestic Saving and Foreign Assistance when Foreign Exchange is undervalued</u>, Center for Developed Economics, Williamstown, Mass., 1969 <u>Pakistan Industrialisation and Trade Policies</u>, Oxford University Press, London 1970
Lovett, A.E.,	'Concepts of Entrepreneurship in Recent Economic Thought', unpublished PhD dissertation, University of Southern California, 1965
Mahfooz, A.,	'Some Aspects of an Interest Free Economy', <u>Monthly Economic Letter</u>, United Bank Ltd, September, 1979
Mallon, R.,	'Export Policy in Pakistan', <u>Pakistan Development Review</u>, Spring 1966
Marsden, K.,	'Progressive Technologies for Developing Countries', International Labour Review, May 1970
Meier, G.M.,	<u>Leading Issues in Economic Development</u>,Oxford University Press, New York, 1976
Nafziger, E.W.,	'Nigerian Entrepreneurship. A Study of Indigenous Businessmen in the Footwear Industry', unpublished Ph D thesis, University of

Bibliography

Illionois, 1967

'Effect of Extended Family
on Entrepreneurial Activity',
Economic Development and
Cultural Change, Oct 1969

'Indian Industrialist - An
Examination of the Horatio
Alger Model', Journal of
Development Science, 1974-5

'Education and
Entrepreneurship, Journal of
Dvelopment Administration,
April 1970

African Capitalism. A Case
Study in Nigerian
Entrepreneurship, Hoover
Institution Press, Stanford,
cal., 1977

Naqvi, S.N.H.,   'Protection and Economic
                     Development, Karachi',
                     Pakistan Institute of
                     Development Economics., 1967

Nulty, T.E.,   'Income Distribution and
                     Savings in Pakistan. An
                     Appeal of Dvelopment
                     Strategy', unpublished Ph D
                     thesis, Cambridge University,
                     1974

Owens, R.,   'Industrialisation and the
                     Indian Joint Family',
                     Ethnology, April 1971

Owens, R.L., and   The New Vaisyas. Entrepre-
Nandy, A.,   neurial Opportunity and
                     Response in an Engineering
                     Industry in an Indian City,
                     Carolina Academic Press,
                     Durham, N.C., 1978

Pakistan: Ministry   Annual Economy Surveys
of Finance   1964-65 to 1980

Bibliography

	Government Sponsored Corporations 1967-8, 1974-5
(PICIC)	Interim Report on Investment 1967-8, 1969
Ministry of Commerce	Pattern of Foreign Trade 1976-77
Ministry of Information	Basic Facts 1978-9
Ministry of Planning	First Five-Year Plan (1955-60)
	Second Five-Year Plan (1960-5)
	Fifth Five-Year Plan (1978-83)
Ministry of Finance	Reports of the Economic Appraisal Committees 1952-1963
Falcon, W.P., and (Eds.),	Development Policy II. The Pakistan Experience, Harvard University Press, Cambridge Mass, 1971
Papanek, H.,	'Pakistan's Big Businessmen. Muslim, Separatism, Entrepreneurship and Partial Modernisation', Economic Development and Cultural Change, Oct. 1972
	Pakistan's Development. Social Goals and Private Incentives, Harvard University Press, Cambridge Mass, 1971
	'Comparative Development Strategis India and Pakistan', Economic Development Report No. 152, Harvard University Press, Cambridge Mass, 1969

Bibliography

Power, J.H.,   'Small Industrialists in
                            Bombay, Delhi and Karachi',
                            Pakistan Development Review,
                            Autumn 1962

                            'Industrialisation in
                            Pakistan. A Case of
                            Frustrated Take-off?'
                            Pakistan Development Review,
                            1963

                            Import Substitution as an
                            Industrialisation',
                            Phillipine Economic Journal,
                            Spring 1967

Punjab   Small Industries Survey
                            Reports

                                Light Engineering 1975-76

                                Small Textile Enterprises
                            1975-76

                                Survey Reports, vols. I   IV
                            1975-6

                                Directory of Preindustrial
                            Surveys, 1980

                                Directory of Industrial
                            Investments, 1980

Rowe, M.P.,   'Indigenous Entrepreneurship
                            in Lagos in Nigeria',
                            unpublished Ph D thesis,
                            Michigan State University,1972

Sayigh, Y.A.,   Entrepreneurs of Lebanon. The
                            Role of the Business Leader in
                            a Developing World, Harvard
                            University Press, Cambridge,
                            Mass, 1962

Schatz, S.P.,   South of the Sahara,
                            Macmillan, London, 1972

                            Nigerian Capitalism,
                            University of California Press,
                            Berkeley, 1977

Bibliography

Sen, A.,

Employment, Technology and
Development, Clarendon Press,
Oxford, 1975

Sharma, K.L and
Singh, H.,

Entrepreneurial Growth and
Development Programmes in
North India, Abinar
Publications, New Delhi,
1980

Singer, M. (ed).,

Entrepreneurship and
Modernisation of Occupa-
tional Cultures in South
Asia, Duke University Press,
Durham, N.C., 1973

Singh, P.,

'Essays Concerning some
Types of Indian
Entrepreneurship', un-
published Ph D thesis,
Michigan State University,
1966

Soligo, R., and
Stern, J.J.,

'Export Promotion and
Investment Criteria',
Pakistan Development
Review, Spring 1966

Smith, N.R.,

'The Entrepreneur and his
Firm. An Explorative
Study to Examine the
Relationship between
Entrepreneurical Type and
Initiation, Maintenance and
Aggrandisment', unpublished
Ph D thesis, Michigan
State University, 1965

Spadoek, H.,

'Manchesterisation of
Ahmedabad', Economic Weekly,
March 13, 1965

Stewart, F.,

'Technology and Employment
in Ldc's', World
Development, March 1974

Strachan, H.W.,

The Role of Business Groups
in Economic Development.
The Case of Nicaragua,
Harvard University Press,
Cambridge, Mass, 1972

Bibliography

Streeten, P.,   'Self Reliant Industrialisa-
                                 tion', paper presented at
                                 international seminar,
                                 Lahore, Pakistan, 1979

Timberg, J.A.,   'Industrial Entrepreneurship
                                 among Trading Communities of
                                 India, Economic Report No.
                                 136, Harvard University Press,
                                 Cambridge, Mass, 1969

Teribe, O., and   Industrial Development in
Kayode, M.O.,   Nigeria, Ibabad University
                                 Press, Ibadan, 1977

Tareen, A.K., (ed),   Directory of Pakistan Cotton
                                 Textile Mills, 1970

UNIDO   Study of Small Scale
                                 Industries in Pakistan,1980

                                 Industry and Development
                                 No. 2, New York, 1980

                                 Industry and Development
                                 No. 5, New York, 1980

Uri, P.,   Development Without
                                 Dependence, Praeyer, New
                                 York, 1976

White, L.J (ed).,   Technology, Employment and
                                 Development, Council for
                                 Asian Studies, Quezon City,
                                 Philipines, 1974

                                 Industrial Concentration
                                 and Economic Power in
                                 Pakistan, Princeton
                                 University Press, Princeton,
                                 N.J., 1974

Wolf, C. Jr.,   'Institutions and Economic
                                 Development, American
                                 Economic Review, December
                                 1955

Yoon, B.C.,   'Korean Development Finance
                                 Corporation', Report read
                                 at the International Seminar
                                 at Manila,Philipines

entrepreneurship,
concept 53;
economists concept 56;
psychologists concept
64; sociologists
concept 64
equality 46
experience 222-3; interface
between training
education and 138;
kinds of firm and 125;
location policy based
on 129; size of firm
and 130;
export led industrialisation
35; small sector 17;
extended family 147

finance sources of 168-71
financial institution
158-62, 227-8
financial intermediary,
joint family as 157

government as catalyst 42;
as entrepreneur 43;
as guarantor 45; as
guide and strategist 44;
role 42; 219-20, 226-7
gross domestic product 5
growth in inherited
industry 84

industrial concentration
37, 219; efficiency 25,
227; strength 228;
choice 18; labour versus
capital intensive 18,
216; large versus small
12; public versus
private 21
industry, reasons for
entering 106
immigrant caste
characteristics 185-7
import substitution 33,95,
219
informal development 223-4
investment 7,23;
non-repatriable 167

joint family 147

labour intensive 18,216
location 32, 218

managing agency
system 103-4
mechanisation effects
of 182-3
Memon community
characteristics 190-7;
competitiveness
192-3; industrial
pattern 190; location
policy 193-4;
management practises
196-7; unity 190-2.
merchant(s):
characteristics 89-90
monopoly houses 38
motives 221

nationalisation 9;
compensation 22

occupation(s) change
101; comparison of
fathers and sons 100;
entrepreneurs
father 78; mobility
85, 86, 108, 223;
options 77,220;
reasons for change
106
opportunity,
environmental 128
Pakistan economy
review 4
Pakistan Industrial
Development
Corporation 21
Pathan characteristics
199-201;
competitiveness 202;
location policy 201;
management practises
203
polytechnic 133
private employment,
occupational
mobility 85
private sector 217

For Product Safety Concerns and Information please contact our EU
representative GPSR@taylorandfrancis.com
Taylor & Francis Verlag GmbH, Kaufingerstraße 24, 80331 München, Germany

www.ingramcontent.com/pod-product-compliance
Ingram Content Group UK Ltd.
Pitfield, Milton Keynes, MK11 3LW, UK
UKHW021831240425
457818UK00006B/154